Neil Marks is a former NSW cri[cketer...] score a century in each of his fir[st...] Born into a sporting family — b[...] Lynn also appeared in first-class [...] time cricket was cut short by illness, but he still became a prolific scorer in Sydney grade cricket, and later a NSW selector and manager on interstate tours.

This is Neil's fourth book, after *Tales from the Locker Room*, *Tales for all Seasons* and *Australian People, Australian Tales*. These books have all featured cricket stories, but this is the first Neil Marks book devoted to cricket.

Neil is known as 'Marksy' to his school and business friends, and 'Harpo' to all in cricket. He has three daughters, two and a half grandchildren and lives in Sydney with his wife Kay ('Herself' in the pages that follow).

GREAT
AUSTRALIAN
CRICKET
STORIES

NEIL MARKS

ABC
Books

Published by ABC Books for the
AUSTRALIAN BROADCASTING CORPORATION
GPO Box 9994 Sydney NSW 2001

First published November 2002
Reprinted April 2003

National Library of Australia
Cataloguing-in-Publication entry
Marks, Neil, 1938- .
  Great Australian cricket stories.

  ISBN 0 7333 1139 3.

  1. Cricket – Australia – Anecdotes.
  I. Australian Broadcasting Corporation.
  II. Title.

796.3580994

Front cover photograph: Cricket at an AIF camp in Darwin, 1943. *State Library of Victoria*
All other photographs in this book are from private collections or from the ABC Archive,
with the exception of Michael Slater (courtesy of Patrick Eagar) and Richie Benaud
(courtesy of Dennis Brennan).

Produced by Geoff Armstrong
Set in 11/14 Berkeley Book
Colour reproduction by Colorwize Studio, Adelaide
Printed and bound in Australia by Griffin Press, Adelaide
5 4 3 2

To Herself
(Who says afternoon tea ladies never get a mention?)

Acknowledgments

I am extremely grateful for the support of the cricket people I contacted in the course of writing this book. Special thanks to Stuart Neal for his enthusiasm and confidence, to Brigitta Doyle, a lovely person with a bubbly personality to whom nothing is too much trouble, and to Geoff Armstrong, a great editor and great bloke (any errors you may find in this book are due to the pigheadedness of the author, not the wise guidance of the editor). And I also appreciate the efforts of Zeena Kirby, Sarah Shrubb, Jo Mackay and Ian Russell, in helping to make this book a reality.

Metrics

You will notice that sometimes in this book I use 'imperial' measures when referring to weights, heights and distances, rather than metrics. My editor tells me this is wrong, that I have to move with the times. However, this is my book so I will use terms and measurements that I understand. Call me old-fashioned, but you have to agree that if something falls 100 feet it falls a whole lot further than if it merely drops 30.48 metres. And how tall is 178 centimetres anyway?

For the record, I give you the following information. Study it closely, while I go and feed my pet dinosaur:

- One inch equals 25.40 millimetres.
- Twelve inches equals one foot.
- Three feet equals one yard, which equals 0.91 metres.
- A pound, as well as being the currency of choice in the United Kingdom, is a measure of weight. One pound equals 16 ounces, and also 0.45 kilograms. There are fourteen pounds in a stone.
- Two miles is the true distance of the Melbourne Cup, not — as it has been since 1972 — 3200 metres (which is 61 and a half feet short of two miles).
- A cricket bat that once weighed two pound three ounces now weighs one kilogram (which is about half the weight of the willow Clive Lloyd used to wield).

Contents

Introduction

Although in other books I have written a number of stories on cricket, I have never felt the need to base a whole book on 'The Summer Game'. To paraphrase the old saying, I believed that cricket books were a bit like buses and girls — there was always another one coming around the corner. Yet now that I've completed my cricket book, I'm glad I did it. Cricket is a game so full of stories, anecdotes and characters that one thing leads to another. As I wrote, I found that a word triggered a memory, a phrase jogged a joke and so on. So I sat down at the computer and, like Adam Gilchrist's batting, I just let it happen!

In a way cricket is a religion but, unlike those religions which have a different significance in our society, we don't address the captains of Australia, 'Your Grace' or 'Your Eminence'. We call them by their given name: Steve or Mark or Allan. Providing we know them well, we may even refer to them by their nicknames, Tugga, Tubby, AB and, going further back, Chappelli, Braddles and 'Mary Ann' — the nickname by which MA Noble was known. (I have a bit of a reputation for calling a spade a 'bloody shovel' but I must confess, even in my most reckless moments,

I could never stoop to addressing the captain of Australia as 'Mary Ann'.)

Yet, unlike the leaders of spiritual religions, the captain of the Australian XI does not don any raiments of office. He is honoured enough just to wear a baggy green cap, and a pair of old-fashioned flannels like the bloke playing C Grade down the park. For we all belong to the same 'congregation' and we all have ownership of the same game. Despite betting, sledging, Bodyline and other scandals that have sullied the game throughout the years, cricketers of the world are of one creed; there is an invisible thread that binds them together, no matter what their nationality, standing or ability. At least, that's how it should be!

This is a book of stories about Aussie cricket and the people who are connected with the game. Tales not just about the stars and superstars whose names and faces are recognised by almost everyone in our land, but also of the lesser lights and those individuals beyond the boundary who are now part of the industry that is cricket. Some of this group of 'non-playing participants' earn their living from the game, while others simply receive joy in serving. Yet all are pulled along in cricket's slipstream, integral pieces of the fabric that make up the summer game.

In writing about the scorers, roomies, administrators and media people, I found a labour of love. I did, however — as is my style — occasionally let my inclination towards nostalgia take control. Thus, sometimes I tend to drift off to yesterday, where I see the world as fair and the days as golden. Maybe they were! Or perhaps it is that I'm feeling my years (and arthritis), and am limping towards eternity supported by the panacea of the past's persuasive propaganda and the crutch of distant memory.

So I wrote of players and umpires and I wrote of barrackers and of sledging (a needless practice which I abhor, but which shouldn't worry any sturdy cricketer). And I also wrote of Bradman and my father. Occasionally, the same character pops up in different chapters and even though this is a book of

Australian cricket stories there are a couple of tales of — and from — the Poms; for they invented the game and were playing it long before we knew it existed (although in those days they had nobody to beat them). If the title of this book seems somewhat presumptuous, please understand that in using it I am referring to the people and events portrayed, not to my writing style. If sometimes my rather quirky sense of humour gets in the way, I hope it doesn't distract the reader from my purpose. For what I really wanted to do was to write yarns that shouldn't be lost and of people who shouldn't be forgotten.

In writing these stories so many memories flooded back and I returned often to the past. As author LP Hartley once wrote, 'The past is another country, they do things differently there.'

Cricket is a game that lives off its past. It reveres the past, it devours the past. Yet in its own way, cricket has always been conscious of the future; the game must go on, the young must replace the old. Cricket's big weakness has always been that, in a strange way, it ignores its present. I remember as a kid, the old timers talking of my idols — Keith Miller, Arthur Morris and Ray Lindwall — in derogatory terms. ('As an allrounder Jack Gregory would leave Keith Miller for dead,' ... 'Warren Bardsley would bat the ears off Arthur Morris,' etc, etc.) Then as I grew older, the roles were reversed. Miller, Morris and Lindwall became the icons and the later generations were treated with scorn. And the same applies today. Only the *names* have been changed to suit the times.

In some pages, I have made my own comparisons. These were written mostly with tongue in cheek, yet I hope I have remained respectful to both the past and the present. There is an adage (more a cliché, really) which says that you can't compare different eras. Whoever made that statement is probably correct but that doesn't mean we shouldn't enjoy trying.

For example, recently I had an argument about the relative abilities of Neil Harvey and Allan Border. I plumped for Harvey while my mate down at the pub picked Border. Who was correct? I really have no idea, but it made for an interesting half hour. And if you asked me to compare Mark Waugh and Norm O'Neill, I don't think I could give you a conclusive opinion. In answering such a question, no doubt I'd wax poetic about their magnificent batting and brilliant fielding. I'd waffle on about technique and of their individual personalities, and compare their eras, peers and opponents — once again wandering down digression's seductive road. Yet, in a way, this is what I like doing most of all. For in memory, I can withdraw to yesterday, where great games were played, everybody laughed a lot and the friendly smells of summer lingered. It gives me an excuse to return to golden days when youth was forever!

Actually, speaking of Norm O'Neill, it reminds me of the time I was batting with Normy, in an up-country game at Boggabri and …

ONE

Tales of The Don

I actually began writing this in the week of Don Bradman's death. In the days after he died, sections of the media turned the event into something of a frenzy, and it seemed to me that for the last decade a significant number of people had been almost salivating over the impending event. Upon the passing of Don's beloved wife Jessie, the preparation for Bradman tributes gained momentum. No doubt the hoardings, 'The Don is Dead', were prepared and placed in a dark storeroom, ready for the time when they would be brought out into the light of day to announce their poignant tidings to a sad, though far from surprised, world.

Only a few days earlier I had been talking to Phil Derriman, author, sporting journalist and Bradman chronicler. Phil and I have become quite friendly over the years, and on this occasion, as we often do, we swapped tales of The Don. I mentioned I had a number of anecdotes about Bradman that were told to me by my father. However, I did not intend to tell these publicly while Bradman was living — not because there was anything damning in the yarns, but because Bradman was a private person and I would feel I was intruding — albeit way back into the past. I was also conscious that this could be construed by some as me (at best) cashing in on the burgeoning Bradman industry and (at worst) being anti-Bradman (which I most certainly am not). Derriman remarked that whatever I decided to do with these stories, I should at least write them down while I am alive and lucid. Well, as we all know, the world's greatest batsman is now dead — and I'm writing them down.

The stories I write come mainly from my father (Alec), a man of honesty, a man without an agenda, a man with a natural, funny and often self-deprecating sense of humour, a man who told it as he saw it — as he remembered it. He told me the stories off the cuff; over a beer at the club; while watching cricket on television; as an aside at a family dinner; as a remembrance over a cuppa in the lounge room. But Bradman didn't dominate the stories. 'Braddles' (as Dad always called him) was just one of the characters involved — a player in the passing parade of Alec Marks' memory who was, for a short period in his cricket life, quite a close friend of my father.

Yet there were other yarns of other people! My father told me of Archie (Jackson), 'Kippy' (Alan Kippax), a bloke he called 'Napper' (Stan McCabe), Bertie (Oldfield) and Arthur Allsopp. He also reminisced about Bill Ponsford, Clarrie Grimmett, Jack Fingleton, Billy Brown and Tiger O'Reilly — a veritable *Wisden* of cricket anecdotes. At reunions, I heard him recount cricket stories to his peers of the 1920s and 30s, as I recount cricket stories to my peers and they to me. As these old stalwarts swapped yarns, the faces of all wore the grin of gracious memory. There were splendid tales of cricket's glory and humorous tales of cricket's imperfection; of dropped catches at a vital time, of bowling with fractured fingers and batting with hangovers, and of sledging (though this was not a term used in those days and no one from the era will now admit that it happened, but it did, though in a far milder form than in the present time). There were yarns of petty peccadilloes which were funny then and stand the test of time. My father, though, never spoke of his fellows' occasional penchant for fast women and slow horses, or of sporadic overdoses of alcoholic stimulants after a hard day's play — cricketers of his era, like later generations, made sure that these stories remained in the lockers when the room attendant closed the door at the end of another cricket day.

(To be honest, my father did tell me *one* story of a player who went to a party. Apparently, this fellow was attracted to someone he thought was a very pretty blonde lady but whom he later found out was actually a transvestite. 'Crikey,' said the cricketer to his team next day, 'I was out the door and down the steps before you could say Jack Robinson.'

'You never could pick a wrong 'un,' one of his teammates retorted laconically.)

He took his bat to a practice

Alec Marks (known to his family and mates as 'Acka') had come to know Don Bradman when Marks was chosen in the NSW practice squad 1927–28, but they were little more than cricket acquaintances; members of the same team practising together but hardly friends. However, just before Marks was to make his first interstate tour, an interesting event happened that brought them closer together. I am not sure exactly when this incident took place, but more than likely it occurred at the last practice held on the Sydney Cricket Ground No. 2 before the team left by train for Adelaide in January 1929. Apparently, Bradman had been unable to make the beginning of this practice session because of some other commitment. (In those semi-professional days, such happenings were not unusual.)

The sun was going down as the practice wound to a close. Alec Marks was packing up his gear, ready to head for the dressing-room, when he heard one of the team's veterans say, 'Get a load of this!' Marks looked up and saw that the man was staring at the gate through which Don Bradman was walking. Bradman was prepared for action. He was wearing his flannels, carrying his bat, was fully protected and ready to make a 'net century': pads, gloves and cap were in place, as were other protective incidentals that are hidden from sight but which all fast bowlers know are there.

Bradman walked the few paces to where his teammates were standing, all of them quiet and motionless. Then Bradman said (in essence), 'Is it all right if I have a hit before it gets dark?' Nobody answered. Slowly, the older players turned their backs, picked up their gear and walked from the ground, while the younger men sheepishly followed. Alec Marks, just 18 years old, was bewildered — as, no doubt, were the few spectators who had gathered behind the nets to collect autographs and watch their heroes practise. While Bradman stood frozen in limbo, the others moved further and further away. [In retelling the story, Alec Marks recalled the lyrics of an old song, *I Took My Harp To A Party (But Nobody Asked Me To Play)*.] Although still a youth, Marks had a strong personality and was never one to just 'follow the leader'. He was also kind. *'I'll* give you a hit, Don,' he called, and picked up a ball lying nearby. Bradman nodded, walked into a net and Marks bowled his accurate, though hardly dangerous, left-hand spinners. He was smashed unmercifully for 10 minutes or so, whereupon Bradman said, 'Thanks, that'll do.' As they walked back to the room, Bradman turned to Marks and asked, 'Who are you rooming with in Adelaide?'

'Gee, I haven't even thought about it,' replied Marks.

'What about rooming with me?'

'Okay.'

[With the benefit of hindsight, all the players involved in the incident on the SCG No. 2 that day were in the wrong. Bradman should not have assumed that he was going to get 'special' treatment because he was late. Nonetheless, he was only 20 and, despite some brilliant performances, had played only a limited number of first-class games and had just begun his Test career. Bradman, from the bush, was learning fast, but was still a long way from being fully versed in the customs and traditions of 'city' cricket. He would never make the same mistake again! On the other hand, those who staged the walkout were teaching the youngster a lesson, although it was a fairly heartless way to do so. It is also probable that there was more than a hint of jealousy in their behaviour. Only a week before, Bradman had made his first Test hundred and was already gaining a huge amount of publicity. Bradman may not yet have become cricket's great superstar but he was well on the way — and what one man gains another man loses!

Yet this incident poses the question: where was the captain? Where were the 'old heads'? Growing up, I was told endlessly by those of the pre-war era, how great was the standard of cricket then and how the traditions and the lore of the game had been emasculated by the players since. Well, let me tell you, this sort of incident would not have been allowed to occur with the likes of Benaud, Chappell, Taylor or Waugh at the helm. Had they been around at the time, these latter-day skippers may have disagreed with young Bradman's action and they may even have let him suffer a bit, but in a quiet spot at the bar that evening they would have explained to him (in a straightforward but sympathetic fashion) the error of his ways. Young players have to learn by experience, but they must also be *allowed* to become part of the team. To some, the era between the wars appears to be 'golden'. Yet it cannot be denied that it was also an era of ultra conservatism, interstate jealousy and rampant sectarianism. (Gold is discovered a long while after it has been in the ground. Those living when it turned to gold didn't recognise it at the time. Only later do others talk of riches!)]

While they were playing in Adelaide, Don Bradman and Alec Marks became closer, speaking to each other of their childhood (which was not that long ago, as Marks had just turned 18 and Bradman 20), their thoughts on cricket, their teammates and their girlfriends. Bradman's steady girl was his childhood sweetheart, Jessie Menzies, while Marks had been going out with Lilian Ward, the eldest girl from a well-known Randwick sporting family. They both claimed that *their* girl was 'the best-looking sort' in the State and agreed that when the tour was over they would double date, so that they could decide who really was the 'best sort'. When the four met, the men agreed that it was a dead heat and often thereafter they went out as a foursome. These occasional 'nights at the movies' graduated to weekends when they would go on picnics, go fishing, play golf and the like.

My father told me of one of these outings, to Berowra Waters on the Hawkesbury River, when nothing went right.

Overthrows

The Hawkesbury River is still one of the most beautiful waterways in the great city of water, although Berowra is no longer a haven for koalas and kookaburras but a part of Sydney suburbia; a place where people with four-wheel drives and mobile phones live before they move to Pymble or Hunters Hill. There were, of course, no freeways in those days and once a motorist and his passengers moved past the uninteresting little railway town of Hornsby, they were in the bush. The old Pacific Highway connected Sydney to Brisbane but to call the main route between two capital cities 'a highway' was tantamount to calling your surfboard 'a ship'. The two lanes of the 'highway' (one each way) wound around the ridges, curved sideways, dropped to the gorges and picked up again. Sometimes the road was made of asphalt and tar and sometimes it was made of rolled-out dirt that had been there since before the Dreamtime — and sometimes it wasn't rolled. In those days, carsickness was an ailment of epidemic proportions.

The trip to Berowra did not start auspiciously. Soon after the two cricketers and their girlfriends had passed Hornsby, the car had a flat tyre. Alec Marks, who was about as mechanical as Merv Hughes is suave, somehow managed to remove the wheel but when he looked at the spare, he found it was old and tatty and certainly not a piece of equipment that you would choose to use except in the direst emergency. Fortunately, there was a garage (as service stations used to be called) just up the hill, so Marks rolled the tyre up the steep incline to see if it could be repaired. In a few minutes, the mechanic had pulled out a sharp piece of metal from the rubber and patched it, and the tyre was ready to go. Flushed with triumph, Marks gave the thumbs up to his companions down the road and began to roll the tyre down the hill while he ran beside it like those old paintings we used to see of polite young ladies playing with hoops. A hoop, however, was built for polite young ladies — a tyre was built for *speed*! As Marks began to pick up pace, so did the tyre, and as the road became steeper, suddenly it bolted. Down the road it raced, roaring along with its new patch coming into view every fraction of a second. 'Braddles, grab the tyre,' Marks shouted as the object gained momentum and hurtled towards the two 'good sorts' and the world's greatest batsman, who were all leaning against the car near the bottom of the incline. But the tyre had gained its freedom and like the wild bush horses from Snowy River it must have seen its 'well loved mountains full in view', for it bumped left, crossed the road, hit a boulder, jumped high in the air and plunged over the side of a cliff. Down it crashed, sweeping branch, bush and bramble from their moorings. Down, down it continued, a hundred feet and then some, before disappearing forever into the dark undergrowth at the base of a forest that had never heard the sound of a human footstep. Meanwhile, Marks, a top schoolboy sprinter, racing down in pursuit of the rampaging tyre, also couldn't stop and was into his follow-through when he passed the passengers who were leaning on the car watching the drama. He pulled up about 50 yards past the vehicle and walked slowly back. Looking straight ahead, Marks reached into the boot and casually remarked to his open-mouthed companions, 'Okay, now let's see how the spare goes.'

Ian Thorpe Braddles weren't!

When eventually the four arrived at Berowra, the two men hired a boat. While the girls retired to the boat owner's bathroom, to freshen up, Bradman and Marks started up the boat and took it out on the river to 'get the feel'. They were out about a hundred yards when the boat's engine coughed and petered out. Anyone who has tried to start an old-fashioned outboard engine with a leather piece of pulling equipment that looked as if it came from a barber shop knows the frustration of the exercise. PPPRRrrr then silence. PPPRRrrr then nothing again. Jessie and Lilian, having finished their 'freshening', walked down the wharf and stood watching as their men tried with muscle and finesse to get the little craft moving. 'Here, give me a look at the motor, Acka, something might be blocked,' Don suggested, and bent over to examine the engine. The sight of the Bradman posterior shoved into the air was too much for an occasional practical joker like Alec Marks and with a quick movement of his left leg, Marks sent his mate over the side and into the Hawkesbury.

On the wharf, Lilian laughed, but not Jessie. 'Grab him, Acka, grab him,' she screamed. 'He can't swim!' As Bradman spluttered and splashed and began going down for the second time Marks dived in, grabbed Don and pulled him into the boat.

Alec Marks later recounted this story to his playing group at the 19th hole at Pennant Hills Golf Club. One of the group suggested that if Don Bradman had actually drowned, then Marks would still be in Long Bay Jail. Another said that he would never have gone to jail, as the next day the headlines would have read, *Bradman Drowns — Marks Lynched at Berowra Wharf*.

Alec, however, didn't agree with this. He felt that the headlines would have read, *Bradman Dead — Marks Moves Up Batting Order*.

The Victor and The Don

On some occasions Don and Jessie would have dinner at Lilian Ward's home in Randwick; later, as Jessie and Lilian became closer, Jessie would stay at the Wards' house for short periods while Don was away on his trips to England. In turn, Lilian would also stay in the Southern Highlands with the Menzies family during this period. (On the day of Jessie's wedding, Lilian was with her, helping her dress.)

[The Wards were a well-known family in Sydney and probably the best-known sporting family in the Eastern Suburbs. Lilian's three older brothers were all first-grade cricketers and had also made their mark in other sports. Cec was hardcourt tennis champion of NSW, Max played Sheffield Shield cricket and Alan played interstate rugby. Their father, Perc Ward, had also played first-grade cricket early in the century, playing against Victor Trumper and Tibby Cotter. He was later in the army with Cotter during World War I.]

Lilian Ward's second brother, Max, who opened the batting for NSW, told of an evening at the Wards' home, after snooker, when the subject turned to cricket — not a surprising topic considering the four Ward men, Alec Marks and Don Bradman were present. Perc Ward was waxing lyrical about Victor Trumper, and as those listening had never seen the great man play, a number of questions were asked. Perc insisted that Trumper was better than Grace and Ranji combined, twice as good as Hobbs and even greater than Macartney — or some such similar exclamations of hero worship which just the name of 'Trumper' seemed to evoke from those of the pre-World War I generation. Bradman said very little, and then he turned to Max Ward and stated quietly, 'Maybe, but have a look at his average!'

Snookered, but not for long!

Once, when a day's practice at the SCG had been washed out, Alec Marks suggested to Don Bradman that they go back to the Wards' home in Randwick and have a game of snooker. When Bradman and Marks arrived at the Wards' this particular day, Marks ushered his mate into the room where the billiard table was situated, grabbed a cue, handed it to Bradman and said, 'You're on!' Then he set up the balls for the game. Though it would be presumptuous to say that Alec Marks was a better all-round sportsman than Don Bradman, he was certainly up there in the same league. Apart from his cricket ability, Marks had won the 440-yards championship at the Combined Intermediate High Schools Athletic Carnival, had played rugby for NSW, was an A-grade tennis player, got to a single figure handicap at golf, was a handy surfer and a most enthusiastic, though very ordinary, fisherman. Thus when it came to snooker he was not only a natural but had spent much of his spare time potting little coloured balls into pockets on his girlfriend's family billiard table. This day Don Bradman was no match for Marks and he was thrashed.

About five years later, Bradman was made an offer to move to Adelaide, for reasons both business and cricket. Soon after this, Marks was chosen in the NSW team to play South Australia in Adelaide. After the first practice session had ended, Don Bradman came over to see his former teammates, and later, in the rooms, over a cooling drink, he said to Marks, 'Acka, would you like to come with me after the game one evening, have a look at our new home and have dinner? Jess said any night would suit.' So when stumps were drawn at the end of the first day Bradman drove his mate home to dinner.

The Bradmans showed Alec Marks around their pleasant suburban home, had a drink and settled down to dinner. When dessert had been consumed, Don asked his wife if he and their guest could be excused as they had some unfinished business to complete. Marks then followed Bradman to another room, which he hadn't been shown on the tour of inspection. The room was large and around the walls were bats, cricket photos and other pieces of memorabilia. In the middle of the room was a full-sized billiard table. 'I saved this room until last,' remarked Bradman, as he set up the balls for snooker. 'Grab a cue,' he said, pointing to the cue rack. Marks helped himself and the game began. It did not take long. Marks was obliterated! 'I've been looking forward to that since the day you beat me at the Wards' five years ago,' said Bradman and grinned. The shell-shocked loser then walked back with the victor to join Jessie for coffee.

Bowling is easy

Alec Marks was a modest man, but when he thought the time appropriate, he told of the day he got Bradman out. People who heard the boast would look at him with a combination of suspicion and wonder, but Marks would then turn silent.

Inevitably, the listener would bite and ask the questions, 'when?' and 'how?' 'Well,' Marks would say, 'it was a grade game between Randwick and St George at Coogee Oval. Braddles was going along pretty well when they brought me on and then with flight and cunning I deceived him. I had him caught on the fence by a magnificent diving catch. He was 246 at the time.'

Wishful thinking

Actually, Alec Marks could bowl a bit! He was a left-hand orthodox spinner who bowled over the wicket and could probably be described as just on the superior side of a change bowler. Strangely, though, at one point in his career there were some in the game who saw him as a possible allrounder for Australia. In the 1930 season, Marks was chosen to play in a trial match played at the SCG. From this game (Jack Ryder's XI versus Bill Woodfull's XI), 15 of the 22 players would be chosen for the 1930 tour of England. Marks was chosen in Ryder's team and Bradman in the opposition. The interest in the game was quite intense as, unlike today, Australia only toured England every four years, South Africa about once a decade and every other place on the globe not at all. Thus every second person in the country was picking his/her 15 players for the Ashes tour. Marks was well favoured to be in the touring party and his odds were shortened by the fact that some influential members of the press were suggesting that not only was he a hard-hitting left-handed bat, but his left-hand tweakers could be used to some effect in the games against county teams.

Though rated as a 'first-class' match, the result of the game mattered little — it was a contest that would eventually be swept into the garbage can of *Wisden's* inconsequential results. In England the game would, no doubt, be called 'a friendly'. However, things are different Down Under. [The last recorded 'friendly' game of cricket played in Australia occurred in 1878, out Brewarrina way, at the Methodist Church Sunday School picnic, and even then a 62-year-old lady scripture teacher was sledged by the wicketkeeper, the organist refused to walk and the parson was accused of cheating.] Nevertheless, no matter the result, what the selectors and fans were looking for was the performance of individual players. Alec Marks made 83 in good fashion, and though he would have liked a ton he was more than happy when one of the Test selectors walked up to him and said, 'You're on the boat, son.' Well, that's one out of three, Marks thought to himself, trying not to become too excited — now if I can only pick up a couple of wickets. The star of Woodfull's team was Don Bradman who, though he started slowly, built up his innings to a crescendo and by the time he had reached 100 was ripping some of Australia's best bowlers to shreds. Then, from Jack Ryder, his skipper, Marks heard the words that every bowler in the world dreaded in such circumstances. 'Have a bowl, mate.'

As Marks measured his run up (which didn't take much time as it was only three paces) he was trying to think positively. He knew that even if Bradman had broken a leg on the way to the wicket and a few seconds later had been struck blind by an act of God, he could never get the little man out. But neither of these things had happened. Bradman was at the very top of his ability. The little batting machine was hitting each ball wherever he wanted and the crowd was roaring for runs — just as the Romans lusted for Christian blood in the Colisseum nearly 1900 years before. The blood that was to be spilled, metaphorically, on one of the world's great cricket grounds this day did not belong to a church martyr but to a 20-year-old left-hand trundler from Randwick. Nevertheless, Marks tried to remain positive.

(Braddles may lose the strike and I could get the other bloke out. Mm, don't think so — the other bloke hasn't had strike for six overs. Braddles could be run out. Not likely, you can't get run out hitting fours. It could rain — yeah, next autumn! Wait a minute, Braddles knows that if I get his wicket I will be a high-priority choice for England — he'll hit me for a couple of fours then jump down the wicket and be stumped. And he's so good that he could do it without anyone suspecting.)

Thus, as he moved in to bowl, Marks was filled with optimism. The first ball was short, spinning away outside off, the perfect ball for a square cut. Bang! It was pulled through midwicket, hitting the pickets before Marks had finished his follow-through. The second ball was pitched on a good length, or would have been, if Bradman hadn't danced four yards down the wicket and hit it on the full to deep mid-on for two. The next ball was again well up, though heading in the direction of first slip. Bradman jumped to it on the full and swept it past square leg to the boundary. Mind you, it was in the air from the bat, three inches above the ground, for a short distance and later in his life Marks claimed that if square leg had dived he may have been able to hold it, providing square leg had elongated arms, hands as big as a steam shovel and X-ray vision superior to Clark Kent. The wider Marks bowled outside off, the harder Bradman smashed it to the on. 'I swear he was belting them out of my hand,' Alec Marks recounted. 'He was so far down the wicket, I reckon he was coming at me from behind.' And so it continued, a sporting massacre without mercy, a cricket blitzkrieg of such terror and precision that those in the Members Stand with a sense of fair play and Christian charity retired to the bar. Meanwhile, the mob on The Hill, overcome by their lust for runs, bayed for more.

Eventually, the over finished and Marks skulked away to the covers, wishing he had taken up finger-painting as his summer sport. In his retirement, Alec Marks said he didn't remember the eight balls from the bowler up the other end but he did recall Jack Ryder speaking three little words which to his dying day filled Marks with fear and foreboding: 'Have another one.'

Marks bowled the next over as if in a slow-motion dream. He could hear the shrieking of the crowd as another ball crashed into the pickets. He was now aiming his leg spinners between third slip and gully. It seemed as if there were nine fielders, plus the 12th man, on the leg boundary, stretching from deep fine leg to deep mid-on, and the only time they touched the ball was to throw it back from the gutter where Bradman had placed it with so much power and finesse. The over dragged on. Marks had been bowling for three days. 'How many left, ump?'

'Four to go.' (Four to go! Eternity! God, please strike me dead!)

After the game, the two teams gathered for a drink and Marks and Bradman came together. Marks made a facetious comment (something like): 'I had you worried, didn't I?' and Bradman grinned. Then Marks mentioned that he thought Bradman was ready to throw his dig away, and he had been hoping that perhaps the prized wicket would be given to the left-hand change bowler who was on at the time. Marks went on to say that if this had been the case, everybody would have been hailing a new bowling discovery and a tour to England would have been his for the taking. Don Bradman looked at Alec Marks with surprise and said, 'It never dawned on me.'

[It would never 'dawn' on Don Bradman to deliberately throw his wicket away. His job was to hit the cricket ball, whoever sent it down. Mateship is part of cricket lore! Mates made on the cricket field remain mates for life. Nevertheless, on the field of battle your mate becomes your enemy, and within the laws and ethics of the game it is your job to destroy him. In Marks' half-joking comment and Bradman's honest, surprised reply we see the difference in the personality and the attitude of the two men. History tells the story of Bradman, the small assassin who was born to hit a cricket ball with more determination, more often and with more effect than anyone who ever lived. Marks was never chosen to play for Australia.]

It was meant to happen

The story told by Alec Marks that best sums up Don Bradman's determination and confidence is the story of *the* bat. In the game against Queensland at the SCG, from Friday, 3 January to Tuesday, 7 January 1930, both NSW and Queensland made low totals in their first innings. After lunch on Saturday, NSW were batting again, and at stumps Bradman was 205 not out. (In those days there was no play on Sundays). On the Saturday evening, Bradman and Marks left the SCG in the latter's car to spend the evening and weekend together (probably) with their girlfriends. As they drove down Anzac Parade, Bradman asked his friend if he had anything arranged for Monday evening and, if not, 'Would you do me a favour?'

Marks answered that he had nothing planned and agreed to do whatever Bradman wanted. 'Next Monday, when the day's play is finished, will you take me down to Mick Simmons?' Bradman requested. (Don Bradman was employed by the sports store, Mick Simmons, in George Street.)

And then the conversation went something like this:

'Why do you want to go to Mick Simmons?'

'To put the bat in the window.'

'What bat?'

'The bat I'm going to use to break the world record score.'

'What world record?'

'The one I'm going to get on Monday.'

On Monday evening at about 7 o'clock, Alec Marks did as he had promised. He pulled his car up in front of Mick Simmons, and Don Bradman got out and was greeted by the manager of the store. Marks watched from the car and in a moment saw Bradman and the manager place a cricket bat in the front of the show window, alongside a photo of Don Bradman playing a shot. Then, in front of the bat and the photo, the manager put a large hand-written sign which announced to the world that in Mick Simmons' window was the bat that had been part of the greatest score in the history of first-class cricket. For on that day, 6 January 1930, using that very same bat, Don Bradman had made 452 not out against Queensland. The game of cricket would never be the same again.

Money is not the only reward

In 1936, Don Bradman became an Australian selector. In the 1936–37 season, Alec Marks was having a good year with the bat and suddenly his name was once again before the public as a Test prospect. Gubby Allen's English team was touring and their toughest match before the Test series began was to be the 'Australian XI' game played in Sydney. The team was chosen and Marks was picked as 12th man. Bradman captained the team.

A few months before this match, Alec Marks had married Lilian Ward. The Bradmans were away and unable to attend, though they sent a wedding present and a telegram which was read at the reception. On the morning of the Australian XI game, Bradman and Marks were changing next to each other in the home side's dressing-room. During the conversation Bradman said (words to the effect of), 'I gave you another wedding present.' Seeing Marks' questioning look, Bradman continued, 'The fee for the match.' (The match fee for an Australian XI game in those days was probably about six times the weekly basic wage.)

Suddenly Marks (the 12th man) realised what his mate, Bradman (the selector), was alluding to. Bradman had done his bit to give the newly married couple a special kind of a kick-start in married life. Marks, a batsman with ability well up to the standard of the team for which he was chosen, shrugged his shoulders, nodded, brushed past Bradman and went out to practice. Bradman stepped aside, surprised at the dismissive response. I believe neither man knew that he had hurt the other!

Little fullback meets The Don

Soon after, war came, and Alec Marks joined the army. After the cessation of hostilities, he returned to peacetime activities and made a good living out of sports' administration (rugby and golf), and for a while continued serving cricket, the game he loved most of all, in an honorary capacity. Marks was a man of many parts and on occasions he did a bit of writing, and some cricket and rugby commentary on radio and lived a useful and happy life. He survived long enough to see his grandchildren into their teens. Don Bradman led the greatest side of all time, was knighted, retired at 40 with an average of … oh well, you know all the rest.

After the war, I doubt that Alec Marks came into contact with Don Bradman more than half a dozen times. I was there on a couple of these occasions, and it was 'Acka' and 'Braddles', and they discussed modern cricket and laughed about the old days.

I first met Don Bradman when his fellow Australian selector, 'Chappie' Dwyer, drove Dad and me home to Randwick after a day's play (I think) in the Test match against India in 1947–48. I was sitting quietly in the back seat with my father when the great man turned around from the passenger's seat and asked me about my school and my sport. I didn't bother to mention lessons (as studies and me were as far apart as The Don's and my father's batting averages), but rushed ahead and quickly told him that I was the opening bat for Randwick Primary School and fullback for the school's 5 stone 7 rugby league team. He seemed genuinely interested and when we reached Chepstow Street he held out his hand and Alec and Chappie both laughed kindly as I hesitated for a moment, and then took it and shook it fiercely. To this day I don't know whether they were laughing at my confidence or my awe.

Ming plays second fiddle

One of the events concerning Don Bradman that stands out in my mind was the first of the four-yearly reunions of NSW cricketers. Every fourth year during the Sydney Ashes Test match every man who has played for 'The Blues' who is still alive and able to hold a glass is invited to gather at some particular venue around the Harbour City. The first of these was held in 1972. The guest speakers were Sir Robert Menzies and Sir Donald Bradman.

It was a wonderful occasion of camaraderie and nostalgia. Yet the thing that struck me that night was the brilliance of Bradman's speech and how in tune he was with the atmosphere.

Bob Menzies was not only Australia's longest-serving Prime Minister, he also loved the game of cricket with a passion and possessed a knowledge of the game which would far surpass some of the first-class selectors I have met over the years. Menzies was either loved or loathed by the electorate, but even his enemies had to admit that he was an orator second to none since Federation. He was eloquent, persuasive, the possessor of a beautifully modulated voice ... and added to all this, he had a superb sense of humour. His dry and incisive wit, though, was probably his greatest asset. In his era, Menzies had been the only person who withstood oratorical comparison with Winston Churchill.

This night, Menzies was his usual brilliant self although, strangely, he seemed a little nervous when he started. Still, who could blame him! Sitting in the audience were, among other immortals, Ray Lindwall, Keith Miller, Bert Oldfield, Bill O'Reilly and Victor Trumper Jnr, not to mention the little man sitting next to him; a man for whose autograph every living Australian would have rushed past Menzies to obtain. But this night, Menzies had even the most rabid Labor supporters standing on their feet clapping. Yet Bradman was better! The boy from Bowral matched 'Ming the Merciless' in his eloquence and wit and bettered him in sense of occasion and thought-provoking content. Only in voice modulation was Bradman behind. Moreover, Bradman was completely relaxed, seemingly at home with the players of the past — a few of whom had made no secret of the fact that they disliked him intensely. The Don was confident and informal, and he let himself reach out to his peers, the huge majority of whom regarded him with respect and, in many cases, devotion.

Early in his speech he thanked his fellows for welcoming a near geriatric cricketer like himself. Then, in a most unBradman-like way, he went on, 'You know what a geriatric is, don't you?' Silence. 'Three wickets in a row by a German.' Everybody roared. The Don might have moved to South Australia nearly 40 years before, but this night he was at home.

Trick shots and Chopin

There is another meeting with Don Bradman that I remember
vividly — and, with the benefit of hindsight, as a privilege. It
began at the Adelaide Oval during a Sheffield Shield match I
was playing. I was alone in the room, nervously padding up to
bat when I heard the famous high-pitched voice behind me.
'Neil, I just came in to wish you good luck and to send my
best wishes to your mother and father.' There he stood,
wearing his familiar grey hat, with his hand out, just as he had
the first time I saw him. I took it, and my nerves dissipated for
a moment.

'Thanks, Sir Don, nice to see you after so long.' Then there was
a roar from the stands, and from the players' balcony in front of
the dressing-room I heard wicketkeeper Doug Ford's voice,
'Harpo, Normy's out.'

Bradman lifted his hand and said, 'Sorry, I'll get out of the way.'
Then, as he moved away, he stated quietly, 'I'm looking forward to
seeing you bat,' and he disappeared through the door. I followed
him, bat in hand, placing my blue cap on my head. I walked
down the stairs and out onto the beautiful ground in a daze. I
must have passed Norm O'Neill on the way out, but I don't
remember doing so. I reached the wicket and vaguely recall taking
block from umpire Egar, 'Give me two legs, Col.' About 45 yards
away stood South Australian speedster, six-foot-six Alan ('Alfred')
Hitchcock, whose intention was to get me out or knock my block
off or both. Yet I wasn't concerned. All I could think of was a little
man in a felt hat with his eyes on me, summing me up, watching
my every batting move.

That evening as I sat in the South Australian dressing-room
having a drink with opposition players Alfred Hitchcock and
Neil ('Nodder') Dansie, the NSW captain, Richie Benaud, sat
down next to me. 'Got a moment?' (When the captain of
Australia asks a 20-year-old apprentice if he's got a moment, it's
Manhattan to a meccano set that the younger guy usually has.)
'What are you doing tomorrow night?'

'I'm taking a girl out.' Then I realised the implications of my comment and rushed on, 'But I won't be home late, B'nord, I promise.'

Benaud grinned and then went on. 'The Don has asked me to dinner at his place and wants me to bring you along, as apparently he and Alec were good mates.' I broke my date as soon as I returned to the hotel — and they say old-time cricketers weren't as dedicated as modern players!

The next evening we arrived at the house in the Adelaide suburb of Kensington. Lady Jessie, with Sir Don, greeted Richie, Jimmy Burke and me at the door. We were taken inside and introduced to their daughter, Shirley, and another guest, Walter Lindrum. [When people assume that Don Bradman was the greatest sportsman that ever lived, I always say, 'What about Walter Lindrum?' After all, Lindrum was so far ahead of his peers that the controlling body of world billiards had to change the rules of the game to bring Lindrum back to the field. An excellent argument could be mounted that Lindrum was Australia's greatest sportsperson, daylight second and Bradman third.]

We had a drink and then sat down to dinner. During the course of the meal I remember thinking how excited The Don and Walter must feel, sitting down at the same table as Neil Marks. After dinner, Jimmy Burke, who was a wonderful jazz and rock'n'roll pianist, sat down at the piano and played and sang, *Shake Rattle & Roll*, *You Ain't Nothing But A Hound Dog* and the quieter, *Down The Road Apiece* (where he whistled some of the melody as well). Then The Don sat at the keyboard and played a Chopin Nocturne: *'How Deep is the Night, Oh Lonely Night.'*

Chopin didn't write those words, and neither did Bradman. The lyrics were written by some Tin Pan Alley hack for a B-grade Hollywood musical, but it was with those words that The Don's beautiful rendition went through my mind that night. The words in my head matched neither the beauty of the melody nor the mastery and feeling of the pianist.

When he had finished, everybody applauded. He sat at the piano for a moment and I called, 'Hey, Sir Don, would you play *Old-fashioned Locket*?'

'How do you know that?'

'My dad told me that you recorded it and he bought the record. I think we have it at home somewhere on an old 78.' Don nodded and played the corny (though pleasant) old tune beautifully.

Later, at the billiard table, Walter Lindrum played some trick shots, shots which, even then, I realised were immensely harder than impossible. Over my short life, I had seen players that could make a billiard ball talk, but let me tell you, Walter Lindrum could not only make it talk, he turned the little white ball into a ventriloquist.

When Walter finished his exhibition, which would have cost me more than my Sheffield Shield match payment if I had gone to watch it at a club in Sydney, I said to The Don, 'Is this the famous table where you gave my old man a belting?'

He looked a little surprised, but he answered, 'So Acka told you about that, did he?' He laughed and seemed pleased.

We left the house about 11pm and caught a cab back to the hotel. I didn't think much about the experience at the time — hell, there were runs to be scored and girls to be taken out. But the experience remained in the archives, among my memory's souvenirs.

Nostalgia

When The Don died and the media brought out all the stories I felt a little sad. I wasn't sad because of his death. He had lived more than a generation past his allotted span and averaged 99.94 — what more could a man want? I guess I was sad for myself, as memories of my father and my youth came flooding back. Probably 'sad' is the wrong word. Nostalgic is how I felt. I hadn't thought of the evening at the Bradmans' house for years, but I remembered it now quite clearly. None of the media, who were now knee-deep in Bradman stories, were at the Bradmans' home that night, but I was. I thought again of my dear old mate Burkey at the piano and the mighty Walter Lindrum playing magic shots on the billiard table where my father once crashed to defeat. I remembered the lovely and hospitable Lady Jessie, I thought of Richie Benaud; B'nord, confident and to those that don't know him, seemingly aloof, but deep down, where it really counts, a compassionate and quiet mentor to his younger players — and as we grew older, a mate who never let us down.

And I thought of my father and his stories. I doubt Bradman told many Marks stories, but then they were different people. Marks was a raconteur, Bradman was a historian. Marks remembered the funny, Bradman the facts. At batting Bradman was both a surgeon and a butcher, while Marks was a heavyweight fighter who threw blows from the first bell and who, on occasions, poleaxed his foes into oblivion — but was often found waking to the count of 10 himself. Yet to compare Bradman and Marks as batsmen is like comparing Field Marshal Rommel with a corporal in the Home Guard. Nevertheless, if you compare them as men you come onto a more level playing field. In life, like all of us, neither was without faults but each did his job to the best of his ability and left the world a better place.

Then again, so do most cricketers!

TWO

You Can't Compare — Or Can You?

During Steve Waugh's team's triumphal Ashes tour of England in the summer of 2001, there were some English critics (with Ian Botham in the vanguard) who were bold enough to suggest that this was the greatest Australian team ever to land on Old Blighty's shores. This statement was greeted with astonishment by old-timers as well as the 'bit younger brigade', all of whom were brought up on a rich diet of succulent tales told about Bradman's intrepid band from 1948. More than 50 years after becoming the only undefeated Ashes team ever, the players from the *Invincibles* have attained a special place in the nation's psyche — far beyond its grudging admiration for Irish bushrangers and just short of its reverence for the First Fleet.

Now suddenly this historic heritage is being challenged. What next? Ned Kelly really *was* a baddie? Phar Lap took drugs? Errol Flynn was celibate?

Whenever such comparisons are raised, the usual clichés are

trotted out by those who wish to be seen as wise: 'You can't compare one generation with another', 'A champion in one era would be a champion in another', etc. Nonetheless, these inter-generational team-choosing exercises have been going on in the pubs and living rooms of Australia since Spofforth first bowled a bouncer, and though averages, styles and types of wickets are all brought into the argument, none of it proves anything. Still, such debates help while away the time over an amber liquid at 'the local' and at a neighbourhood dinner party they have the added advantage of reducing the opportunity for the lady opposite to bring out the photos of her daughter's wedding.

So, in the hope of causing some controversy and a flood of letters and emails (or at least a couple of rude Christmas cards), I will endeavour to choose a composite side from these two fine groups of cricketers — which, remember, played nearly five and a half decades apart. (When chosen, this team will play five fantasy Tests against a composite English side of the same periods.) The only criteria for selection are (a) that the players are to be judged on their form in the months that they toured England in 1948 or 2001 and (b) that such a composite team would play matches under the 2001 laws — eg the present lbw law, 80 overs before the second new ball, etc.

There will, however, be some by-laws that must be sorted out:

- Are helmets allowed? NO! And *won't* that sort the men from the boys!
- Will a match referee be appointed? NO! We are playing cricket, not football.
- Is lost time to be made up? YES! This is an excellent rule and has had an enormous effect in decreasing the number of boring draws.
- Will the wickets be covered? YES and NO! Two of the Tests will have wickets covered, two will be uncovered and the players will vote for the final Test. Boy, I wouldn't mind being a scrutineer at that vote — especially as I'd make sure it was decided by a show of hands.

- Will the games be played under lights? NO! The games will be played during the daylight hours but lights will be switched on if the ball becomes hard to see. And I don't care if the Poms *do* object.
- Will there be neutral umpires? YES! The games will be officiated by two very competent and independent umpires — Steve Bucknor and ... and ... golly, I'm struggling a bit now.

In choosing such a team I am reminded of the time that former Test bowler, journalist and painter Arthur Mailey was asked by his editor to choose his greatest team of all time. Mailey proceeded to do so and a few days later the team was published. Within 24 hours, letters began to stream in to the paper. Arthur Mailey had forgotten to pick a wicketkeeper! When called into the Editor's office to explain, Mailey justified his decision by saying that, after some consideration, he believed the bowlers he'd chosen weren't much good. Actually, he reckoned that they were such a poor lot that none of them would ever beat the bat — so he didn't bother with a keeper.

As I sit at my desk choosing the players, I must admit that I am slightly agitated by the fact that I could well be bombarded by lightning bolts sent down by Bill 'Tiger' O'Reilly, who, no doubt, is of the opinion that the 1934 side would have beaten *both* these teams by an innings and plenty.

To remind the reader of the players involved, I list below the following candidates. You pick your composite team and I'll pick mine.

Opening bats: Morris, Barnes, Hayden, Slater, Langer.
Batsmen: Bradman, Hassett, Brown, Miller, Harvey, Ponting,
M. Waugh, S. Waugh, Martyn, Gilchrist.
Allrounders: Miller, Loxton, Gilchrist.
Wicketkeepers: Tallon, Gilchrist.
Opening bowlers: Lindwall, Miller, Johnston,
McGrath, Gillespie, Lee.
Medium-pace bowlers: Toshack.

Spin bowlers: Ring, Johnson, Toshack, Johnston, Warne.
Captains: Bradman, S. Waugh.
Coach: Buchanan (2001 side) — and, no doubt, there
would be many others applying for the job. The '48 side
didn't have a coach (though they had a brilliant manager
in Keith Johnson) but that does not preclude readers
from choosing their own coach.

[You will notice that there are a few names in more than one
group. This is for the reader's edification and to show the
adaptability of players in both sides. For example, Toshack and
Johnston bowled two types of delivery, while Miller and Gilchrist
are genuine allrounders who were accomplished enough to be
included in their teams even if, for some reason, they could
perform only *one* of their outstanding skills.]

Opening batsmen

I know that I'm in the minority but I have always believed in the
theory that openers are just the players who walk through the
gate first. Any good batsman should be able to open and any
good opener should be able to bat down the list. To illustrate
what I mean: if you are listed at No. 3 and one of the openers is
bowled second ball — what's the difference? None! Except that
the bowler has one under his belt and is now tearing in, ripping
them down, flat out. Anyway, with that little homily out of the
way, let's look at the five players on offer.

In his first innings of the 2001 series, Michael Slater leapt from
the blocks like an Olympic sprinter who was being chased by his
creditors. He played an innings of such overwhelming power and
viciousness that England's lately won, and unexpected, confidence
from its fight-back in the first innings disappeared in 20 minutes.
Though Australia had a lot of work to do from then on to win the
series, for those students of portents and body language, the Ashes
were ours once again. However, by the end of the series Slater was
dropped. From the starting blocks to the chopping blocks!

At the other end, Matt Hayden proved his comeback was no fluke and showed himself to be a hardworking and often dominating player who grabbed his chance and, on occasions, performed brilliantly. Moreover, Justin Langer made the most of his one chance and began his own batting restoration. These two astonishing comebacks forced Slater out of the side and Lazarus into the minor leagues.

Yet no matter how you look at it, the opposition to these three fine players is just too strong. Arthur Morris and Sid Barnes were an opening combination close to the greatest the world has ever seen. They must be considered with Ponsford and Woodfull, Hobbs and Sutcliffe and Greenidge and Haynes. Morris topped the averages in '48 and Barnes averaged 82.25. Morris was chosen in Bradman's greatest team of all time and although Barnes' detractors are quick to point out that he played only 13 Tests, his peers speak of him with awe; he was an impenetrable opening bat and, when the occasion demanded, a player who could pulverise any attack. To judge a player, look at his statistics and then investigate his standing with his peers. If you continue to remain uncertain of his ability, take note of the latter.

First wicket

Bradman. Any arguments?

Second/Third wicket

This is where selection starts getting difficult. It's a matter of who you leave out. Bill Brown would have walked into a world side before the war but he was not quite the same player after it. Damien Martyn has seen the error of his ways and turned from a confident individual of potential to a resolute team player of ability and responsibility. He would make most teams over the eras but just can't quite make this one. The same can be said of Ricky Ponting. Ponting was born with the eye of Rasputin and the reflexes of a hyperactive snake. Despite this, his footwork and the angle of his bat don't always match his other assets — but he is exciting and dangerous, and the fact that he would bat at five here would certainly help his cause. His wonderful all-round fielding, which is up to the standard of Neil Harvey and his mate, Mark Waugh, would also help. Still, try as I may, I just can't squeeze Ricky in.

This leaves the two Waughs, Harvey and Hassett. Harvey was only 19 on the '48 tour and it took him a while to settle. However, in his first appearance in the series, in the fourth Test at Headingley, Harvey made a brilliant and vital hundred. By 1949 he was being mentioned as the best batsman in the world. He *must* be included in this side and will bat at four.

So it now comes down to the twins versus the greatly respected and lovable Lindsay for *one* position. In '48 Hassett hadn't passed his 'use-by date' but the edge had probably just gone from his pre-war form. A tough decision, but I leave Lindsay out. Thus 'Tugga' and 'Junior' remain. As a fan of both, this is not an easy decision. If I was lying on the sand at Cronulla and I heard that Mark Waugh was playing cricket with some kids on the beach at St Kilda, I'd catch the next plane to Melbourne to watch. Mark averaged 86 during the 2001 Test series, but the one player who beat him in the averages was his brother, who had a Test series that any batsman in history would have been satisfied with. Therefore, Steve Waugh will bat at five.

Fourth wicket

The perfect place for a genuine allrounder to bat is six. Keith Miller is the choice. Once again, any arguments?

Wicketkeeper

There are many knowledgeable critics and players of his era who say that Don Tallon from 1946 to 1948 was the greatest keeper the world has ever seen. Though I was only a callow youth in those days, I'm inclined to agree. Conversely, I'm not including him in this side. Tallon was a better keeper than Adam Gilchrist, of that there is no doubt, yet Gilchrist is a keeper of high international standard and a keeper/batsman beyond compare. In the history of cricket there have been some great keeper/batsmen (Don Tallon was a fine bat himself), but there has never been a keeper who could be classed as the best bat in the team. (Perhaps Clyde Walcott could be regarded as the greatest batsman of the West Indies teams of the 1950s. This would be a well-earned compliment, although debatable. Yet to be honest, though the great Sir Clyde was a batsman of immense ability, he was little more than a backstop behind the stumps.)

Moreover, one would not need to be Perry Mason to argue that Adam Gilchrist was the best batsman in the 2001 side. Gilchrist goes into this team. Imagine it, Miller and Gilchrist in partnership. The pulse races!

Bowlers

The great advantage of having class batsmen down to seven is that it leaves the way open to choose specialist bowlers. Therefore, even a fine old-fashioned allrounder such as Sam Loxton is not needed.

The only weakness in the '48 side was the lack of a top-class spinner. Colin McCool did not play a Test, Doug Ring was handy, Ernie Toshack was tight and versatile but needed some assistance from the wicket to be dangerous, and Ian Johnson was, at best, just adequate. Therefore Shane Warne really has no competition and would walk into a composite team without raising anyone's hackles.

When speaking of the attack of the '48 side, people are nearly always inclined to mention the names Lindwall and Miller before all others. Yet the bowling star of the '48 team was undoubtedly left-hand pace and swing bowler Bill Johnston. He achieved 102 wickets on tour and averaged 23.33 in the series. Johnston had the added advantage of also being able to bowl medium-pace left-hand leg breaks when the occasion demanded. His hostility, versatility and sheer natural ability make 'Big Bill' a certainty for this team. Opening bowler Keith Miller is already in the team, as a batsman, and no team in history could leave out Ray Lindwall. If the TAB ran a box trifecta on the greatest Australian opening bowlers ever, Ray Lindwall would be the 'standout'. A different type of bowler from the others, but a champion nevertheless, is Glenn McGrath. His accuracy, bounce and ability to seam the ball would provide the perfect foil for Lindwall and Miller — or maybe, they would provide the perfect foil for Glenn McGrath

So there we have it, an unbeatable team:

A. Morris
S. Barnes
D. Bradman
N. Harvey
S. Waugh
K. Miller
A. Gilchrist
R. Lindwall
S. Warne
G. McGrath
W. Johnston
M. Waugh (12th man)

Bradman would be captain and if a vice-captain was needed, Steve Waugh would do the job admirably.

I see a problem, however. Who would bat at No. 11: Bill Johnston or Glenn McGrath? Both men are eminently suitable. Perhaps a coin should be tossed, as it would be a devastating insult to each to be forced to bat after the other.

Finally, let me talk about the need for a coach. In thinking of the possibilities, I'll let my imagination take hold and envisage the following conversations occurring between coach and team. I reckon they would go something like this:

Coach: Keith, there will be an early cross-country run this morning. We will have fielding drills until midday and then a full net session this afternoon.

Miller: Practice!! Be buggered we will! I'm meeting an old airforce mate of mine, at 10, for a few beers at a pub in the Strand. Then I'm off to Ascot in time for the first at 1.30.

Coach: Sid, I'm a little worried about your square-cutting. I am of the opinion you're overdoing it, Sid.

Barnes: And who did you bloody play for, mate?

Coach: [In dressing-room] You bowled beautifully today, Ray. Now go and warm down — and remember, no alcohol for an hour.

Lindwall: Hey twelfthy, bring me three bottles of real cold beer and make it quick.

Coach: Don, I'm ready to discuss tactics whenever you are.

Bradman: (Stares at coach with a withering glance) Excuse me, I have an appointment.

Coach: Arthur, I just popped in to let you know that the team dinner is to be held in the hotel dining room at seven o'clock tonight. As it is the night before the Test I have taken the liberty of excluding the customary wine with the meal.

Morris: Dear boy, you are ill. Now you just sit quietly, while I call the hotel doctor.

Coach: Steve, the team meeting is just about to start and I can't find Bill Johnston or Neil Harvey. Do you know where they are?

Waugh: They've just left for golf.

Therefore, I have not chosen a coach. Readers must understand that, deep down, I am a compassionate man who would detest the sight of a broken and bleeding body lying, prostrate, outside the dressing-room door.

THREE

Scrapbooks and Autographs

Sometimes fans can be hard on players and often they are downright rude. In large stadiums sheltered by the crowd and anonymity, individuals can get away with lewd and defamatory comments that would have them arrested on the street. Yet, as a gnarled old cricketer once said to me at the MCG after I had undergone the educational experience of fielding for an afternoon in front of Bay 13, 'Son, don't let 'em irritate you. It's just their way of saying g'day.'

Of course, sometimes the reverse can apply. Cricketers full of self-importance and insecurities can sarcastically deride somebody who is just being polite. There are also times when *both* the players and fans can be accused of teetering on the brink of unacceptable behaviour. 'How many runs are you going to make today?' people sometimes ask as the players are walking along to their room. A well-known player from my era would answer this inane inquiry with one word. 'Seven,' he would say.

It can also be quite embarrassing to all concerned when a batsman, storming through the gate after having made a duck, is approached by fans for an autograph and suddenly refers to the scriptures by telling them to 'go forth and multiply'. Indeed, if you are tired of this cruel world and want to end it all, don't bother to head for The Gap or overdose on knockout pills swallowed with a rum and Bonox chaser. Simply stroll up to a batsman who has just been robbed by the umpire, and as he slams the gate behind him say, 'Why did you play a stupid shot like that?' Not only will you achieve your aim, but your demise will be seen on the six o'clock news and at 11 o'clock on the cricket highlights as well.

Yet, unheralded and unsung, players often go above and beyond what would be normally expected of them. They spend hours signing autographs and coaching kids without looking for remuneration; they visit the sick and support charities, seeking neither publicity nor kudos. Like humans the world over, cricketers are not without frailties, but in the main, beneath a crust of tough individuality and cynical banter lies a good heart and a man who is thankful for the gift bestowed on him: a person who tries to help when he can.

At a game some years ago, I was sitting next to Steve Waugh in the players' viewing area when the carer of a physically handicapped lad leaned over the rail and handed Steve a hard-covered drawing book. The book contained press cuttings and photos of Steve Waugh's career which had been put together under what must have been very difficult circumstances but, undoubtedly, with great love. Interspersed between the pages were rudimentary drawings of cricket scenes and underneath were such captions as, 'Steve, hitting a four' or 'Steve, taking a catch'. The great cricketer slowly turned the pages and examined the book intently. When he reached the end he passed it over to me said, 'Have a look at this', picked up his batting gloves, walked down the stairs and over to the concourse where the lad was sitting in a wheelchair. Waugh kneeled down beside the boy and they talked for a while. Then he signed the gloves and handed them to his new friend. At that moment, there was a yell from the centre of the ground. Somebody was out and it was Steve Waugh's turn to bat. He rubbed his hand through the lad's hair, turned and jogged up the stairs. Grabbing his bat and a fresh pair of gloves, Waugh hurried out to meet the enemy. As he left, I noticed Steve's eyes glistening and couldn't help but wonder whether he would be able to see the first ball.

*   *   *

Fans are not constantly wide-eyed with rapture when they meet players, though; nor are they always encouraging. Bruce ('Roo') Yardley, well-known Australian cricketer of the late 1970s and early 1980s, often used to tell a story of meeting a fan in the West Indies who was hardly overawed by his presence.

During a break between games, Yardley was lying on a beach in Barbados, soaking up the sun and endeavouring to put all thoughts of cricket as far back in his mind as possible. Out of the corner of his eye he saw a shadow cover the sand. He looked up and saw an attractive young Barbadian girl, standing, staring at him. 'G'day,' said Yardley.

The girl kept looking down at him for another moment and then asked, 'You an Aussie cricketer?'

Yardley sat up and nodded, 'Yeah.'

'Which one are you?'

'I'm Bruce Yardley,' replied 'Roo'.

'Yardley!' replied the girl in a sarcastic tone, 'Yardley!' Then she began to laugh.

'What are you laughing at?' asked the surprised Australian.

'Yardley,' (laugh), 'Yardley,' (laugh). 'Man, when Andy Roberts, Joel Garner and Michael Holding finished pounding you with their bouncers, you won't be called Yardley — everybody will call you Inchley.'

*   *   *

During the 1948 Invincibles tour of England, so the story goes, Don Bradman was at a cricket dinner, seated next to a local political figure and his wife. The politician, ecstatic about sitting next to the great cricketer, besieged him with questions, while beside him sat his dutiful wife, nodding at the appropriate time. Eventually, Bradman turned to the lady and asked, 'And are you interested in cricket, ma'am?'

Without a great deal of conviction, the lady declared that she was and then continued the conversation. 'So are you having an enjoyable trip, Mr Bradman?'

'Most certainly,' answered The Don. 'Everybody has been most kind.'

The lady seemed happy with the response. Then she asked another question which caused her husband to cringe, the Master of Ceremonies to choke on his soup and the pigeons nestled on the nearby windowsills to hurriedly flutter off to more predictable climes. The lady said, 'Now tell me Mr Bradman, what do you do — bat or bowl?'

[Don Bradman was a well-mannered man, so, despite the question, the reply was, no doubt, well considered and polite. However, let me pose a supplementary question to readers. How would you answer that question if *you* were Don Bradman? Obviously, those who are cynics and have a 'goonish' feel for occasion could not possibly just let the question pass with an 'I bat — a bit.' Here a few comebacks for you to cogitate upon:

- Well, I once bowled Wally Hammond out.
- Neither, I'm in for my captaincy.
- I do a bit of both, plus drive the bus, assist the scorer and style Keith Miller's hair.
- Actually I'm over here as a tourist: explore the Tower of London, watch the changing of the Guard, catch a show in the West End, see Sissinghurst in spring, have lunch at a pub in the Cotswolds — the usual sort of thing!
- My coach believes that I will one day be as fast as Larwood but I'm thinking of changing coaches.

- Why is everybody always asking me *questions*? How do I know *what* I do — how does *anybody* know what they do? The selectors picked me and I'm doing my best — that's *all I know*! Get off my *back* will yer? (Break down and sob.)
- Madam, Bradman's the name. Read my lips — Bradman. D-o-n B-r-a-d-m-a-n!
- I'll answer that question in a moment. First tell *me* something. Do you always attend cricket dinners on roller skates, wearing a little pointed hat with a bell on it and dressed like Po Po the Puppet?]

*   *   *

NSW was playing a first-class game at the Newcastle Sports Ground. There was a large crowd in attendance and, as was the custom in Newcastle, the Blues had agreed to supply a player to sign autographs during specified hours. A chair would be placed on the walkway in front of the pavilion and the ground broadcaster would make an announcement. 'In five minutes, Mark Taylor (or Brad McNamara, or whoever) will be out to sign autographs.' Then out would come the player and the line would form on the right. This situation led to a moment that I will never forget.

In the chair signing autographs this particular day was hard-hitting NSW batsman Richard Chee Quee. 'Cheeks' wasn't an international but he was particularly popular with fans because of his swashbuckling batting style, his strong build, good-looking face and the fact that he was the only player in first-class cricket who was of Chinese origin. Thus the queue for the Chee Quee autograph appeared to stretch back past the town of Woy Woy. About 50 places from the front of the line stood a chubby little boy of Chinese extraction, about nine years of age, carrying a cricket bat. You did not have to be an expert in human nature to work out who happened to be the lad's favourite cricketer. I don't know how it started but I guess somebody in the grandstand must have noticed the little boy and pointed him out to the person next to them and so on. For by the time the chubby youngster was about 10 places away from his hero, the grandstand was abuzz with expectation. Nobody was watching the game; everyone was waiting for the moment when the little boy and the cricketer came together.

Gradually they got closer. Four to go. Three to go! At this stage, Chee Quee was oblivious to what was happening. He was only going through the motions: 'Thanks, mate' … 'Good luck, dear,' he kept saying as he signed away with all the enthusiasm of a worker on a production line who is suffering from a hangover. His eyes must have been aching and his fingers throbbing. 'Richard Chee Quee' would not be the longest autograph in the world to sign, but it's long enough, and by the look on his face this day, while sitting under the hot Newcastle sun, I reckon Cheeks was regretting the fact that his name was not Dean Jones or Reg Duff.

Two to go! One to go! Then a cheer went up, the likes of which had not been heard on the Newcastle Sports Ground since that wonderful day in 1946, when Newcastle beat Gus Risman's previously undefeated British rugby league team. Cheeks was about to sign the back of the bat when the crowd's roar broke through his trance. He blinked for a second, saw the boy and realised what had happened. Then Cheeks hoisted the boy up onto the chair and raised his small arm above his head, as if he were a referee in the boxing ring announcing the winner.

The crowd cheered again and light bulbs flashed. Hardened sports followers ran down the stairs to get a closer look. For a few inspiring moments the cricketer and the fan stood and posed for the people. At that moment in Newcastle it felt good to be an Australian!

FOUR

Blind Man's Bluff

I'm often asked who was the best batsman I've ever seen, the fastest bowler I've faced, the greatest allrounder, the best stumper, etc. However, I don't think I've ever been asked my opinion on the best umpire. To be truthful, I'm not sure what my answer would be if I was asked such a question. I guess, like most batsmen, I still continue to rage over all those 'wrong' decisions that went against me, just as I take as my inherent right those that were granted in my favour. I speak on occasions at umpires' dinners and hit them with the usual one-liners: 'Could somebody please tell me what's on the menu — unfortunately, I can't read Braille.' And: 'I didn't so much mind the ump giving me out lbw when I was four yards down the pitch, but I did object to his seeing-eye dog trotting over and piddling on my pads.' Yet deep in my heart I have a soft spot for umpires and have found that, on the whole, the umpiring fraternity is no different from any other group in society whose hearing is impaired, whose judgement is warped and whose dogs urinate in the wrong places.

Nevertheless, cricket lore is filled with stories about umpires and about the caustic confrontations that have occurred between them and players. There are some who say that such encounters should never happen; there is even talk of bringing in yellow and red cards for such unsporting behaviour. Admittedly, sometimes incidents that are not in keeping with the standards laid down by our forebears do occur, but I have been around the game for a long time and some of the funniest cricketing stories concern umpires. Let's hope that by acting the part of headmaster over what happens in the middle, cricket administrators don't inhibit the flair and fun that has been part of the game for so long. Show me players and umpires with a sense of humour and I'll give you a game that will be enjoyable and amusing, where after stumps are drawn, the drinks will flow and friendships will be established and cemented.

Allow me to reminisce and tell a few of these stories. Some I have experienced personally and others have been regurgitated over the years. There are so many good cricketing yarns floating around the world but you will never find them recorded in *Wisden*; alas — only statistics reside there. Thus the yarns are eventually forgotten. This is a pity, really, because when we first start playing we are taught that cricket is a team game to be enjoyed. We are not told to concentrate on making our batting average high. This comes later, and many of us pursue the task with vigour and purpose, but in the end we are at risk of forgetting the instructions we received when we started and thus in danger of missing the best part of the game.

There'll always be an umpire

In recent years, we Australians have been found guilty of speaking scathingly of English cricket and we never miss the opportunity of rubbing it in. It is true that in modern times, Aussies have been very successful in a number of sports and world champions in a few. Yet the sport in which we have held the gold medal longest — and will, I believe, continue to hold it for years to come — is the sport of 'gloating'. While in England last year, Herself and the writer were invited to lunch at a friend's home in the scenic rolling Chilterns area of Buckinghamshire. Over a cleansing stimulant the conversation turned to sport. Soon we were arguing about the ability of Michael Atherton. 'A dedicated and gutsy opening batsman, nothing more, is how I would describe him,' I stated pompously to my host.

My friend hit back. 'I believe that posterity will regard Atherton as one of England's great cricketers,' he countered.

Seeing an opportunity to slip in a 'gloat', I responded, 'The term you used — "England's great cricketers" — isn't that an oxymoron?'

My friend slumped back in his chair and had a large gulp of his alcoholic beverage. 'Gee you're tough, Marksy. You're always having a go at we poor old Poms.'

'Sorry, mate, I couldn't resist a chance for some Pommy-bashing. Forgive me, it's just an integral part of our Australian culture.'

My friend looked at me quizzically and replied. 'Australian culture? Isn't that an oxymoron?'

English cricket has its faults, but there is one facet of the game in which the Poms are way in front, and always have been … umpiring! In the main, the English umpires are not only competent but also funny.

The basic reasons given for the English being so proficient as judges of the first-class game is that (1) they are almost all former first-class players themselves and (2) they umpire every day of the week. As a matter of fact, they umpire so often that sometimes they want to 'get on their own bike' and go home. (In a county match a few years ago the No. 9 and No. 11 batsmen were hanging on desperately in the last hour of the game to salvage a draw. The No. 11 propped forward, was hit on the pad and there was raucous appeal, 'HOWERZAT?' Umpire Sam Cook looked at the batsman's leg, which was well outside the off stump, then quickly raised his finger. As he did so he said, 'Bad luck son, but I've got to catch the six o'clock train to Tetbury.')

I would give two other reasons for English umpires being the world's best: their professionalism and their humility. Watching

English umpires in county games is an interesting exercise. They go about their duties with the minimum of fuss. Spectators don't notice them until they have to make a decision, they dress differently from the players but without flair or fancy uniforms, and they give the impression that they are just an appendage to the game going on around them, not the centrepiece. (This is in direct contrast to their counterparts, British rugby referees, who seem to believe that 70,000 people turn up to watch *them* alone and that the teams are chosen simply to *play* rugby because none of the 30 players is intelligent or athletic enough to be a referee.)

English umpires never seem officious but they keep good control of the game; no doubt because the top international players regard them with respect. Yet such respect works both ways. Good umpires admire a great player, but can put that out of their minds when he is batting or bowling. Good umpires also treat captains with respect, but never with awe. Nor do they allow a captain's charisma and status to sway any on-field decisions. (The fine English umpire Arthur Jessup was once controlling a one-day county semi-final between Lancashire and Gloucestershire. Because of weather and a number of other hold-ups, the game dragged on well into the twilight, and as the clock headed towards 9pm the Lancashire captain walked up to Umpire Jessup and growled, 'Hell, it's getting dark, Arthur. What about going off for the light?'

Jessup pointed to the sky. 'You can see the moon, can't you?'

'Yes, of course,' answered the captain.

With a shrug of the shoulders, Jessup replied, 'How far do you want to see? Play on.')

When I speak of the expertise of English umpires, I speak of the first-class game only, not of the umpiring down the ranks. Over the years I have seen quite an amount of club and schoolboy cricket in England. Unlike the Australian system, where independent and qualified umpires are allotted to club cricket, the English way, in most cases, is to allow each club to provide its own umpire. This leads to many farcical situations and an occasional punch-up at the back of the grandstand. In

English club cricket, the definition of playing for strike is not to face the easier opposition bowler but to reach the end where the decisions are made by your *own umpire* — or to put it another way, to get away from *their* bloke.

There is a story told of two villages in Nottingham playing a grudge match against each other. While the game is progressing an Australian tourist stops his car, hops out and walks around the little ground, soaking up the village green atmosphere. By the time he returns to his car he has seen five wickets fall — all lbw.

The Aussie walks up to an elderly man sitting in a deck chair. 'Which team is batting?' he asks.

'Our village team,' said the man.

'They're not going so well,' remarks the Aussie. 'But to be honest, you've had a few rough lbws. Who is the umpire?'

'He belongs to the other team,' the villager answered in a resigned manner.

'Boy, he's quick with his finger.'

'The old man nodded in agreement and replied, 'Yes, he is that. As a matter of fact, I've heard it said that on a dicey wicket he can be almost unplayable.'

Take your pick and take your time

If modern umpires were to be seeded by ability, I guess that the Aussies would be rated second, if only because they don't have much to beat. Nonetheless, it would be true to say that there seem to be a number of other cricket nations who regard our white-coated custodians with the same confidence with which a canary regards a prowling cat. Meanwhile, umpires on the subcontinent have been improving. (While Venkat was close to the best in the world a few years ago, the others still have a long way to go). Aussie umps are now looked at with suspicion, but those from the subcontinent were once regarded with terror. (Former Australian wicketkeeper Brian Taber was once batting in India. He jumped down the wicket attempting to swat the ball over midwicket. He missed it by half a metre and was hit on the pads. The ball flew high in the air and the bowler followed through, dived and grabbed it before it hit the ground. There was a huge appeal from the Indian team and 40,000 voices in the stands. 'Out,' said the umpire emphatically.

Standing four yards down the wicket and knowing he didn't hit it, Taber asked, 'How was I out? Caught or lbw?'

The umpire, still with his finger in the air, replied, 'Take your pick, Mr Taber, take your pick.')

My favourite umpire at the moment is neither English nor Australian, it is the West Indian Steve Bucknor. Beneath the sunscreen, Steve Bucknor's relaxed and smiling countenance exudes a quiet air of confidence and expertise. He is undoubtedly the best West Indian umpire of the last decade and today one of the top three umps in the world. 'Unflappable' is the word often used to describe Steve. He moves around the grounds and stadiums of the world with a gait so laid-back and unhurried he could easily be mistaken for an undertaker on sabbatical.

A friend of mine recently described Steve Bucknor to me this way: 'I was at the Test match last week with a mate. About three o'clock I went to the toilet and while I was in there I heard a loud appeal for lbw. I then walked to the bar, bought a couple of beers and returned to where my mate was sitting. "What happened while I was away?" I asked, as I handed him his beer.

'"Not much," he replied. "Bucknor's still making up his mind on the lbw."'

Crazy decisions

There are some players who take little notice of umpires, regarding them merely as a necessary adjunct to the game, like the heavy roller or the ladies who make the afternoon tea. Others see umpires as the devil's disciples dressed in white coats, sent to Earth to spoil pleasant, sunny Saturdays. Some cricketers (mainly bowlers) go even further, imagining the umpire to be a dictatorial Prime Minister and seeing it as their duty to play the role of Leader of the Opposition.

One such player was Kevin 'Crazy' Cantwell, from the Petersham Club in Sydney.

Crazy Cantwell was a far better than average first-grade allrounder. He often opened both the batting and bowling for his club and was a member of the NSW Practice Squad. An excellent baseballer, Crazy was also chosen as catcher for the All-Australian baseball team. In his battle with umpires, what made Crazy a little different from most of his fellow umpire-baiters was that despite his being a stylish sledger of individual brilliance, there was always a touch of humour lurking just beneath the tough surface of the Cantwell personality, and a joke would often follow an expletive. On one occasion back in the 1960s, Northern District were playing Petersham. The 'Districts' had an express opening bowler named Bill 'Jingles' Jocelyn. When Jocelyn was on line he could be a handful for any opening bat, but there were times when Jingles was known to stray from the bowler's straight and narrow and when this was the case, the keeper would be made to cover more ground than a theodolite. This particular day, Jingles was bowling to Crazy and I don't think there was much love lost between the two. As ball after ball hurtled over the top of the batsman's skull or to first slip or leg gully, Cantwell kept calling, 'Hey, ump, that's a #&%#! wide.' The umpire remained unmoved. When the keeper took the next ball by diving outstretched to his left, Crazy feigned to move towards the pavilion. 'Can I be excused for a couple of minutes?' he asked.

'Where are you going, Kevin?' queried the ump.

Crazy replied, 'Well the only way I can reach this bugger's bowling is on my surfboard, so I'm going out to unstrap it from the roof-rack of my car.'

On another occasion, Crazy was bowling to my brother, Lynn. I was up at the bowler's end, where the umpire was a cheerful bloke named Fred Tilley. Lynn attempted to smash the ball into next month, missed and was hit on the back pad. 'Howzat!' screamed the bowler. In the manner of the era, Fred Tilley was bent over staring down the wicket, weighing up the options. Crazy spun around and growled, 'Well, put your finger up!'

The umpire remained motionless. 'Up what?' said Fred.

During Crazy's time in first-grade cricket there was an umpire named Jack Scarborough, who was proficient enough to umpire some first-class games. In the winter season, Jack was also a first-division soccer referee. Sydney soccer in the 1960s and '70s was comprised of many clubs of European background. Thus, when two politically or religiously opposed teams met, the tension was high — and this occurred somewhere in the city nearly every weekend. Fights would occur between opposing factions in the crowd and the referees often had to have police protection to get back to the safety of their rooms.

One such incident occurred at a suburban ground where punches flew, missiles were hurled and the police had to protect linesmen and referees. Apparently, Jack Scarborough was the referee on that day. Early in the next cricket season, Jack was umpiring a Petersham match and Crazy Cantwell was bowling from the end where Jack was standing. According to the Petersham captain, Clive Johnston, who told the story, the batsman got a thick edge to the ball and there was a loud appeal from all, led by Crazy. 'Not out,' said Jack Scarborough. Cantwell said nothing but walked back to bowl, shaking his head. At the end of the over, Crazy took his cap from the umpire and as he did he muttered, 'You know, Jack, you've just helped me understand why people throw bottles at you all bloody winter.' To his credit, Jack Scarborough walked away chortling.

The wisdom of Solomon

In grade cricket in Sydney there used to be an umpire named Cyril Solomon — known to everybody as 'Sol' or 'Old Sol'. Sol was one of the game's characters. He loved the theatre of a cricket match and wanted to be one of the lead players himself. In the early 1930s Sol was drawn to umpire the Balmain v St George game at Birchgrove Oval. Nothing unusual about that — just another game of grade cricket. WRONG! The fact of the matter was that Sol was umpiring and Bradman was batting for St

George. Nothing unusual about that — so Bradman is batting, so somebody has to umpire, so what? SO THIS! In the days leading up to the game, Sol had informed everybody who was willing to listen that he was going to give Bradman out lbw the first time he was hit on the pads. And everybody listened! An old player of the era told me that for the first time in the history of the city of Sydney, the Department of Transport had to double the number of trams to the suburb of Birchgrove, for just a humble club cricket match. The people poured in. Three hours later they crowded back onto the trams again, satisfied with a wonderful day's batting. Bradman had made a poultice of runs in under even time and not one ball had missed the middle of the bat — let alone hit the pads. 'He can bat, that little fellow,' said Sol to the press afterwards.

Sol umpired well into the 1950s and my first experience of him officiating was in a Green Shield (under 16) game when Northern District were playing Manly at Manly Oval. At the last moment the other umpire had called in sick, so the two team managers got together and agreed to ask my father, Alec (a former state player and a current State selector), who was there as a spectator, to perform the task. He agreed and the game began. The wicket turned out to be a sticky and after 20 minutes, Northern District were 4 for 17 and I was batting, with my father peering at me from a position down the wicket, 22 yards away. The bowler who was causing all the trouble was the Manly captain and future international, Peter Philpott. Bowling up the other end from Philpott was a lad who was quite fast but who had an elbow action which suggested that he would be far more at home pitching outcurves for the New York Yankees than bowling inswingers for Manly Green Shield team. My father picked up this fact quickly but as a 'guest' umpire he did not feel it his duty to call the boy for throwing — especially as on this nasty wicket the bowler had been causing the umpire's 12-year-old son great discomfort and bruising him in most of the bodily areas between his dandruff and tinea. So Alec Marks walked over to his fellow umpire and said quietly, 'Sol, I don't want to do anything about it, but keep your eye on the lad bowling at my end. He is a blatant no-baller.'

'I'll have a look at him,' said Sol and walked back to his position at square leg.

The next over, nothing happened, so Alec Marks just shrugged his shoulders and let the game continue. However, the first ball of the 'chucker's' next over there was a raucous yell from square leg, 'NO BALL!' The same call the next ball and the next, 'NO BALL!' Nothing happened for the next four balls, then 'NO BALL!' Eventually, the over finished and Sol turned and walked over to my father. 'You were right, Marksy,' he said, 'that bloke's dragging over by at least a yard and a half.'

A few years later I was playing in a Poidevin–Gray (under 21) match at Mosman Oval (since renamed Allan Border Oval) and fielding at square leg next to Sol. Apart from being the centre of attention, the thing Sol loved to do most on a cricket field was have a chat. So there he was, yapping away, talking to me about how much better the players of the 1930s were compared with the players of the present, when the batsman hit the ball through mid-off and ran three. I remember the shot well, because threes on the small Mosman ground are few and far between. As the batsmen raced up and down, Sol continued his nostalgic discourse on yesterday's players, taking no notice of what was happening in the game. As the ball was returned to the keeper, Sol stopped speaking, turned towards the scorers and put his fist up to his right shoulder. 'One short,' he called.

I shook my head and said, 'Gee, you're a bit tough, Sol! You were talking to me all the time they were running and you weren't watching the crease at all.'

Sol grinned as he replied, 'True, young Marksy, but that's just the time those sneaky batsmen try to put one over you. One short,' he called again, just in case the scorers had missed it the first time.

During the same season I was playing in another Poidevin–Gray game and again Sol was the umpire. I had struggled to about 15 before I was hit on the pad and there was an appeal. Sol's hand shot from his hip with a speed that would have made Wyatt Earp envious. 'You're out, young Marksy,' he called loudly, 'and about time. You didn't bat nearly as well as you did against North Sydney when I had you last season.' Sol was not only an umpire, he was also a critic.

A rocky decision

I must admit that although I always tried to play within the ethics of the game, there were one or two occasions when I showed a little anger at umpires. For instance, there was the time I was captaining the Northern District team at Waitara and the umpire was a good mate of mine named Rocky Harris. I was fielding at a short-cover when the Sutherland opener got the thickest of edges and the ball headed straight for our wicketkeeper, Vic Gray. It was hardly necessary, but I spun around and yelled, 'Howzat?' to the umpire. Rocky Harris hesitated for a minute and then shook his head.

'What?' I screamed.

'Not out,' said Rocky.

I continued with my tantrum, 'Bloody hell, Rocky, I knew you had trouble with your glaucoma but I didn't know that you were profoundly deaf as well.'

Rocky shook his head. 'Not out.'

'But he not only snicked the ball, he bloody well drove it.'

'I know he did.'

'Well, why didn't you give him out?

Rocky then moved from behind the stumps, stepped towards me and said, 'Harpo, let me explain to you one of the most important rules of cricket. For a batsman to be given out caught, the ball must be held in the hand, not dropped onto the ground. If you'd held back your appeal for a fraction of a second you would have seen that your keeper missed the catch.' I turned my head and saw Vic Gray standing with his hands on his hips staring guiltily at the ground. 'Er, er, I, er, sorry, Rocky, er, I didn't notice the finish, er, that is ... How's the light?'

That wasn't the end of the incident. Cricket being the game it is, some of my teammates wouldn't let me off the hook There were a couple of real stirrers in the team, great mates, named Billy North and 'Toot' Byron, who subtly kept the pot boiling. They didn't overdo it, just a little dig here and there. Comments like, 'Don't worry, Harpo, we'll give you a long session at the nets next week and we'll work on your appealing.' There were also remarks to the umpire: 'The trouble with your umpiring, Rocky, is that you're too technical. Fancy giving a batsman not out just because the keeper spills the catch!' For the rest of the day I kept shouting, 'Will you blokes pull your bloody heads in and shut up!' And between balls Vic Gray just stood with his hands on his hips and stared guiltily at the ground.

The game's the thing

Let's return for a moment to the man I believe was the best umpire I ever played under. Some cynics I have played with would say I have a choice between Tweedledum and Tweedledumber, but this is not fair. I have played under many umpires who were a lot better at umpiring than I ever was at batting. So after some consideration, I opt for George Borwick.

Firstly, George was a kindly man who was vastly experienced. He umpired Test cricket for a period of 16 years, including the Bodyline series, and he was steeped in the lore and the tradition of the game of cricket. When I was starting in grade cricket, George was ending his career, but even though George was then quite an elderly man, he still went about his job with profound efficiency and a minimum of fuss. Because of his name and record, George had an aura about him, a respect that had been earned. He also looked the part and what is even more important, he never gave me out when I wasn't. I do believe, however, that my opinion of George may be coloured a little by a story once told to me by my father.

The game was a minor representative match played on the now extinct Sydney Cricket Ground No. 2. I don't know the names of the teams involved but it could have been a Country v City game or a Possibles v Probables State selection trial or something of that ilk. Anyway, early in the afternoon, George was umpiring at the bowler's end while overhead the clouds were low and rain appeared to be only moments away. As the bowler ran in to deliver the ball, the heavens opened and the rain bucketed down on the Eastern Suburbs of Sydney. Lubricated by the rain, the ball slipped from the bowler's hand, becoming a rank long hop. In an effort to smash the ball into Kippax Lake 200 metres away, the batsman opened his shoulders and swung at the ball. Apparently, he hit the ball pretty well, but he connected with it 'on the up', which instead of causing it to go 'long', forced the ball 'high'. Up it sailed into the storm-blackened sky … underneath it was the man fielding at midwicket, waiting for it to start its descent. Cricket may be one of the world's great team games, but it was every man for himself that stormy day at the SCG No. 2. Batsmen, fielders and one umpire raced for the cover of the pavilion; the only two left on the field were the man at midwicket waiting for the ball to come down and George Borwick watching him. Eventually, the soaking fielder took the catch and he and George headed quickly for drier places.

The storm passed over in a matter of moments, and soon the players returned to the ground. As George was taking the sweater from the bowler, he heard some terse words coming from the other end. He looked up to see the fielding captain arguing with the batsman who had been caught at midwicket just before the interruption. 'Listen, mate, you've been caught out! Now clear off,' the skipper yelled.

The batsman smirked at the captain. 'There was no appeal,' he replied.

'We don't have to appeal when the batsman's caught off a skier.'

'Yes you do.'

'All right then,' said the captain and he turned to George. 'Howzat?' he asked.

'Not out,' said Umpire Borwick. Then George went on to explain. 'The laws of cricket say that a batsman cannot be given out if there is an appeal after a break in play. The stoppage for rain is defined as a break in play, therefore, technically, the batsman is not out.' The captain swore but George took no notice, though he turned and said something to the bowler.

The first ball bowled after the resumption was sent down to the 'technically not out' batsman. The ball was wide down the off side and the keeper had to dive across in front of first slip to gather it. The bowler then turned to George Borwick and asked softly, 'Howzat?'

'Out,' answered George.

The bemused batsman, whose bat had not gone within a rowing oar's length of the ball, stood his ground and called up the pitch to George. 'How was I out?'

George smiled as he answered, 'The scorebook will record that you were caught behind, but the *real* reason I gave you out is that you do not understand the true meaning of this great game and your recent action brought it into disrepute.'

I guess that is why George Borwick was the best umpire I ever played under. George always kept the concept of sportsmanship at the forefront of his mind and he never forgot the true meaning of those oft-quoted words — words that are now mostly considered a cliché, or even corny, yet which still have meaning for the honest sporting purist— 'It just isn't cricket.'

Umpires must be impartial and Egar

I was sitting at a Test match with former international umpire Lou Rowan recently. 'Lou, what do you think of the idea of appointing neutral umpires for every Test in the future?' I inquired.

Not a man to beat around the bush, Rowan replied, 'Bloody rubbish! It's an insult to every international umpire in the world.' Then he went on. 'Did you know that my good mate, Col Egar, and I, umpired 19 Tests together?'

I said I didn't know. 'Well we did. And not once was our impartiality ever questioned.'

'And neither it should be,' I replied indignantly.

Lou Rowan smiled broadly as he said, 'Mind you, there were times when people questioned Egar's competency.'

Umpiring is not that Tuff(ers)

Finally, let me tell one more story about an English umpire. Phil (Tuffers) Tufnell was bowling in a county game, and standing in that encounter was Test umpire Ray Julian. After Tuffers had measured out his run and handed his cap over, he said to Julian, 'Do you know, Ray, I only need one more victim to achieve 1000 wickets in first-class cricket.'

To which Julian replied, 'Well you've come to the right end, son — I only need two more for 3000 lbws.'

Umpires may be blind, deaf, inconsistent and pedantic, but they make you laugh.

FIVE

Easy as ABC

Television is our master, radio is our friend! Television is formal, radio laid back. In the case of sport, we often watch it on television with others; with radio we mostly do it on our own. (Think about it – does anybody ever say to you, 'Come over to my place and listen to the footy on the radio?') Television operates from a specific viewing point, but we just pick up our little 'trannie' and take it in the car, down the beach and from room to room. In the magical world of communication we live in, television is the wizard in his castle, while radio is the leprechaun on our shoulder.

In the days when I was growing up, radio *was* actually our master. Though in those times radio was more than a little pretentious. Some saw radio as an extension of the theatre, and fantasised that the audience was watching as well as listening. On the Sunday, 8pm, Lux Theatre, actors would perform in front of studio audiences. The ladies would wear evening dresses and pearls (in the winter months, fur coats as well), while the rugged male heroes would stand resplendent in dinner suits, reading lines from *Moby Dick*.

'Grab the tiller, Bosun.' ('Splash, splash' from the sound effects booth.) 'Here comes the huge monster again. Quick, give me the harpoon.' ('Splash, splash.')

We would listen, transfixed. Meanwhile, back at the studio, Captain Ahab and his gutsy crew would be reading into the microphone from typed scripts, their shirts immaculately starched, bow ties bristling and shoes so shiny that you could comb your hair in them. The closest they got to water was the studio bathroom.

This throwback to the mores of the Victorian age may be seen as ridiculous from our present perspective, but it gets even worse. Down at the ABC studios, the climactic event of the day's broadcasting was the 7 o'clock news. The names varied, but in front of the microphone there would always sit a man with voice mellifluous and accent Oxford. He would take the plum from his mouth, pop in a watermelon, and inform the Australian people of the news of the world in a tone so sombre that a communiqué about a gruesome murder was almost light relief. To add further to this attitude of gravity and pomposity, the newsreader would dress in a dinner suit, to deliver his austere tidings. The British Empire's influence on our land came from within as well as from without!

In today's broadcasting industry, sport is a big-money player. This was not always the case, but from the end of World War II, sport has evolved from a recreation to a profession; from a sideshow to the main event. Seventy years ago, cricket commentary really began it all and remains, still, an important part in the mega-business that is broadcasting. Cricket may no longer be the leading light in sport's broadcasting family, but it is still the wise old patriarch whose traditions are respected, initiatives emulated and ratings envied.

*   *   *

When we read of, or listen to, the history of Australian radio, there is always a chapter or segment on cricket's synthetic broadcasts (the describing of the game by means of radio telegrams). This was a pantomime; clever for its time, but a fake! Ball by ball description is what cricket broadcasting is all about. At its worst it is informative, at its best it is an art form. It began in England in the 1920s and has developed in reasonably ordered sequence to the modern day.

[Although I do recall hearing a reproduction of a BBC broadcast from the 1930s where the announcer was so far behind the play that it would have been quicker to let him read the telegrams: 'The bowler bowls.' (Pause — clunk of leather on willow, crowd applause — pause continues — somebody close to microphone clears his throat.) 'Woodfull hits it for a single.']

Let us skip over the early days of the stop-start call and the histrionic synthetics and go straight to the Golden Age of cricket broadcasting, which began in the mid to late 1940s. By that time, the war had destroyed half a world but it had been the cause of great improvements in science and technology, and radio was among the beneficiaries: microphone and receiver knowledge had improved enormously.

In Australia, despite an occasional incursion by a commercial station, the government-owned Australian Broadcasting Commission (ABC) was the prime broadcaster of first-class cricket. The same applied in Britain, where the BBC was always in control. Yet when the war ended and cricket was broadcast worldwide, the styles of the two cricket-playing nations' broadcasters remained quite different.

Most of the BBC cricket broadcasters seemed to be 'Oxbridge' graduates who worked full-time for the BBC and who, during an interruption for rain, you would expect to pop over to Westminster Abbey and comment on a coronation. Only John Arlott was different. He was part of the BBC's perfunctory effort to appear egalitarian: a way of placating those people of the British Isles who made themselves understood in the dialects of their great-grandparents. In other words, those who didn't speak 'posh'.

Arlott, though, was not just an example of early cricket tokenism. He was a most interesting character, a fine journalist, author, poet and a cricket connoisseur. He spoke with a distinctive, lilting West Country burr, which conjured up images of Farmer George, the village green and peaceful Somerset summers spent sipping cider. Arlott had a wonderful turn of phrase and could paint a word picture which was a form of poetry in itself ...

Umpire Bird signals a bye with the air of a weary stork ...

Gilmour bowls and Lloyd hits him high, way over midwicket for four — a stroke of a man knocking a thistle-top off with a walking stick.

You can sense the warmth of the applause for this young man [David Gower]. He's captured the enthusiasm of English crowds, looking almost frail with a half-sleeve shirt clinging closely to a not very substantial physique. He passes Boycott, who's got the helmet underneath his arm: like a knight at arms, alone and palely loitering.

Although the broadcasting style of Arlott may have been poetic, it was hardly exciting. He described the game quietly and accurately — John Arlott was there to inform, not to arouse. (He was broadcasting a county match where Viv Richards was batting and his commentary was characteristic of his style: 'Richards, on 94, faces the next delivery' ... pause ... 'and this stroke brings up his century.') Later in Arlott's career, the style of broadcasting in England moved from the Arlott, studied 'ball-by-ball' calling, to the informal, 'We have just received a delicious iced chocolate cake from a kind lady listener in Chorley Wood', conversational style of the Brian Johnston mould. Apparently, John Arlott detested Johnston's buffoonery. Cricket was a serious business and there was no place in it for iced chocolate cakes, nor indeed, for any kindly ladies from Chorley Wood.

[There is a famous cricket story told of John Arlott, cricket writer and wine critic for *The Times*, and the fabled Neville Cardus, cricket writer and music critic for the *Manchester Guardian* at lunch. 'You know, Neville,' remarked Arlott, 'I've got the best job in the world. I watch cricket all day and drink wine at night *and* I get well paid for it.'

Cardus looked at his friend for a moment and replied, 'You're wrong, John. *I've* got the best job in the world. I watch cricket all day and at night I sleep with sopranos — and as well as getting paid, I claim expenses.']

Meanwhile, back in Australia, the Golden Age of cricket broadcasting was well under way. Radio-cricket rode this non-competitive wave for about a decade and a half. During this time, television was just something that was 'coming', a type of Jules Verne prediction that was heading into our lives, though from far away. Radio was the medium of the masses and the man who towered head and shoulders above the others (and did so for the next 40 years) was Alan McGilvray.

In his early days on air, McGilvray was part of a triumvirate of famous cricket callers — the others being Vic Richardson and Arthur Gilligan. Richardson was a famous sportsman from Adelaide, who not only captained Australia at cricket but also captained South Australia at Australian Rules football, played baseball for South Australia and participated in top-grade lacrosse, tennis and basketball in Adelaide. To really top off Vic's career, he eventually became grandfather to three reasonable cricketers named Chappell. Gilligan was a former captain of England, an old-fashioned amateur and a lovely English gentleman. These three were to radio-cricket what Benaud & Co. are to television today. Their ratings were enormous and their sayings became part of our everyday language. You could be standing in a bar where a couple of regulars in blue singlets would be arguing about some sporting matter, when one of them would turn to a third and in a pseudo polished accent say, 'And what do you think, Arthur?'

One of the differences between the cricket broadcasters of the middle of the 20th century and the radio (and television) broadcasters of today, is that the latter don't drink during the day's play. Such microphone sobriety would have been seen as an intrusion into their working day by Vic, Arthur and Alan —

and also by John Arlott, who viewed alcoholic abstinence with the same delight as retail butchers regard vegetarians. Not that a little nip from time to time ever affected the performance of these great commentators. In all my years of listening, I have never heard a word used out of context or a phrase slurred. Mind you, during the afternoon sessions, the vowels were a little more rounded and the consonants more precise than they were before lunch — just in case!

Today the ABC is still the only provider of ball-by-ball commentary on radio and although there are sometimes complaints from listeners that regular programs are interrupted during the summer, radio-cricket still rates highly. (Over the years, some of the better ratings that early morning programs have received have been during the Ashes series in England. People go to sleep with the radio on the cricket and wake up next morning to the ABC Breakfast Program.) If the ABC wants to promote a new, or flagging program, they find the best time to do so is during cricket season, when more, and new, people are listening.

Cricket broadcasting is still an art and, like the game it describes, is ever changing. Eighty years after it first began, it is now also a part of our heritage; a friendly, informal, portable sound, with us wherever we are.

*   *   *

When Alan McGilvray (Mac) retired in 1985, Jim Maxwell had been on the scene for 12 years. In the broadcasting sense, Jim was an 'allrounder' — he was more than proficient at calling rugby and athletics, but his love and specialty was calling cricket. As a schoolboy, Jim had wanted to get into sports broadcasting, although it had been assumed by the Maxwell family that Jim would study law and go into his father's business. Jim's dad, Ian, had a law practice, specialising in probate matters; 'a dead business', as his son now describes it. But the call of calling was strong within young Maxwell. He auditioned a couple of times for a broadcasting job with the ABC and eventually was given the position. Jim is thankful that Bernie Kerr, then head of ABC Sports Broadcasting, took a liking to him. Kerr's encouragement helped Jim greatly in the formative years of his career and his advice about breathing while speaking into the microphone was invaluable to the apprentice caller.

In the early days, Jim made a point of listening: good broadcasters are good listeners! He listened to other callers, asked for suggestions and read diligently about his profession. One particularly pithy piece of advice that sunk deep into Jim's psyche was a comment made by the great Welsh rugby five-eighth, Cliff Morgan. (When he retired from football, Morgan took up broadcasting and eventually became head of BBC Sport.) Morgan said, 'Broadcasting is a privilege, not a right! A broadcaster's duty is to his audience, not to his ego.' This became Jim's motto for his broadcasting life and remains to him as relevant today as it was 30 years ago.

The man Jim listened to most of all was Alan McGilvray. When he was not on air, Jim would sit behind the great broadcaster and watch the game, noting the way Mac went about his job. He had a resonant, polished Australian voice, which helped listeners gain the impression that they were hearing a man in control of his craft. Mac brought much to broadcasting, but Jim noticed that his main strength was that he was in front of the game. For example, when Mac said, (1) 'Lillee runs past umpire Crafter and (2) bowls to Boycott', he was anticipating the fact. What was really happening was that (1) Lillee had *not* reached the umpire but was only halfway through his approach and (2) Lillee had *not* bowled the ball but had only just run past the umpire. Thus, Mac had an extra fraction of a second to lift his eyes and concentrate on Boycott. The important thing was not Lillee's approach to the crease but what happened when the ball reached Boycott.

Jim also noted that Mac accentuated likely happenings. In the Lillee/Boycott scenario, Mac would stress two things: the fact that the new ball was swinging around and the cordon of slips waiting for the edge. In this battle of the titans, Lillee would have slightly the upper hand, as he was fresh, the ball was new and he was a champion. Mac would therefore describe the game almost from the perspective of the bowler and the anticipation of wickets. The listener would become quickly involved, waiting each ball for a catch behind the wicket. If Boycott survived, began to accumulate runs and was facing Ray Bright, Mac would call from the batsman's angle. 'Boycott looks around the gaps in the field. He is showing the broadest of bats to Bright and is waiting for the chance to dispatch a loose one.' The listener was now anticipating Bright copping a bit of a hammering.

Jim Maxwell doesn't quite possess Alan McGilvray's dulcet tones, though he has a most pleasant and relaxed accent and an inflection which, even in the dullest of cricket moments, never comes close to being either monotonous or patronising. It is the voice of Australia's educated middle class. Though Jim's cricket broadcasting technique is the 'Maxwell style', it is based on much of Mac's method of 'getting involved yourself' and 'involving the listener'. To that, Jim has added his own brand of light humour; he has also broadened the language of the broadcast box to include colloquial cricket terms and onomatopoeic words. 'Gilchrist gets a short ball from Pollock and (punches/crunches, smashes/thrashes, carts/blasts, towers/powers) it eight rows back into the George Giffen Stand.'

Unless one of the commentators is lost in the cavernous wastes of the MCG or is having a fight with his wife and arrives late, each broadcasting segment lasts for 20 minutes. Thus, barring rain, a commentator will broadcast six segments a day. At some time in each segment, Jim endeavours to read right through the scoreboard of the day's play — it must be remembered that cricket listening is a switch on/switch off pastime and audiences are coming and going all day.

The other thing that Jim tells himself before each stint is, 'Remember who you're talking to.' A match between countries will be heard all round the world and most of the audience will be listening with a parochial ear. So while some 'trannies' are blasting away on the sands of Noosa and Maroubra, others are doing the same on the sands of Barbados and Cape Town. Jim has been broadcasting too long and is too professional to be anything but impartial, but he is always conscious of emphasising each team equally.

[Let us, for just a moment, take a look at the Maxwell style of broadcasting. The scene is a Test match in Johannesburg and Australia is on top of South Africa.

'The score is 5 for 555 ... Ntini rattles in from the golf course end, unwinds ... and Gilchrist *carves* him through ... no ... *over* point for four ... a searing, scorching stroke that would've torn the skin off Gibbs' hands at deep point if he'd got near it ... but he didn't, as Gilchrist found the gap with a cleanly airborne half-drive half-cut that powered away like an Exocet missile ... one bounce and then over the boundary ... that's Gilchrist's 13th four. He's 157 and Australia, going at eight an over, are now 559 ... Ntini doesn't know where to pitch the ball 'cause there is no such thing as a good length to Gilchrist in this devastating, explosive form ... Ntini tries again ... and ... *Gilchrist* ... pulls between mid-on and midwicket for yet another sizzling boundary ... we are seeing power aplenty today ... he just banged that ball away with a short, crisp pickup and a contemptuous wave of his bat ... what a shot, what an *innings* ... Gilchrist to 161 and Australia have smashed 110 since lunch in just an hour and a quarter ... it's 5 for 563.' (Cue for demoralised South African commentator to lament how well Gilchrist is batting and ask what poor old Ntini can do next.)]

*   *   *

Due mainly to the efforts of the Australian team, the way international cricket is played has changed over the past decade. To the Australians, attack is seen as the best means of defence and 'backing yourself' under all circumstances is the motto of the team and the players. In all his 30 years of broadcasting cricket, Jim has never seen a team as focused as the present Aussie group of players; nor has he ever found the game itself more attractive.

Transmitting cricket from all corners of the Earth is a fascinating experience for a broadcaster. To meet the wonderful people, share the laid-back lifestyle and watch the brilliant cricketers of the West Indies is a superb experience. For Jim, it was like having a holiday while working. Jim's trip there in 1984 is one of his happiest memories. It was actually the last hurrah for the cricket journalists from the afternoon press. (In the years to follow, Australia's afternoon papers were shut down and lost to the street corners of our cities, leaving newsboys without employment and fish shop owners without wrappings). The journos from these dailies could see the writing on the wall in the West Indies in 1984, so they made up then for the future tours they would never have. Jim, on his first tour of the Windies, was dragged along in the slipstream.

Broadcasting cricket from the beautiful, cosmopolitan, but sometimes dangerous African continent offered a huge contrast to the West Indies. As far as cricket broadcasting is concerned, the SABC is far more haphazard than the ABC. On his tour there in the early months of 2002, Jim often found he had an 'expert' broadcaster sitting beside him whom he hadn't even met. One particular day, Jim had former international Lee Irvine beside him. Irvine apparently took his appointment very seriously, and was so passionate with his comments on the South African team as a whole that he went on speaking about this as the play continued. For example: 'One of the problems with the South African team is [pause] — he bowls, pushed out to cover [end pause] — is that the batting order, etc, etc ... The bowling has also been disappointing [pause] — Oh, he snicks it! He could nearly have been caught at third slip [end pause] ... Getting back to the bowling, the new ball has failed to make an impact and, etc, etc.' Meanwhile, Jim sat back, gazing at the cloud formations and letting the rest of the world go by.

Nonetheless, Jim loved his time in South Africa. He remembers once playing golf in Johannesburg, with a local caddie as his guide around the course. When his caddie asked him what he did for a living, Jim replied that he spent most of the time behind a microphone. The caddie looked quizzical, so Jim explained, 'Well it's sort of my office.' On the first green, Jim had a winding 15-foot putt for a birdie. 'Aim six feet to the right,' said the caddie. Jim shook his head, and commented that it *couldn't* be that far. The caddie looked him directly in the eye and replied, 'Six foot, Boss, you're in my office now.'

The most fascinating place in the world to broadcast (though certainly not the easiest) is the Indian subcontinent. Here, broadcasting in often archaic conditions, with the crowd screaming, chanting and occasionally on the verge of rioting, a broadcaster's adrenalin never knocks off for lunch. Out in the centre, the wicket is spinning, the fielders are clustered around the bat and raucous appeals are the order of the day from 75,000 patriotic spectators. The dust and the smells add to the atmosphere and to make matters worse, it is almost an odds-on bet that the cricket authorities will have failed to link up the broadcasting line or haven't connected electricity to the box or won't let the broadcasters into the ground or … you name it, it will happen! On many occasions, Jim has had to resort to broadcasting from his mobile phone to get the description to the world. Yet being there among the most fanatical of cricket fans, in the hot, dusty mayhem, was an experience for which Jim will be ever thankful.

Somebody once said, 'England would be a better place if only they had put a roof on it.' Yet despite the weather, the slump in the standard of English cricket and the difficulty of negotiating the cones along the motorways, England remains a wonderful place to watch, and broadcast, cricket. And no matter how much we Aussies brag about ourselves and sledge the Poms, it is still the home of cricket and forever will be.

Jim has always been welcomed by the English broadcasters, though he believes he is only tolerated by the British audience as just another bloke from Bondi with a nasally twang, whose segment will be over in 20 minutes. Jim has great respect for the cricket broadcasters in England and he sees in former England bowler, Jonathan Agnew, a broadcaster with a great future. Agnew is a man who balances knowledge, practical experience and humour in his lucid and pleasant commentary style. [Jonathan Agnew! Isn't that a perfect name for a cricket commentator from the BBC?]

If there is a weakness in the British commentary box at the moment, Jim feels it is the fact that the commentators are talking about peripheral issues and failing (or afraid) to come to grips with the deep-seated problems that beset English cricket. So they applaud Australia, make remarks about being beaten by a better team and go on to the next season where, in all likelihood, the same thing will happen.

It's different in Australia, where Jim Maxwell is a popular (albeit self-effacing) personality on the Australian radio scene. Letters and e-mails from all over the land flow into Jim's office all year round. Just about all of these are positive, many offering suggestions. The general tenor of this correspondence is one of appreciation for the ABC product and for cricket in particular. Surprisingly, many of these people regard cricket not so much as a sport but as an old friend; their mate for the summer and often, nowadays, their companion for the cold and lonely winter nights.

So given that a recent survey found cricket Australia's most popular team sport, what category of person is your typical ABC radio listener? Jim is not sure of this. The obvious answer would be people who are keen on sport, but Jim says that if he were to take a line from those who correspond with the station and contact talkback radio, he reckons he could come up with some interesting classifications:

- A person over 60 who spends a lot of time at home. *She* regards cricket and the ABC as a partnership.
- People over 40 who knew radio-cricket before the advent of World Series Cricket.
- Men who watch television with the sound down and the radio on.
- Teenagers and 'young marrieds' on the beach, boating, picnics and the like. Not so much for the ball by ball but in the background, to keep up with the score.
- Farmers doing the harvesting in their large machines. Jim believes the ratings in this category would be 99 in every 100.

- During the last Ashes series in England, *all* those television viewers of sport who were disgusted by Channel Seven's decision not to televise the first session of play.

Jim has no doubt that there is a huge closet audience for cricket on radio. He is continually astonished at the people of all ages and walks of life (and both genders) who say that they listen to the cricket on radio. An example of this was when the Archives Department of the ABC realised that they did not have the recording of the last overs of the tense Test in 1997, between South Africa and Australia at Port Elizabeth — the one in which Ian Healy hit the six to win the series. Recently, during a cricket broadcast, Jim took a long chance and asked if anyone had recorded the last over of the game. Within minutes, a farmer from Colac in Victoria rang in and said that he had it, and that if the ABC would like the last two hours of the game, they could have that as well.

The formal manner of McGilvray and Gilligan has now given way to the more conversational style of the present: describe a ball and then cross to the 'expert' commentator. This seems to be popular with audiences, though it is probably more difficult than the older style — the teamwork and timing between the two commentators must be sharp and the verbal 'baton changing' precise.

During his years behind the microphone, Jim has worked with many 'experts'. He has liked just about all personally and enjoyed working with them, but his favourite was Jimmy Burke. Among others for whom he has a respect and affection are Norm O'Neill, Ian Brayshaw and Bob Massie. One of the expert commentator's jobs is to sum up the two hours of play at the end of each session. Jim is continually surprised at the ability of cricketers, with knowledge but no radio experience, to perform this task so proficiently, off the cuff. Two of the best 'summers-up' Jim has heard are Lindsay Hassett and Peter Roebuck.

Occasionally, Jim has worked beside other than ex-cricketers. Politicians, entertainers and people of other sporting persuasions have sometimes made guest appearances. John Howard and Bob Hawke have been in the broadcast box on a number of occasions. One particular incident that Jim well remembers was the time Prime Minister Bob Hawke was spending a few minutes describing a ball-by-ball segment of a Test match in Perth and happened to be on air when Merv Hughes claimed the third wicket of a hat trick. Bob was nearly as excited as Merv! Some cynics have said that luck played a big part in Hawke's premiership and that this was just another example. Maybe so, but it was certainly something that Malcolm Fraser and Paul Keating could never do!

In a career of broadcasting, a person would have to make a few mistakes and Jim has made his share. Such as the Test against England in Melbourne in 1982-83, when Australia were nine wickets down overnight, still needing 37 to win. Allan Border and Jeff Thomson were at the crease and, with the match (apparently) a forgone conclusion, the Australian Cricket Board opened the gates next morning and allowed the crowd in for nothing. However, Border is one the greatest fighters ever to pull on the baggy green, and nothing fazes Thommo. Gradually the score was whittled away and eventually the crowd had built up to 20,000. In the box, Jim could sense history in the making as he broadcast this potential boilover to his listeners in the following terms: 'Thomson drives at a half volley ... it hits the edge ... squirts between slip and gully ... and races down to the third-man boundary for ... *FOUR*!! Australia need 16 to win. Bay 13 is humming. My word, this large crowd, that has been allowed in for free, is certainly getting its money's worth.'

Even before the days of the great cricket barracker, Yabba, the crowd in the outer has been an integral part of Aussie cricket. One of Jim's favourite stories is about Merv Hughes and the bloke in front of the Scoreboard Bar in Adelaide.

Although Merv Hughes had bowled well that particular summer, he had done so without luck, and by the time the fifth Test, in Adelaide, arrived he had only taken one wicket since taking 13–217 in the second Test of the series, at the WACA in

Perth. After bowling his first over, Merv retired to the fine leg boundary at the Cathedral end and the mob were into him. One man in particular kept calling out, 'How many wickets have you got since Perth, Merv?' Merv completely ignored the question and went about his business in the outfield. However, this didn't discourage the questioner. 'How many wickets have you got since Perth, Merv?' Merv continued to bowl, without luck and without a wicket, and the insistent barracker continued the same call for the next three hours. Merv just pretended he wasn't there.

Getting close to tea, however, the question was becoming a bit slurred and scrambled (remember, the bloke was standing next to the Scoreboard Bar!). 'How got many wickets have ya since Merv, Perth?' By this time, the frustrated Merv Hughes had had enough, and with a deft flick of his wrist, both the pointer and index fingers went heavenward, in a gesture that Winston Churchill would have envied. The crowd close by cheered and Merv waved to them — that'll make the bloody stupid nuisance shut up! Then as the crowd grew silent and Merv turned back to concentrate on the game, his nemesis had the last word: 'Wrong answer, Merv — ya still only got one.'

Jim has never really considered 'going commercial'. Nor is he ambitious to work his way up the rungs of the ABC ladder. But once he did apply for a quite senior position in the Sporting Department, and it so happened that he was chosen as one of the final two applicants. He well remembers walking into the meeting room for his interview with the ABC's 'heavies'.

> *First Question (from 'heavies'):* Maxwell, if you were to be given this position, how would you go about handling your department's budget?
> *First Answer (from Maxwell):* I'd spend it first and worry about it later.
> *Further Questions:* Nil.

Jim Maxwell is a born broadcaster. Why would he want to do anything else? Horses for courses! With the ABC's 200 network stations, Jim has friends in the farthest reaches of this continent, most of whom he has never met. He travels to famous and exotic places throughout the world, watches the game he loves from the best seat in the house and discusses it with mates, while others listen in. All this and it's commercial free! On his days off, he can play golf with Test cricketers on some of the world's most famous golf courses. (He'll probably be hustled out of his money by the cricketers but no matter — he'll be treated as a VIP by the golf authorities.)

Jim has job satisfaction and is paid for it. Yet it is more than that. Jim Maxwell informs, performs and entertains, while always remaining true to his audience — never to his ego. If they were alive today, Neville Cardus and John Arlott would envy him and Cliff Morgan would be pleased. And what would Arthur think? I am not exactly sure, but my guess is that dear old Arthur Gilligan would be a little envious and more than a bit proud as well.

SIX

Parking Rites at Bushy Park

There is an old saying, 'If you want to be different — live in England.' To go even further, it could also be said, 'and to be even more different, play cricket'. Michael Welch does both.

Known to all as 'Welchy', this man *is* different! He is a person you can't quite stereotype, although in English cricket there may be still one or two others of this breed roaming wild and free around the cricket grounds of the land. He is a throwback to the *Age of the Amateur*, circa 'Percy Chapman' or early 'Ingleby-Mackenzie'. These days Welchy does not play the game himself; he is a cricket organiser, the man behind the scenes. Yet to say that Welchy is 'behind the scenes' is an inappropriate designation — like saying that Laurel was Hardy's assistant. For Welchy is not only in front of the scene, he is often the lead in the show.

It is not only in cricket and not only in England that Welchy is known and appreciated. In Australia he is loved. Welchy has contacts everywhere and can get you into places that the Prime

Minister would miss out on. (Once when in England, I was bemoaning the fact that I couldn't get tickets to a rugby international at Twickenham. It had been booked out for months and scalpers were buying tickets from scalpers. 'Leave it to me,' said Welchy. Next day he came to me with a long face. 'I got you two tickets, upstairs in the front seat of the Western Stand but it's about 10 seats from the halfway line. Terribly sorry, old fellow.' Amazed, I reached for my wallet, 'Oh no charge, no bloody charge,' he said.) Wherever you go, there's Welchy: at Epsom racecourse, sitting on the top deck of a parked bus near the winning post; in the committee room at Lord's, drinking a gin and tonic with the Chairman of Selectors and the Duke of Rutland; at Wimbledon, sitting with the girlfriend of the fifth seed; at the Melbourne Cricket Ground, in the Australian dressing-room, having a beer with the Australian team, most of whom are his mates and most of whom, over the years, he has helped.

Welchy speaks with the accent of an Old Etonian auditioning for the position of newsreader on the BBC. He is not being pretentious, it's just the way he speaks. His vocabulary is extensive but spiced with the vernacular of upper-crust England ('dear fellow'), though he uses 'mate', in the Australian sense, quite regularly. To Welchy, nobody has a first name. People are referred to by either their last name or their nickname. ('I say, Harpo, have you seen Wacky, Junior or Radford lately?' Interpreted, this means 'Neil, have you seen Warren Saunders, Mark Waugh or Bob Radford lately?') Nor is Welchy reticent about using the occasional expletive to make a point. This he does with the composure of an Oxford Don quoting Shakespearian sonnets. You could be sitting having high tea with Welchy, your elderly maiden aunt and the local Wesleyan parson when, in the course of a discussion about church architecture in Dorset, Welchy will drop a few purple profanities. To your surprise, the conversation will continue unabated and not a serviette will be ruffled. I guess Welchy pronounces the obscenities so beautifully that nobody ever takes offence.

Welchy looks typical of the friendly, laid-back, fun-loving Englishman that he is. He has a round, cherubic, smiling face, fair skin and light brown hair that flops uncontrollably over his forehead. You could not describe Welchy as 'good-looking'; 'attractive and charismatic' would be a more appropriate appellation. I'm not sure of my facts, but I suspect that Welchy wears a tie in the bath — why not, everywhere else he goes he wears one? The ties vary, but his favourite is one of the egg-and-bacon coloured MCC variety — knotted at an angle, pointing over the left shoulder. His coat is usually slightly crushed and loose fitting. Welchy dresses well enough to be admitted to any exclusive club in town, but it's always in an upper-class, dishevelled, British sort of way.

The passion of Welchy's life is cricket or, to be more precise, the Teddington Cricket Club. At Teddington CC he holds many portfolios. I don't know if the positions are official, but it seems Welchy is president, patron, treasurer, fundraiser, barman, selector, match organiser, social secretary and cleaner of one of England's best organised and most charming cricket clubs.

Just on the outskirts of Greater London, in a fertile area called the Thames Valley, lies Hampton Court, the former home of Henry VIII — a humble little abode of about 400 rooms and extensive gardens that must cover half a small county. Nestled in behind Hampton Court lies Bushy Park, one of those lovely recreational regions which abound in England, where elms and oaks grow thick and large and where deer graze, graceful, protected and pampered. Within this lovely park there is a special place set aside for cricket grounds, and these are rented out to the Teddington Cricket Club. Actually, Bushy Park is officially owned by Queen Elizabeth II, but those who use the facilities of the park do so for free — the Teddington Cricket Club pays only a nominal or 'peppercorn' rent each year. Nevertheless, I would imagine that in her usual thorough way, Her Majesty would make sure that everything is up to date and, come the end of the financial year, she would no doubt summon the Chancellor of the Exchequer and say, 'Hey Fred, has Welchy sent in his peppercorn yet?'

There are many young cricketers from Australia who owe Welchy a great debt. During the southern hemisphere's winter months, they come over and play for Teddington, in a club competition that is reasonably strong, and many of them have stayed at Welchy's place. For some of these youngsters, whose eyes are firmly fixed on a future in the game, it is their first taste of cricket under English conditions and some of Australia's best-known players owe much to the hospitality of the Teddington Cricket Club and the exceptional kindness of Michael Welch. The four Waugh brothers have all played at Teddington and the Australian XI have played on this lovely ground in Welchy's version of a cricket pro-am. Thus it is that Welchy has been adopted by Australia and is beloved by all who know him.

There are a thousand 'Welchy stories', but let me tell just one that sums up this happy, easygoing man who treats cricket as a game, opponents as friends and life as a gift to be enjoyed.

I was sitting with Welchy one beautiful spring day at the quaint White Swan Hotel, drinking lunch. The pub is wonderfully situated on the banks of the upper Thames, in the pretty Richmond area and as we consumed our pints and watched small craft cruise slowly by, I asked my friend a question that had often set me wondering. 'Tell me this, Welchy, why is it that you don't own a car?'

He grinned. 'I'll get us another pint and I'll tell you,' he replied. He returned with two glasses of that thick, dark, warm liquid that passes for beer in the thatched watering holes of the British Isles; a libation which, frankly, I believe should be drunk with the assistance of a knife and fork, while holding one's nose. My friend took a sip and in a subdued, almost melancholy, way he told me the following story:

'Well, I used to own a car once but it's gone now. Although I miss it every now and then, I guess I'm better without it.

'On Saturday morning I'd take it down to Bushy Park and set things up for the game and then sit back and watch the cricket. In the course of the day I'd have a few drinks and when stumps were drawn I'd go in and have a drink in our dressing-room to celebrate a win or drown the sorrows of a loss. Later we'd join our opponents and before you knew it, it was midnight. So I'd get a lift with somebody reasonably sober or call a cab.

'Next morning there would be a Sunday League game to be played, so I'd stagger down to watch, fully intending to take the car home that afternoon. Yet before I realised, the hours had flashed by and I was pissed again. So I'd leave my car in its place for another night and cadge a lift home or call another [expletive] cab.

'With my bloody hangover for company, I'd walk to work on Monday and get a cab down to Bushy Park late in the afternoon. On arrival, I'd notice a few of the boys standing in the bar having a "hair of the dog" from yesterday's celebrations — for all I knew, some of them had been there all night. "Come and join us, Welchy," they'd shout. Realising that I probably needed a "pick me up", I'd stroll over and attach myself to the group. Later, I'd somehow get home, take a couple of Panadol and get into bed. Then I'd remember that the bloody car was still down at the ground. "[Expletive]," I'd say as my head hit the pillow.

'Next morning I'd wake up determined that in the afternoon I'd get a taxi down to Bushy Park, hop out of the cab, jump into my car and take it straight home. But you know how things are, Harpo, when I'd arrive, there would be a few of the fellows having a net and I'd get out of my car and watch them. They would not play for long, because nets are hard work and cause a terrible thirst to develop, and I would get a thirst just bloody well watching them. So I'd join them at the bar. Three hours later — home in a cab!

'On Wednesday evening I'd go to the pub with some colleagues from work and by the time we'd finished I would be too tired to do anything but just go home.

'On Thursday, I'd go down for the club practice session and of course we'd adjourn to the bar when it finished and I'd get another cab home. At this stage my car had been standing at the ground for six bloody nights and was on first-name terms with most of the deer who live in the park.

'On Friday, I'd grab a cab at lunchtime. There would be nobody around, the bar would be closed and I'd hop into the car and drive it home.

'Early on Saturday morning I'd get into my car, drive down to the ground, set things up for the game and then have a heart-starter before the toss. Before I knew it, it was Thursday and the whole bloody thing had happened again.

'This occurred for two or three seasons. There was one year I filled the car up with petrol early in April and it was still three-quarters full by the middle of September. I spent more money on cabs than I spent on booze. So I sat down and thought of the alternatives.

'I could build a garage in Bushy Park, hire a chauffeur or stop drinking. Obviously the last option was unthinkable. Also, it seemed stupid to put a nearly new car into a type of "vehicle nursing home", plus the authorities would probably stop me building a garage in the Queen's parklands. Finally, I couldn't bloody well afford a chauffeur. Anyway, a chauffeur would have to be practically teetotal and who'd want to be driven around by a chap with whom you couldn't have a drink?

'So I sold the car. Not a hard decision really!'

SEVEN

Santa Claus is Coming to Slog

had just visited a client in the Sydney suburb of Epping, a suburb which, a quarter of a century ago, realtors inclined to hyperbole used to describe as 'leafy'. (Twenty-five years later, a more explicit one-word description would be 'concretey'.) The time was about 1pm and, after visiting a client, I was heading up the main street to grab a quick snack at a coffee lounge I knew. It was the month of December and Epping was in a Christmas mood, with bunting fluttering in the hot westerly wind and from a loud speaker provided, I guess, by the Epping Chamber of Commerce, came a rendering of *Good King Wenceslas*. I must admit, it made an incongruous scene. The traffic roared along the busy highway while the people in the street hurried forward 'in their rush and nervous haste', never deigning to make eye contact, let alone wish each other Merry Christmas. Meanwhile, the crackling carol played on, conjuring up visions of a wintry British evening with Dickensian urchins wailing at the top of their voices about some fellow (obviously on the dole) who was 'gath'ring winter fu-oo-el'. And here was I walking unenthusiastically through the streets of northwest Sydney while the Fahrenheit thermometer headed into the mid-90s and my shirt was just about ready to spring a leak from the area of the armpit. A far cry indeed from a cool and bright Bethlehem sky and a holy baby in a manger!

To throw another ingredient into this boisterous bouillabaisse of discord, I then saw Santa Claus coming towards me, ringing a bell and 'ho-ho-hoing' left and right to various uninterested citizens of Epping. Behind him, tugging at his rather tattered red ensemble, was a group of the *local* urchins — or what passes for urchins in the more stylish and salubrious suburbs of Sydney. As Santa came closer, I noticed that his garb was thick and heavy, and sweat was pouring down his face and disappearing into his stringy beard like an overflowing drainpipe in a hailstorm. The sun beat ferociously down on the Harbour City and I shuddered for the poor bloke. He must have been dressed by the sadistic commandant at the prisoner of war camp on the River Kwai. 'G'day Santa,' I said as I passed. 'I haven't been good this year, but if you could find it in your heart to forgive me, I'd like a bike and a Lego set.'

Santa began to 'ho ho' again, then did a double take and yelled, 'Marksy!'

I must admit that to be recognised by an icon like Santa Claus makes a meek and lowly fellow like myself feel somehow important. Mind you, I'd had brushes with fame before. Once I shook hands with our local Federal member of Parliament (whose name escapes me for the moment), and many years ago I was in the same room as Victorian left-hand slow bowler Ray Bright — though I never actually spoke to him. However, to have Santa Claus address me, in an informal way, was indeed the highlight of my day, so far.

'Marksy,' Santa repeated loudly. I must have looked a little bemused. Santa lowered his beard so that he could be identified, causing a gasp from a few of the urchins behind. I immediately recognised Santa as Jim Mathers Jnr, one of life's sporting characters and a former Northern District Cricket Club teammate of mine. 'What are you doing now?' he asked.

'I'm just going to grab a ...'

Santa/Mathers interrupted, 'Well, I'm dying of thirst. Let's go to the pub.' He laughed a laugh I recognised from cheerful days long past. 'The Epping Pub is just down the road and they serve a bloody good drop there,' he said. I mostly made a conscientious effort to desist from having a drink during my working hours, but this was different. You could feel the Christmas spirit in the Epping air (providing you looked particularly hard and had a fertile imagination). What's more, the day was hot, and I could see that unless he had a large liquid intake very soon, my red-garbed companion would soon wilt away and turn into a spot of perspiration on the pavement. Furthermore, it's not every day that a bloke receives an invitation to have a schooner with Santa! It was an offer I couldn't refuse.

*   *   *

Jimmy Mathers was typical of a few top-class sportsmen of his day — he was an allrounder. Nowadays, Australian sport has become a genuine career path for talented sportspeople, and lucrative amounts of money (varying from plenty to obscene) can be earned by those with talent. However, in gaining these riches, Aussie athletes have forsaken their all-round skills and concentrated on specialisation. In the past it was not uncommon for a great surfer in summer to be a household name at football in winter, or for a Sheffield Shield cricketer to also represent his state in tennis or football. Not so now. Whatever sport modern athletes choose becomes a 12-months-a-year religion and the altar at which they worship is the training ground.

It is perhaps going just a bit far to describe Jimmy Mathers as a 'great' allrounder, but he was 'very good', and as a team man, second to none. Jimmy played first-grade cricket as a wicketkeeper/batsman with the Northern District Club and first-grade rugby as five-eighth and centre for Eastwood. I once saw Jimmy marking that magnificent Wallaby centre, Trevor Allan, in a club match at Eastwood Oval and though Mathers didn't make any breaks, he held Allan in check for most of the game, which is something a host of famous players failed to do. Although he later played interstate rugby for Western Australia, Jimmy Mathers was probably a better cricketer than footballer. He was a thorough, no-nonsense wicketkeeper, without the flamboyant style of most of the keepers of his time. No flannelled *pas de deuxs* behind the stumps for Jimmy Mathers. He would just throw the ball back to the bowler and get on with the game. No ear-piercing appeals either, just a quiet 'Howzat, ump?' that was not much louder than a clearing of the throat.

Yet, in my mind's eye, when I think of Jimmy Mathers, I always see him at the batting crease. He was normally placed seven or eight in the batting order and if there was ever a better No. 8 in Sydney grade cricket, I can't name him. Jimmy played with the straightest of straight bats when the occasion demanded, but Jimmy rarely believed that the occasion demanded it. He was an exponent of the swashbuckling innings, a maker of glorious 30s and 40s. No matter what the situation, Jimmy would stride to the crease, take centre, look around the field, pull his left-hand batting glove up with his teeth and then drag his hand across his chest, looking for all the world as if he had wanted to genuflect but had slightly miscued. All the time he would be laughing. Well, not exactly laughing — sort of smiling aloud.

When Jimmy was in the groove, no bowler could contain him. I even saw him thrash the legendary Alan Davidson for a few overs (something that hadn't happened to 'Davo' since Len Hutton gave the game away). Jimmy wasn't orthodox in his batting, but neither was he crude. He also had two other things going for him: a great eye and a longstanding and passionate affair with Lady Luck. Like his wicketkeeping, Jimmy's batting was not flashy. If you saw him at the crease while you were driving past Waitara Oval, you'd never mistake him for Norm O'Neill. Yet he hit the ball with power and mostly in the middle of the bat. When he was on song, Jimmy loved to play his favourite shot and repeat it again and again. Let me tell you, this shot was definitely not from the MCC coaching manual. Then again, when has any reasonable Aussie batsman ever read the MCC coaching manual?

In cricket, it is not at all unusual for the side sitting in the pavilion to concentrate on other matters for a while: read the form guide, surreptitiously look at a mate's new girlfriend or engage in earnest conversation with the chairman of selectors. Not so when Jimmy Mathers was batting. His team watched every ball he faced and waited with growing anticipation for Jimmy to pull his signature shot from his locker of unorthodoxy. When he did, even jaded old pros would cheer and laugh. No matter the pace of the bowler, Jimmy would move onto the front foot, drop his back knee and, in a position of a lawn bowler about to bowl, sweep the ball just forward or just backward of midwicket. The closest thing to this shot in modern cricket is Steve Waugh's 'slog-sweep'. Yet whereas Waugh's stroke is played with the bat about three-quarters straight, Mathers' bat was exactly horizontal. Test opening bat Jim Burke used to call it 'The Mathers Hoick', though probably a 'slog-slog' was just as good a description.

Each time Jimmy played the shot and the ball crashed into the pickets, he would laugh and the bowler would fume. Yet he didn't laugh to tease the bowler in any nasty way. Jimmy used to laugh because he loved playing cricket and was happy to have hit a four. Upsetting the opposition was the furthest thing from Jimmy Mathers' mind. After all, he was going to be drinking with them after stumps were drawn and this session could go on for many hours. It would be stupid if there was to be any disharmony in this après-match celebration. Cricket was too good a game for all that nonsense!

The Mathers family is steeped in sport. Jimmy's son, Mick, played second row for the Wallabies and Jimmy's dad, Jim Snr, known as 'Old Jim', was one of Australia's most famous sporting writers. Old Jim was senior sporting journalist for the *Daily*

Mirror, his specialties cricket and rugby league. As Jimmy's batting could never be mistaken for Norm O'Neill's, neither could his father's journalism ever be confused with Neville Cardus'.

Through old Jim's pen flowed vitriol and his typewriter ribbon was made of arsenic and barbed wire. Mind you, Old Jim could write well if so inclined, but that wasn't the *Mirror's* policy. To criticise, carp, censure and condemn was the order of the day on the back pages of the *Mirror*. Not even the gods of sport could escape the verbal tirades of the paper's writers, and men such as Keith Miller and Clive Churchill copped it nearly as much as did every high-level administrator who ever sat down to a free lunch. In fact, Old Jim criticised everybody and everything — *except* the Northern District Cricket Club and (without mentioning his name) the Northern District wicketkeeper.

Sadly, the season after he was a most important cog in the first Northern District team to win a First Grade Premiership, Jimmy was dropped to second grade; an injustice, most people thought, but these things happen. Suddenly, the *Mirror* (courtesy of Old Jim Mathers' pen) painted the Northern District selectors as pariahs and the sporting public, who had previously taken as much notice of club cricket selections as they did of the Bullamakanka greyhound trials, was told of the foul deeds that were being perpetrated at the very heart of the country's national sport. Jimmy then moved to Perth to pursue his sporting career. Some years later, when he returned to Sydney and the Northern District club, Jimmy was brought back into the team and helped win another premiership. Old Jim was happy again and implied in his column that six to eight of the NSW Sheffield Shield team should be dropped and replaced by the young and enthusiastic Northern District youngsters. This, of course, didn't happen, but we continued to have a lot of fun and Jimmy continued to stoop down behind the stumps and kept laughing.

*   *   *

For some time, that hot afternoon, I stood at the bar of the Epping Hotel, eating a sandwich and drinking a beer with Santa. I had expected that, being in such illustrious company, I would at least be given a discount on my purchases — and perhaps a 'freebie' every now and then. However, publicans throughout our land are not known for either their generosity or their public relations. 'Want another, mate?' Mine Host asked Santa, offhandedly. (Mate?? Mate!! What sort of hard-hearted scoundrel would call Saint Nicholas 'mate'? It could well have been a relation of this short-changing beer-puller who owned the pub in Bethlehem and said to Joseph, 'No room here, mate, and get that smelly donkey out of my beer garden.')

Santa took no notice of the insult, kept talking of the great players of our era and ordered again. 'Two schooners of Tooth's New, thanks.' The publican scowlingly obliged. 'Bloody good drop they serve here,' Santa said.

Eventually we left the pub, shook hands and Santa picked up his bell. In the meantime, the Chamber of Commerce had given *Good King Wenceslas* the flick and had put a scratchy red-nosed reindeer in his place. The urchins began to regather. While his younger sister stood tentatively behind and his mother hovered in the background clutching a pram, a young lad, aged about seven, brazenly walked up to Santa and said, 'Hey, Santa, can I have a soccer ball for Christmas?'

'*Soccer* ball!' shouted Santa. 'You tell your old man that Santa doesn't deliver *soccer* balls. Santa only brings *rugby* balls to boys in Sydney.' Then he turned to the shy little girl, 'And what do you want, sweetie?'

'I don't know, Santa.'

'Well you tell your mummy that I'll bring you a doll. Is that your brother or sister in the pram?'

'My little brother.'

'Okay, I'm going to bring him a pair of wicketkeeping gloves for Christmas. And tell your old man that Santa said not to forget the inners.' I laughed. Santa 'ho hoed' a couple of times and rang the bell as I walked away.

Jimmy Mathers is now gone, as are many of my former teammates. The catches they made and runs they scored, now all but forgotten, are only numbers in fading old scorebooks stowed away in some cobwebbed basement. Cricket, though, is a game of statistics and sometimes these old books are taken out and the facts are pulled together and turned into club histories. But statistics don't reveal the unorthodoxy and the flair or explain the mistakes and the courage or show the disappointments and the pride — and with statistics you never hear the laughs.

*   *   *

Epping is now mutilated by a freeway and I haven't stopped there for years. It is just a place through which I drive to get somewhere else. Nor have I been to The Epping Hotel since that last drink with Santa Claus. Maybe I'll pop in one hot summer's day and down a cold one for old time's sake. They used to serve 'a bloody good drop' there. I suppose they still do!

EIGHT

Age Shall Not Weary Him

A few years ago I was sitting next to Bill Brown at the first day of a Test match in Sydney. As a former great opening batsman, he naturally wanted to see the early overs of the day, where the new ball swings past the edge of the bat and bounces at the throat and the tension is so apparent that you can touch it. A couple of overs went by, tense but without any noteworthy happening. Then without warning, Michael Slater wound up and launched himself into a cover drive that, but for the fence, would have travelled across the road, over Moore Park and through the doors of Sydney Boys' High School. As the crowd roared, Bill exclaimed, 'Good heavens! What time is it?'

Surprised, I replied, 'About 10 past 11.'

Shaking his head, Bill muttered, 'I am amazed. Surely this young man has been taught that, at the commencement of a Test match, an opener *never* plays a cover drive before lunch.'

Bill Brown should know. He toured England three times (1934, 1938, 1948), played 22 Tests for Australia and averaged just on 47. His greatest performance was to bat right through the innings in a Test at Lord's to make 206 not out. If you were to throw a party for the players who have scored 200 in a Test at Lord's, the venue need not be too vast. A large phone box would suffice — providing you placed the keg outside.

Since the death of Don Bradman, Bill Brown has moved to a rank he certainly didn't seek and doesn't covet — Australia's oldest living Test cricketer. Bill makes light of the position and laughs at the publicity it has engendered. Yet as Australia itself grows older, its traditions become more important and to be cricket's elder statesman is indeed a position of national importance and respect. There is no more respected man in sport than Bill Brown.

Unlike some, Bill will not be drawn into comparisons. When asked how he compares the 1948 side with Steve Waugh's 2001 team, Bill merely states that both teams were well balanced and had depth. 'All Australian teams are strong. Sometimes one comes along which is *very* strong.'

When talking about the game he loves, Bill Brown prefers to speak of his own era, not because he feels the players then were better than those of other eras, but because he believes he has a right to comment only on men he played with and against.

Earlier this year we sat over a cup of coffee as Bill, well spoken and erudite, reminisced about cricket, before and just after World War II. Bill Brown is a gentle man who talks of these halcyon days with understanding and kindness but always with a glint in his eye. His mind is agile, his affection for his time and his contemporaries obvious and just below the surface lies the Brown sense of humour, always ready to spring into action. This ageless cricketer smiles as he recalls the joys of yesterday and is thankful.

The subject is cricket. The time is yesterday. The words are Bill Brown's.

Best batsmen

Oh, Bradman of course. Nobody close. He was dynamic. He hit fours off balls that others couldn't snick. I was batting with him on a very nasty wicket against Farnes [England's fast bowler who was killed during the war]. I was ducking and weaving, playing and missing and really struggling. In a style exactly opposite to mine, Bradman was cutting and hooking when they were short and driving them through the covers as soon as they were pitched up. There was I, lucky to just survive, and he was murdering them.

I don't suppose you would describe Don and I as close mates. 'Braddles' didn't get too close to many. After the game he would go off to his room while most of us had our feet up in the vicinity of the bar. I remember though, during the war, when I was in Adelaide on leave from the air force, my wife, Barbara, came down to join me. Don and Jessie couldn't do enough for us.

In 1938, when Bradman achieved 1000 runs before the end of May, we threw in for some champagne to celebrate. On the train that evening, we all got stuck into the bubbly and Braddles joined us and had his share. I wouldn't say he was intoxicated but he had a whale of a time, as did we all.

Stan McCabe, in my opinion, was the most attractive batsman I've ever seen. He was always perfectly balanced and hit the ball with enormous power. To go with his skill as a cricketer, Stan was also a terrific bloke.

Len Hutton had the best defence of any player I've played against. I stood in the field at The Oval in 1938 while he made his world record score of 364. In 1948, when we played Surrey at The Oval, I took some of the team out to the spot where I was fielding for Hutton's innings. I pointed to the ground and said, 'I am most attached to this piece of turf. Ten years ago I stood here for three bloody days. So you blokes be careful how you tread on it.'

In 1948, Arthur Morris was magnificent. Probably the best bat in the world at the time. I was captain of Queensland when Arthur made his debut for NSW. In the first innings he scored a brilliant hundred. As the most experienced player and the captain of the Queensland side, I gave the team a lecture about the way they bowled against Morris. I told them that we had bowled too straight and this fact made it easy for him to work the ball both sides of the wicket. I went on to say that in the second innings we must concentrate on bowling on and outside off stump and restrict his range of strokes. The bowlers bowled exactly to plan. I was pleased. So was Arthur! He made another brilliant hundred in the second innings. So much for experienced captains!

I played in the game against an England XI in 1934 and Jack Hobbs opened the innings for them. He didn't play particularly well by his standards but what I saw showed me what a great bat he must have been. I was the youngest member of the Australian team, but for reasons known only to him, Jack took an interest in me and was very helpful. He was one of the most humble fellows I've met. He was a great man, as well as a great batsman.

Best captains

Bradman was the best on-field captain, Vic Richardson the best off the field. Bill Woodfull was a great all-round skipper, though more conservative than the other two, but he looked after each member of the team and never played favourites.

In South Africa, our team was a lot better than the home side, so the trip wasn't that hard on the field and was good fun off it. Vic Richardson made it a joy to travel and the team spirit was great. I remember our manager came down to Vic one morning at breakfast and said, 'Vic, Arthur Chipperfield is not well. He reckons he has the flu and can't play today.'

'What are his symptoms?' Vic asked.

The manager replied, 'Arthur says he feels nauseous, has a thumping headache, and every time he gets out of bed he feels dizzy.'

Turning back to his breakfast, Vic growled, 'You go back and tell Arthur that he's playing. I feel like that every morning!'

When I was selected as captain of the Australian team to tour New Zealand in 1946, a friend of mine said to me,

'Congratulations, Bill, but how do you think you'll handle Bill O'Reilly? He seems to be noted for his rather headstrong ideas'

I told my friend that *I* was the captain and I'd quickly tell Tiger what I thought. 'How will you do that?' asked my friend.

I explained that I'd be very firm and wouldn't mince words. 'As soon as I walk on the field, I'll stroll over to Tiger, look him directly in the eye and say, "Here's the ball, mate, take whichever end you like, set your own field and start bowling. When you reckon you've had enough, hand the ball back and I'll give somebody else a bowl until you're ready to go again."'

The '48 side

Well it has all been said, really. We were a well-balanced team, well led, and had some of the greatest batsmen and bowlers of all time. We had a good spirit. Most of us had been through a war and, after the game, we'd like to put our feet up and get close to the bar. The only thing I'd like to mention is that I believe Ernie Toshack has been underrated by cricket historians. Ernie fitted into Don's plans perfectly. He came on, kept it tight and picked up the occasional wicket. But most of all he plugged away while Ray [Lindwall], Keith [Miller] and Bill [Johnston] were rested. Yes, we were a good side.

Mankading

[During the Indian tour, in the summer of 1947, there was a minor furore caused when Bill Brown was run out by bowler Vinoo Mankad after he backed up too far at the bowler's end. The first incident occurred during the Australian XI match at the SCG. I was very young at the time but I was at the game and can recall the incident clearly. Bill was backing up, in a normal manner, when suddenly Mankad stopped and held the ball close to the stumps with Bill out of his ground. Bill scrambled back and nothing happened. A few balls later, Mankad stopped again, but this time removed the bails with Bill about a yard and a half out of his ground.

A few weeks later, while batting in the second Test in Sydney, Brown was warned again by Mankad. Déjà vu reared its ugly head and shortly after the warning, off went the bails with Bill again well out of his ground. However, this time Mankad didn't stop — he held on to the ball and ran the batsman out during the bowling action. (In baseball terms it would be called 'a baulk' by the pitcher). The media were quick to pounce on the incident and the headlines read, *Brown Mankaded*. The words *mankaded* and *mankading* are now part of cricket's lexicon.]

Oh yes, that caused a bit of a commotion. I was happy enough to turn and go in the Australian XI game but in the second Test Mankad ran me out at the completion of his action, which was different from the first time. I looked at umpire George Borwick. George didn't say anything, he just put his finger up. So off I went again.

The Australian and Indian teams were staying in different hotels in Sydney. That evening a few of our boys were in my room having a drink. I didn't want to hold a grudge, nor did I want any bad blood between the teams. One of the boys suggested that I give Mankad a ring and ask him round to join us for a drink. So I did.

The switchboard put me through to his room and he answered. I said, 'Vinoo, Bill Brown here. A few of the Aussie team are having a drink in my room. What about joining us?'

There was a pause and then he said, 'Oh, hello, Bill.' Another pause.

'Vinoo, there are no hard feelings on my part. Come over and have a drink.'

'Thank you, Bill, but no. You see, I don't drink.'

'That's okay, Vinoo, come and have a softy.'

'No, if you don't mind, Bill, I won't.' There was another pause and then he said, 'But Bill, about what happened today, I'll never do it again.'

There is a sequel to this story. I was batting in the fifth Test in Melbourne. I hadn't been in the best of form but I started to see them all right and had reached 99. Neil Harvey pushed the ball to point and called and there was a run in it. Yet when I was a couple of inches from the crease, I saw the bails fly. As I walked off, I looked up to see who the fielder was. It was little Vinoo Mankad. He had hit one stump from 35 yards out, side-on, and had run me out for 99. I guess I should have been backing up further.

Years later, I spoke to an Indian friend who was very close to Vinoo Mankad. He told me that Vinoo regretted what had occurred. He also mentioned that Vinoo went through the rest of his life detesting the term *mankading* and would become very upset when he heard the word. I'm sorry it haunted him. So far as I was concerned there really were no hard feelings.

Best bowlers

In my era, two stand out. Bill O'Reilly was the best bowler of my time, the best I've ever seen. One of my lovely memories is of the great battles that Bill had with the tough English left-hander, Maurice Leyland. Perhaps Tiger didn't bowl quite as well to left-handers. Ray Lindwall would be my second choice to O'Reilly. Clarrie Grimmett was also a wonderful bowler. I used to love to see him bowl to the Englishmen. He had a different plan for every batsman. For instance, he was low and quick to Hammond, but threw them up a lot higher and slower to Herbert Sutcliffe.

Room mates

I had some great fellows to room with; great characters. For part of the 1948 tour I roomed with Sid Barnes. Now *that* was an education! The room was full of stuff that Sid was selling as he travelled around England. Cricket gear galore, and just about everything else. I answered the phone once and the man at the other end said, 'Sid, I've decided to buy the crockery.'

One of my favourites was your father, Alec. We roomed together on a trip to Western Australia, in the train back and forth over the Nullarbor and in Perth itself. The trip must have lasted a month or so. We had a wonderful time together and became close mates.

The trip didn't start very well, however. The week before we left, we were both playing in a Shield game in Sydney. Our captain moved Alec Marks from cover point to extra cover and told Alec to push me around to mid-off. (Now let me explain — at that stage of my life I was an objectionable, swollen-headed young brat.) Alec jogged towards me at extra cover and said, 'Move to mid-off, Bill.'

I replied, 'I'm not moving. You're not the captain!' One word led to another and the next thing you know we were shaping up to each other in the middle of the famous SCG. Fortunately, keeper Hammy Love saw what was happening and dived in between us, otherwise we would both have probably been banned from the game for life.

You can imagine how Alec and I felt some weeks later when we saw we had been made 'roomies' for the long trip to WA. So we sat down and talked things over. Alec told me some home truths about myself and he was right. From then on, we got along like a house on fire and had great fun. When I look back, I realise that Alec had helped me.

[Not long before he died, my father told me of an incident that occurred during the trip across the Nullarbor. Each time the train stopped for water, my father would get out and go for a run. At one stop, he was running through the desert, about half a mile from the train when he heard the whistle blow and the train start to move off. Apparently, one of the NSW team had persuaded the driver to pretend that they were departing before schedule and therefore leaving Alec Marks to fend for himself out in the Never-Never. He broke the Olympic 800-metre record getting back on board. Nobody ever admitted to being the culprit. Dad roared with laughter as he recalled the incident and said, 'But I *know* who it was — Billy Brown!'

Nearly seven decades on, Bill denies any knowledge of the incident. And who am I to argue with an Australian icon?]

Best fieldsmen

The best fielder I played with was Ernie Bromley. He had a great pair of hands, was very quick over the ground and had an arm like a rifle. When Ernie had the ball, nobody wanted to take the bowler's stumps. Players would scatter for their lives because Ernie could put the ball right through you.

Harvey and Fingleton were great in the covers and Don Bradman was the best outfield I ever saw. Braddles had a fast and accurate arm and was responsible for many run outs, especially in his early days. Later, when he became captain, he moved to the infield to be closer to his bowlers and to have more control of the game. It worked, of course, but it was a great loss to our outfielding.

Favourite ground

Lord's. Though I'm not sure whether it was because I scored runs there or because it is the home of cricket. I guess probably the latter. It is a wonderful feeling to open the batting in a Test match there.

I also loved the Gabba for its wonderful wicket and fast outfield. It was my favourite Australian ground.

Allrounders

Oh, I suppose I'd have to say Keith [Miller]. He could do anything. A tremendous player. Arthur Chipperfield was also a fine allrounder. Arthur was very highly regarded by the players of his era.

Keepers

In my time, two stand out. Bertie [Oldfield] and Don [Tallon]. Bertie was neat, correct and great to watch. Still, I firmly believe that Don Tallon was the best of all. Up on the stumps, he was like a striking snake. He appeared to move his hands towards the ball and meet it on the way.

I remember captaining Queensland at the Gabba against South Australia. Bradman was batting on the Saturday afternoon and the ground was full. Medium pacer Geoff Cook was bowling and Tallon was standing up. The ball swung down the leg side and Braddles tried to glance and missed. For a brief instant he raised his toe and then dropped it back again. But in that instant Don Tallon took the bails off, in a superb piece of keeping. We all appealed and the umpire put his finger up. The crowd groaned. Then suddenly the umpire realised he had wrecked the day for thousands of people. So he changed his mind and, with his finger in the air, said, 'Not out.'

I walked over and inquired, 'Excuse me, umpire, is Mr Bradman out?' (We were very polite in those days.) The ump, now red in the face, answered, 'He is not out.' Strangely, as he said it, he still had his finger in the air. I walked back to my fielding position and the crowd was able to enjoy another Bradman century.

Status

I used to be well known because I played for Australia. When I retired, I slipped quietly back into obscurity. Then, unfortunately, my old skipper died and suddenly I'm well known again.

Fancy gaining kudos just because you're old!

NINE

Press-Box Allrounder

If thoroughbred horse racing is called 'The Sport of Kings', an epithet for cricket could well be, 'The Sport of Words'. For surely no other game in history has had so many articles, essays, poems, journals and books penned about it as has cricket. Cricket libraries abound and it is not uncommon for cricket books to top the bestselling lists in the non-fiction category. In fact, I've read a few cricketers' autobiographies that were obviously placed in the wrong category. They would have more correctly been classified in the 'Fiction Only' section. Famous writers such as Charles Dickens, Alfred Lord Tennyson, Arthur Conan Doyle and Banjo Paterson have all delved into cricket's fascinating lore and customs. (For the record, Alfred Tennyson's grandson, also a lord, captained England, although his exalted status depended on ancestry rather than ability. The press of the time was far more inclined to make mention of his poet grandpa than to wax poetic about his batting. To be frank, the young Lord

Tennyson's record was not one that would place him side by side with the game's immortals — or even the also-rans. Nevertheless, from all accounts, he enjoyed feminine companionship, looked the part, played as an amateur and made many a splendid after-dinner speech.)

As cricket progressed through the last two centuries, it spawned its own fine writers and journalists. These scribes developed from scribblers recording scores to artisans describing the beauty of the game. The latter group came into their own in the late 19th and early part of the 20th centuries. Soon after World War I, they were joined by others; in England, some of the great cricket writers were RC Robertson-Glasgow, John Arlott and of course Neville Cardus, the doyen of descriptive cricket writing. In Australia there were Jack Fingleton, Ray Robinson and Arthur Mailey, among others.

Yet the real historians of cricket are the working journalists, who season after season churn out the facts of each day's play and offer to those who are unable to attend cricket matches, and to subsequent generations, a word picture of events. In the era when I was playing, journalists such as Tom Goodman, Phil Tresidder, Keith Butler and Percy Beames brought to the readers well-written and incisive accounts of cricket matches. These men, and others of their ilk, were respected by the players and the public at large, while often being regarded with suspicion by insecure administrators.

Continuing this tradition, there are many fine cricket writers in Australia today. Despite the fact that the number of newspapers is declining and cricket is now a round-the-year industry, the print media remains an enormous influence on the game of cricket. Led by the knowledgeable and tenacious Phil Wilkins, the Australian corps of cricket journalists is, in the main, a very professional and committed group. Hard-hitting writers such as Malcolm Conn 'keep the bastards honest', while Greg Baum is a journalist of great flair and instinct. Peter Roebuck, a writer in the Cardusian mould, continually produces articles of exceptional quality and style. Though he recently became an Australian citizen, Roebuck is an Englishman who has a wonderful feel for the game of cricket, says what he thinks and remains unbiased. This is a combination not readily found in press boxes — nor in many other places in the cricket world. Though the faces in it now change more frequently than of yore, the Australian press box remains strong, as old stalwarts and ambitious youngsters, all with different approaches and different styles, continue serving the game and informing the public.

*   *   *

Then there is Mike Coward! The most travelled of all cricket journalists, Coward knows the sweeping grandeur of the game's mountaintops as well as the nooks and crannies of its controversial back lanes. He understands what lies behind the headlines and where the bodies are buried. Erudite and forthright, with a brilliant turn of phrase, Coward is the respected 'allrounder' of cricket journalism. He is a man of firm opinions and impressive ideas, and now, after nearly 40 years in cricket journalism, he sits comfortably at the top of his profession. In his four decades in the game, Mike has seen enormous changes; changes that the grand old men of cricket journalism could not possibly have imagined two generations ago, as they sat in the musty confines of their boxes and depicted the seemingly ever-unchanging rites of bat and ball.

When it comes to cricket, Mike Coward is a paradox. He regrets the passing of the old, yet welcomes the new. He loves cricket with a passion, but becomes angry with its inconsistencies and its mistreatment of its own. Mike revels in detail and analysis, and then, with a slight lift of his head, can gaze outward and see the big picture with the vision of a prophet.

Mike grew up in Adelaide in the 1950s. Adelaide then was hardly more than a very large country town. People knew each other and heroes lived close to those who revered them. The adage that Adelaide was more British than other cities probably had a germ of truth in it, and few places were more parochial, a trait that was part of Adelaide's charm. This 'Britishness', ironically, denied a hereditary sporting culture that had pervaded this pretty place for a century. With no surf worth talking about and water sports well down the pecking order, Adelaide was, per head of population, arguably the team-sport capital of the land. With parks and grounds second to none, sports such as Australian Football, cricket and tennis thrived. Suburban Adelaide was the embodiment of Australian life in the 1950s; a wonderful place for a boy to grow up and get around.

[Herself, who hails from the 'City of Chappells', continues to remind me that Adelaide was the town of free settlers — thus implying that my descendants were from the dregs of society, dressed in chains and given a stimulating dose of the cat o' nine tails every so often to keep their bodies tuned and souls refreshed. From anecdotal family history, I don't believe that any of my relations were convicts. If their progeny's predisposition for alcoholic beverages is any indication, they were more likely to have been members of the Rum Corps.]

In the days of his youth, Mike Coward rode his bike around Adelaide and enjoyed the normal pleasures of a suburban boy's childhood. In winter he marked and kicked, in summer he batted and bowled. Didn't every kid? Young Mike had two idols. The first was Les Favell, opening batsman and later captain of South Australia. 'Favelli', as he was known, was the personification of Australian cricket: a tough competitor with a swashbuckling blade and a heart of gold. Although one of the most respected cricketers in Australia, Favelli reckoned that God never created a bowler who could actually *bowl*. When a leg spinner came on, he would jump down the wicket singing 'Happy birthday to me' and proceed to hit the ball to places unguarded and far away. On one occasion, Favelli and his batting partner were walking onto the Adelaide Oval to open an innings. As is the custom, the opposition was warming up by throwing the new ball around, when the keeper misjudged a catch and the ball bounced over towards the incoming batsmen. In one movement, Favelli picked the ball up and slammed it backwards into the pavilion. As the fielding side watched aghast, Favelli said, 'It's in the George Giffen Stand, near that lady wearing the straw hat.'

Mike's other hero was the tough, yet genial, high-flying ruckman from Norwood, 'Big' Bill Wedding. Later in life, Mike got to know both his heroes. As he says, 'I idolised two men from afar. Then, later, I got to know them as friends and found them exactly as I had imagined. Neither of my idols had feet of clay.'

As a youngster, Mike watched Garfield Sobers play on the Adelaide Oval — so it was a case of starting at the top. To this day, he has not seen a cricketer who could better the cricketing genius from Barbados.

Mike Coward: *'Sobey' is the greatest cricketer I have ever seen. Yet when we talk of the past we must put things into historical perspective — in the context of the time. For example, Worrell did more than anybody for West Indian cricket and Allan Border may not be regarded as the best batsman or captain Australia has ever had but it is not going too far to see him as the saviour of Australian cricket.*

I am drawn to those who defy the odds. That's why I have enormous respect for 'AB'. He did not want the job but took it on and gave it his all. Australian cricket was in a turmoil and it was an emotional time. He went through personal pain, made all the more dramatic because of the constant failure of his team. It was as close as I've seen to an Australian captain having a nervous breakdown. If Australia had lost the Tied Test in Madras, Border would have resigned as skipper. When they called him 'Captain Grumpy' it offended me. Allan Border played 153 consecutive Tests, 93 of them as captain. Ian Chappell was a magnificent leader and his contribution to Australian cricket cannot be overestimated. Yet Allan Border did even more with far less resources. His courage was exemplary.

Greg Chappell was a wonderful player and an underrated captain. Some critics regarded him as a little harsh on his players. Greg was never harsh on those who did their best, he was only critical of those who abused their talent. Like AB, Greg Chappell would be classed as a champion. Yet they both had the work ethic of lesser players striving to make the top. They never took their talent for granted …

When he was a lad in primary school, Mike had the itch to become a journalist. He would spend a day at the cricket or football and then rush home to tap out his analysis of the game on an old Royal typewriter his mother kept in the back room. At school he would 'broadcast' playground games through a make-believe 'microphone', which was actually a broken torch. Mike got his broadcasting down to such a fine art that he would call games in which he was actually playing. During one football match, Mike was in full swing, playing his heart out for his team and also shouting a volley of words into the broken torch. 'The ball goes to Murphy, who kicks it to Coward. Coward takes a brilliant mark, weaves through the pack and lines up …' WHACK!!! The tough little ruck rover from fourth class had hit the broadcaster with a tackle that not only buried Mike in the dirt but buried the microphone through half his lip as well. Still, a few stitches in the lip couldn't stifle this young reporter! Mike's fate was sealed. His destiny was journalism.

There is an adage in the newspaper game: 'To learn the industry, a person should do one or more of three things: work for a news agency, work for a country paper, work for an afternoon daily.' Young Mike Coward began as a copyboy for *The News*, the afternoon paper in Adelaide. To work for *The News* as a copyboy was to fast-track experience. This was a place for the improviser, the jack of all trades and those who weren't afraid of getting their hands dirty. It wasn't long before the copyboy moved up a rung to cub reporter. Soon he was doing the rounds of the lesser news: court reports, club cricket and the wool sales. Oh those wool sales! Nightmares are made of this! Compared with wool sales, gazing out on a suburban cricket ground as the rain poured down was a dramatic event and covering the annual general meeting of the Angaston Branch of the Country Women's Association was a scoop.

It was at *The News* that Mike learned the sense of urgency that is part of a good journalist's make-up. These were the times of typewriters and carbon paper; the days of hard-nosed, hard-drinking reporters who, while typing, closed one eye to avoid the smoke from his cigarette and in the meantime dropped the ash all over his copy. It was the era when the newsboys jumped on and off buses and trams with the latest edition under their arms. ('Pa-yer, pa-yer, get ya last race pa-yer.') Mike recalls the time with nostalgia: 'It's easy now with mobile phones, faxes and emails. Yet we always got the copy through. They were great days!' Mike shakes his head. 'Days long before the cult of celebrity ...'

> **Mike Coward**: *In Britain and the United States they say, 'If you want to be somebody, be a sporting journalist.' In Australia, there seems to be a type of cultural cringe in regard to writers in sport. In spite of this, in my time in the profession there have been some superb practitioners of the art of sports journalism. I can name dozens, but let me just mention Brian Mossop and Peter McFarline, two of my favourites. Because we all wrote for morning papers, somebody dubbed us 'The Morning Mafia'.*
>
> *Players complement the profession of journalism — Adam Gilchrist is doing a terrific job with* The Australian. *However, the players must remember that they can't pick up large amounts of cash for writing and then turn on the press when they are justifiably criticised. This diminishes and devalues the profession that is earning money for them and their team mates. In this instance, their responsibility extends to our profession as well as to theirs and the game ...*

In his boyhood winters, Mike had played Australian football from dawn to dark, but in 1970 he took his biggest punt. Having left Adelaide to spend two years with *The Herald* in Melbourne, he then set off for Britain and Europe in the hope of getting a job and adding to his experience. He had little money and really no idea where to start, but he was armed with references from some highly regarded people in the industry. After a short time as a subeditor with *The Sun*, in London, he was appointed to a position as reporter for the news agency AAP.

The big break of Mike Coward's career came in 1972, when AAP assigned him to cover the 1972 Ashes tour of England. For an ambitious young cricket writer to be given such a break is tantamount to a 19-year-old interstate cricketer being rushed into the Australian XI.

[Nobody has ever doubted Mike's passion for the game of cricket. Yet if there is a fragility in his personality it would be the modicum of self-doubt he retains concerning his ability to write about the technicalities of the game. Such self-criticism is groundless. Nobody who ever lived has fully understood the game. Connoisseurs can be too technical, while others can look at it too simply. Cricket is a team game like no other, yet it is a game for specialists. Mike played nowhere near the top standard of cricket but this is counterbalanced by the fact that he has watched more cricket in more places than almost any person living. Furthermore, he understands the lore and ethos of cricket and he sees that big picture. I'll back such people, any day, against quasi coaches who rely on buzz words and catchphrases, and self-important selectors who sit round the table saying nothing, waiting to see which way the argument is heading and then jump on the bandwagon of the majority.]

The Ashes tour of 1972 was one of the most interesting and exciting ever. The series ended two all, with one draw. Moreover, it was the resurrection of cricket from the dull days of the 1960s. It was the start of the Chappell era — attack became the order of the day and Australia began to dominate again. For Mike Coward it was the real beginning of his career in cricket.

Mike was very insecure when he first walked into the press box in 1972. There, confidently pecking away on their portables, were 'the Royals' of the press box: Jack Fingleton and Richie Benaud from Australia, and 'Jim' Swanton and John Arlott from England. If Mike felt vulnerable when he saw Fingleton and Benaud, he had a feeling somewhere between veneration and apoplexy when he gazed on the celebrated countenance of John Arlott, journalist, poet, wine-taster and cricket broadcaster extraordinaire. For in Mike Coward's catalogue of heroes, John Arlott had been raised to the same level as Big Bill Wedding and Les Favell. (Mike is quite renowned for his John Arlott impersonation. Not that Mike is the only one. If, during John Arlott's lifetime, a promoter had held a 'John Arlott Impersonation Contest' and Arlott had entered it himself, the result would probably have caused a shock. It would not be unreasonable to suggest that Mike Coward would have come first, Bob Massie second and John Arlott third.)

The young journalist's insecurities were quickly laid to rest. The Royals of the press box all had the common touch and they welcomed Mike to their critics' castle. Richie Benaud was particularly helpful and John Arlott took Mike under his wing. No matter what else went wrong, this alone made the tour worth it.

Mike Coward: I have been lucky. I've seen matches that will be remembered as long as the game is played. The second Test at Lord's in 1972 was one of the greatest. This was a watershed in the history of Australian cricket, the beginning of our rise to the ascendancy. Massie took 16 wickets. Lillee bowled with searing pace and Greg Chappell made 131 — an innings, I believe, that was the best he ever played.

Then there were two last wicket partnerships. Firstly, between Border and Thomson against England in Melbourne. And the time when May and McDermott went within two runs of winning the Frank Worrell Trophy in Adelaide. Extraordinary games!

Australia's winning of the World Cup in Calcutta was another game that will live with me forever. In my opinion, however, the greatest game ever played would have to be the Tied Test in Madras in 1986. The game was played in the steamy cauldron of the MA Chidambaram Stadium. The excitement built up and in the end the game was almost unbearable to watch. It was here that Dean Jones played the greatest innings I ever witnessed. He made 210 in conditions in which others would drop with exhaustion just walking to the wicket. [Jones was later rushed to hospital and put on a drip to combat his dehydration.]

I remember a number of wonderful cameos. Lara's innings in Sydney. Shane Warne's coming of age in Colombo when, after Australia looked beaten, he came on late and cleaned up the Sri Lanka middle order and tail and saved us from humiliation. Steve Waugh's innings of 200 in Jamaica, when he took on Curtly Ambrose and Courtney Walsh, was another superb knock. That innings was another turning point in Australian cricket …

In 1972, as the apprentice of the press corps, Mike was concerned about the attitude of the players towards him. Again, his worries were unfounded. The captain, Ian Chappell, often invited Mike into the Aussie room for drinks and a yarn. As is not uncommon with Australian cricket teams, the definition of 'drinks' was not a little nip of sherry before they left for their lodgings. Three hours after stumps were drawn, it was customary to find the members of the team still with their fists around a bottle or a can, having a singalong. On occasions, the booming baritone voice of Mike Coward would lead the chorus.

Mike was in Europe for three years. For the young journalist, this was an experience that money couldn't buy. He was there at the Munich Olympics with its magnificent sporting spectacle and its cataclysmic ordeal of massacre and suffering. He was also sent by AAP to cover the Kangaroos' rugby league tour of France. As Mike was a fanatical follower of Aussie Rules, this was tantamount to having an atheist stand in the Cathedral pulpit every Sunday to give a sermon. To overcome his lack of knowledge of rugby league, Mike leant on 'opposition' journalists such as the *Daily Telegraph*'s Ian Heads. Mike could not have found a more principled journalist, a better teacher or a more dependable friend.

Heads remembers the trip to France with much pleasure. 'Mike Coward was a great companion, a wonderful bloke who enlivened our group. He has a fine baritone voice and often,

Mike, the late Ernie Christensen (from *The Sun* newspaper), Bill Mordey (from the *Daily Mirror*) and I would go to a restaurant for dinner. We'd have a few drinks and Ernie would talk Mike into entertaining the diners. To the surprise of management and patrons, suddenly this big man would walk up the front and belt out *The Impossible Dream* or *If I Were A Rich Man*, in English. Then off he'd go on his Gene Pitney impersonation. I reckon Mike toured the circuit of Parisian cafés that season with a medley of his hits.'

These days Mike watches only the 'big occasion games' of rugby league and admits to having 'no feel for the game'. He believes that 'you care passionately only about the games on which you are breastfed'. In Mike's case, these games were, of course, cricket and Aussie Rules.

These were great sporting years for Mike and he now sees them as 'the break of his life'. As well as cricket and rugby league, he covered golf's Eisenhower Cup and the fight between Australia's Johnny Famechon and Vincenti Saldivar of Mexico. (Mike was not a boxing fan and had only been to the fights once before, but with a confidence that only comes from youth, he performed his task with aplomb and nobody seemed to complain.) Also, it was a great thrill to cover two Wimbledon tournaments. To make it even better, in 1971, the Men's Final was won by John Newcombe and the Women's Final by Evonne Goolagong. Mike could not believe his luck! Outside the courts there were Aussies begging for tickets from scalpers and here was a young journalist, still wet behind the ears, strolling into the holy of holies, sitting in the best seat in the house and rubbing shoulders with immortals. Mind you, the strawberries and cream were a bit overrated.

It was a time he would never forget, but Mike's ambition was to be an Australian journalist, and for that to happen he had to return to his homeland. So in 1973, after three years overseas, Mike returned to Adelaide to take up the position as a cricket/football correspondent for the only Adelaide broadsheet and morning paper, *The Advertiser*. At *The Advertiser*, Mike played second fiddle to Keith Butler, one of the most highly respected men in the trade. A few years earlier, at *The News*, he had worked with another outstanding reporter in Lawrie Jervis, whom Mike today refers to as his 'mentor'. From such people the enthusiastic young Coward was given a hands-on education, as he was instilled with the discipline of journalism and a respect for the craft and those in it. The best advice he ever received, he says, was given to him by Lawrie Jervis: 'Son, be a journalist before you become a sports writer.'

Mike achieved his ambition in quick time. In cricket, particularly, he felt he became not just a reporter but a participant on the periphery. If not exactly a mover and shaker in the national game, Coward was at least a close observer of cricket's glorious uncertainty and occasional ignominious skullduggery.

John Arlott used to say, 'Cricket is a microcosm of society.' The 1970s was an agitated decade in the history of the world; it was also one of cricket's most turbulent times. Mike believes it was the beginning of the period when cricket's very gradual rate of change quickened. 'The game leapfrogged over the rest of the 20th century and landed feet first in the next century.'

Over the next 30 years, Mike toured the world watching cricket matches. In the 1980s he moved to Melbourne, to work at *The Age*, and then to Sydney, where he became the chief cricket writer for the *Sydney Morning Herald* and later cricket commentator for *The Australian*. His insights into the game were respected and noted by players and 'the powers that be' alike. During this time, Mike began an emotional liaison with the Indian subcontinent, a place he loves dearly. (His book *Cricket Beyond the Bazaar* is a superb work, combining cricket with a commentary on the culture and customs of a continent that is home to over a billion people.) Mike was one of the first in the old cricket establishment to realise that in the 21st century, the power, money and influence would come from this area.

Mike Coward: *We have to get away from Old World thinking and start understanding New World rationale. Cricket in the* subcontinent is huge. *The money coming from advertising and television rights for the World Cricket Cup alone is enormous. Within a generation the South African team will have a majority of black players. Soccer is still the sport of the indigenous people on the African continent but cricket is moving forward. It is held back a bit by the parents and grandparents of kids who see cricket (and rugby) as the sport of their former oppressors. Also, all you need for soccer is a pair of shorts and something to kick. And I guess you don't even need a pair of shorts …*

English cricket doesn't know where it is or where it is going. The English are being left behind. In the days of colonial expansion they built up their territories and took the game of cricket with them. Now the Raj and government from Westminster have disappeared. Yet the irony of it all is that the game of Empire has outlasted the Empire.

Cricket is part of Australia's identity. It used to be part of England's. Unfortunately, in the new century, I'm not sure that this is so …

Today's newspapers are diminishing in number, and they are also changing, quite significantly — television, with its all-encompassing eye and 10-second 'grabs', is seeing to that. The old 'ball by ball' journalism has been diminished (and not just in cricket), to be replaced by more contemplative and vigorous pieces. In one matter, though, I disagree with Mike. I've never felt the existence of a 'cultural cringe', either within the journalistic ranks or from the Australian readership. In the main, Australian cricket journalists are reliable, perceptive and proud. Their writing is entertaining, and on occasions rises to the rank of classical prose.

Mike has become an integral part of the game he has known for nearly four decades. This fact must surely make discerning cricket fans wonder why the governing authorities of cricket (such as the ACB and the toothless ICC) don't make more use of journalists such as Coward, Wilkins and Conn. Such people should be regarded as adjuncts to cricket's administration, not as the enemy at the gates or mere kite-flyers for some ambitious official's devious agenda. There is a wisdom in the press box that should be utilised, a resource that should be tapped.

Cricket, with its faults and virtues, seems, somehow, to bring the best out of many diverse types. As long as this continues and the game produces influential people with the ability, integrity and, most importantly, the passion of Mike Coward, it will rest in safe hands — and the sound of leather on willow will remain the intrinsic background music to each Australian summer.

TEN

Playing by The Book

ricket is a sport of statistics. It's a numbers game and a game of numbers. Football, in all its various guises, is war as sport. The release of man's animal instinct, within certain ordered rules, created the sport of boxing. Golf is nature and sport cohabiting. Yet cricket is a sport like no other. It is a game of mathematics played over 22 yards.

Grab one of the many books on cricket statistics and, if you are so inclined, you will learn which two batsmen hold the eighth-wicket record for Queensland against Victoria at the Gabba. (If the book is any good it will also tell you from whom the present holders took the record and thus achieved their enduring fame.)

When I was a little kid in infants' school, my father was captain of the Randwick Cricket Club, and the man who kept the book for the first-grade team was the Bradman of Australian scorers, Dave Sherwood. Dave would later became scorer and baggage man for a number of Australian teams on Ashes tours to England. As an eight-year-old, my life revolved completely around sport and although my ambition was to represent Australia, I don't believe that I ever harboured even the mildest desire to represent my country at scoring. Nevertheless, I spent many happy and interesting hours at grade games, sitting next to Dave and watching him at work. He was a champion in his field.

One Christmas, Santa Claus brought me a scorebook. It was a big green book, about the size of the morning broadsheet, and inside was leaf after leaf, all of the same content and design. A few days later, I took it out to the SCG and, before the game, went up to the scorers' box to show it to Dave, who was the main scorer for the Shield match being played there that day. He told me how lucky I was and gave me a few pointers on the art of scoring and how to look after a scorebook. Then I went back to my seat, took out three pens (blue, green and red) and settled down for a day of concentration and statistics. After five overs I was bored witless. I shoved the book under the seat and just watched the cricket. That evening I took the book home and never opened it again. From that day on, I never trusted Santa.

Twelve years later, I was playing for NSW against England. I had batted adequately and made a reasonable score. I was sitting having a post-match beer with one of my teammates when Dave came in. 'I thought you might like this, pal,' he said and handed me a diagram of the shots I had played during my innings (a 'wagon wheel', as it is now described).

I don't know where the old scorebook is now and the wagon wheel has long gone to the recycling bin for, unlike some, I don't go in for memorabilia, even when it concerns me. Yet four and a half decades later I still remember that moment, the look on Dave's face and the words, 'I thought you might like this, pal.' I guess he remembered the old days.

Dave Sherwood departed from us many years ago, but the tradition of Sherwood, Bill Ferguson (Fergie) and other dedicated scorers remains. The computer has come to scoring and wagon wheels are now on television. Yet one of the biggest changes of all is that a gentle type of affirmative action has come to scoring. There are many women now wielding the pens and driving the wagon wheels. What's more, the old green scorebooks have disappeared forever — which is a damned good thing, I say!

*   *   *

In her career as a scorer, Merilyn Slarke received a flying start. At the age of 15, after one game as scorer for the Hawkesbury Cricket Club third-grade team, she was promoted to scoring for the first-grade team. If the same thing happened to a young batsman, the pundits would be proclaiming the advent of a child prodigy — a new Harvey or Waugh emerging from the cricket club at the foot of the Blue Mountains. In a way, such a comparison is not out of place, for in her own field, Merilyn *was* a prodigy, a star on the horizon of cricket's complicated science of statistics, a shy but extremely talented young kid headed for the top — a new Dave Sherwood!

Merilyn had cricket in her blood. Her father, Owen Earle, was a keen player of the game and her grandfather, Snowy Smith, was a renowned cricketer in the area. Once, playing at Richmond Oval, which is set in the middle of the pretty Hawkesbury River town of Richmond, Snowy hit a ball from the wicket, over the trees, over the road and onto the railway lines. A thump that would have challenged Adam Gilchrist or even Keith Miller in his prime. Merilyn's brother Bruce played cricket all his life and represented Hawkesbury in first grade for a number of years. At family get-togethers cricket was a dominant topic and, as happens in many families, the girls couldn't help but become interested.

Actually, Merilyn started scoring long before she reached her teens. Bruce Earle and his mate Dave used to play backyard cricket against each other and as is normal between young 'backyarders', there were the usual doubtful decisions and disputed scores.

'Don't be stupid. You haven't won yet. I got 48 and you're only 46!'

'That last shot didn't reach the jacaranda tree, so it wasn't a four. You're cheatin'.'

So to bring a semblance of fairness to the contest, the boys called in Bruce's little sister to adjudicate. They also made her

scorer. Mind you, they didn't ask her to play or be an umpire —
c'mon! She was a girl! You can't ask girls to enter into a serious
'knock 'em down drag 'em out' contest like backyard cricket.
Anyway, she should feel honoured to score! So Merilyn became
scorer. (Don't you feel sorry for girls who don't have big brothers?)

A few years later, Bruce Earle was chosen to play for the NSW
under 16 team in a tournament in Melbourne. The scorer for the
team was Kim Stephens, a 19-year-old scorer in local district
matches. Kim was going on her own, so the team management
asked 13-year-old Merilyn if she would like to accompany Kim as
companion, roommate and deputy scorer. Merilyn didn't have to
score, but by the end of the tournament she realised that she had
fallen head over heels in love with the game of cricket.

From then on cricket became a passion with Merilyn and she
knew that for the foreseeable future she wanted to be associated
with the game in some form or other. She found the outlet for
her passion in a scorebook.

A couple of years later, she attended a Debutante ball and
remembers the embarrassment when the invitees were
announced. (You know the sort of thing: 'I am pleased to present
Ms Vera Splunge, who on leaving school wishes to become a
world-renowned journalist, climb Everest and raise albino
goldfish.') When it came to Merilyn's turn, the announcer called,
'Ms Merilyn Earle, whose ambitions are to obtain a degree of
Bachelor of Business and be scorer for the Australian cricket
team.' Everybody laughed. Yet by the age of 26, Merilyn had
achieved the second part of her ambition — and to the best of
my knowledge Vera Splunge has not yet even begun the long
climb up her mountain, nor does she own a goldfish bowl.

Now, at 31 years of age, Merilyn has achieved most of her
ambitions in cricket and her passion for the game has not waned.

*   *   *

Merilyn Slarke looks out from the scorers' window through large,
attractive eyes. She is slim and blond, with pretty 'girl next door'

looks and a smile that lights up the room. She is now more confident of herself and the future, and though 'conceit' is a word that could never be associated with Merilyn, she realises that she is respected in her field. She is not afraid to speak her mind and her early shyness has been replaced by a polite and gentle assurance.

It really all began in her first first-grade game. Though this was the beginning of Merilyn's cricket life, it happened to be the last game of the 1985–86 season. Merilyn slept fitfully the night before and when eventually she did drop off, she kept having a dream. In the dream — more a nightmare, really — she was sitting at the scorers' table trying to watch the match, but somehow she was down in a ditch and couldn't see the game. No matter how much she struggled to look over the top of the ditch, she just couldn't. So runs were being made and wickets were falling but the scorer couldn't record them.

The game was played against Western Suburbs at Benson's Lane (Hawkesbury's home ground, known colloquially as 'Benson's'). Conditions for scorers have recently improved in Sydney grade cricket, although they started from a low base. Fifteen years ago things were very archaic indeed and there were some ovals in the competition which even Burke and Wills would have considered too torrid a place to take a scorebook and pencil. For this particular game the scorers were sitting in the open, between a couple of rusty 44 gallon drums. A wooden plank had been placed across the gap between the drums to create their 'table'. The sun was beating down and though Benson's is a well-cared for and attractive ground, it was once a dairy. When the weather is good Benson's is an enjoyable place to watch cricket, but when the wind blows from a certain quarter the flies arrive to search, in a nostalgic way, for the smorgasbord of cows' leftovers that were once their staple fare. When this happens, you would rather be anywhere else in the world. So here sat 15-year-old Merilyn Earle, nervously pencilling in the leg byes and 'dot balls', keeping the sun from her eyes and busily engaging in the 'great Aussie salute' every couple of seconds.

Then came the words that Merilyn will remember forever: 'Excuse me, scorers, we will have to take this plank from you so we can set up the afternoon tea.' Suddenly scorebook, worksheets, pencils, calculator and personal items were all sitting in Merilyn's lap — while the game kept going and the flies kept coming. Eventually the plank was returned, but for Merilyn this was hardly an auspicious first impression of Sydney first-grade cricket. What made matters worse was that the game was a thriller. Set 317 to win, Hawkesbury were making a real fight of it. There were boundaries galore, overthrows, sundries from no balls, the kids on the scoreboard fell behind the official count, followers of both camps kept racing up to check the scores and ... you name it ... it happened at Benson's that day. As the match headed towards its climax, the little blond 15-year-old scoring her first game, hunched over a wobbly plank, was the centre of attention. If this was what it was like in a grade match in outer Sydney, between two clubs on the bottom rung of the competition ladder, what would it be like scoring at the MCG in a close day/nighter with 75,000 people baying for blood and raising the decibels to deafening? Merilyn concentrated as she never had in her life and relied heavily on her co-scorer.

As luck would have it, her co-scorer, Malcolm Gorham, from Wests, was one of the best scorers and nicest people in the game. As the scores got closer Malcolm seemed to grow calmer. While the people on the sidelines were yelling and screaming and the players were running around the field and up and down the wicket like hyperactive kids playing in the park, Malcolm was in complete control. Merilyn wasn't, but she tried to look as if she was! The scores grew closer, 312 ... 315 ... 317, 'He's out. It's a tie — what a game!!' Now will each book balance? They did. (You reckon cricket's a tough game to play? Try scoring, mate, try scoring!) Merilyn leant back; she'd done it.

Yet there was something different, even surreal, about this match. The year was 1986, Hawkesbury's first season in the competition. They had not been very competitive and had never looked like gaining a competition point. In this, the last game of the season, Wests closed at 5 for 317. Using previous performances as a guide, Hawkesbury would be lucky to get a third of that score — everybody would be up the pub by 4.30. Then a young girl from the mountains appears, nervously clutching a scorebook, and suddenly Hawkesbury come back from an almost impossible position and gain the first points in their history by means of a tie. Now ties in any form of cricket are unusual but this tie was extraordinary. Both sides made the same number of runs off the same number of balls (524). The players instantly looked at Merilyn in a different light. Was it just coincidence or was the new scorer a portent from a Higher Authority? Nobody knew. But one thing was for sure: Merilyn would be sitting behind the wobbly trestles and versatile plank for as long as she wanted.

Thus, next season, Merilyn, not yet 16, was appointed regular first-grade scorer for the Hawkesbury club. Apprehensive at first, she soon became more comfortable as the team quickly took her under their collective wing, making sure she had a ride to each game and generally looking after her as they would their little sister. Her youth and shyness did not, however, exempt her from the banter and friendly sledging that the players inflicted on each other and she had to take it like the rest. The important thing to Merilyn was that she was part of the team.

Obviously, Merilyn never entered the dressing-room unless all players were respectable (if Australian grade cricketers can ever be described as 'respectable'), but apart from this she went everywhere with them. She became a part of the fraternity that is a cricket team so quickly that the players soon forgot that their new scorer was young and female and that she did not talk the way they did. For cricketers use language and speak about subjects that would never be imagined, let alone mentioned, at your wife's Thursday afternoon Bible study group. Off-colour stories, oaths and four-letter words roll from players' tongues with a constancy and a rapidity that make a race caller sound as if he has an impediment. The language and invective that comes from a just-dismissed batsman who believes he has been robbed is wondrous to the ear and his description of the umpire who was the perpetrator of this heinous crime is almost Shakespearian in its venom. Merilyn at first blushingly pretended to ignore it. Then, as the months went by, she *did* just ignore it, without either pretending or blushing. These days it's like water off the pitch covers to Merilyn, just part of the background noise, as insignificant as a dot ball in a century partnership. Yet to the best of my knowledge, and despite her close contact with cricketers, Merilyn doesn't use bad language herself. Her vocabulary remains polite and her demeanour ladylike. There are times, though, when a Hawkesbury batsman comes storming off, polluting the atmosphere with the smoke coming from his ears and the words coming from his mouth. When this happens, Merilyn will turn to her fellow scorer and the opposition supporters close by and say, 'I apologise on behalf of my team and my club.'

*　　*　　*

For the next season and a half, Merilyn continued to learn more about her favourite hobby. As games came and went she began to see that scoring was more than a hobby, or even an occupation — it could be an art form.

In this period of Merilyn's scoring 'education', David Lemon, scorer for the University of New South Wales, introduced her to the 'Linear System'. Sitting in the grandstand at Waverley Oval, gazing out over the rooftops onto the blue Pacific in the distance while, on her left, the traffic hurried down to Bondi Beach, the Linear System was explained to the teenage scorer from Hawkesbury. A whole new world opened up to her — Bondi Road proved to be Merilyn's scoring road to Damascus.

Merilyn refined her way of working with the Linear System, combining it with some methods of her own. Basically, the Linear System can tell you just about anything you want to know about the game of cricket you are watching. Apart from the usual total, individual scores, bowling analysis and so on, it can also give details of how many balls each batsman faced against each bowler; how long since Kallis had strike against Warne; which ball of what over saw the last sundry; how many twos were run in the last eight overs, and more. I don't know for sure, but I'm of the opinion that the Linear System could also tell you how many returns Jonty Rhodes threw to the bowler's end, what the opening batsmen had for lunch, the winner of the last race at Caufield and who killed Cock Robin.

As her scoring became more proficient, Merilyn realised that her earlier ambitions in cricket may not have been as far-fetched as some would think. She was becoming well known among her peers and those with influence in umpiring circles, and even a few top administrators domiciled in the lofty towers of the New South Wales Cricket Association were beginning to take notice of this young girl's efficiency and dedication.

As Merilyn moved around from suburb to suburb and ground to ground, she met and formed friendships with other scorers and learnt from them. For unlike the game of cricket itself, where men might play against each other a number of times and never speak, scorers sit cheek by jowl for six to eight hours at a time. If both scorers aren't pleasant and helpful to their co-worker they are in for a long and tough day indeed. Thus, close friendships are often formed by Saturday afternoon between two people who were strangers on Saturday morning.

Looking back on her career so far, Merilyn is thankful for the people beside her. People like the late Ernie Cosgrove, for many years the State's No. 1 scorer and for every day of his life a Balmain man from the soles of his feet to the race form in his back pocket. She enjoyed the company of former first-grade player and gentleman Dave Evans from Gordon, who always wore a tie. And how could Merilyn ever forget the renowned 'Silent' John Sandes, who continually darts in and out of the box but still doesn't miss a ball. As his name implies, Silent is never short of a word on cricket or, for that matter, any other subject you would like to mention. Females now make up about 50 per cent of the scorers in Sydney grade cricket. All are worthy of mention, but among some of the more experienced 'ladies of the

Linear' are the enthusiastic Julia Coote of Sutherland, and Robyn Sanday from Northern District, who by means of a computer, not only scores at the table but works the scoreboard as well. Two of Merilyn's closest friends are Ruth Kelleher and Chris Bennison. With Ruth, who is from Manchester, Merilyn has formed a wonderful rapport in the score box. In January 2002, Merilyn and Ruth were appointed to score the Test against South Africa — the first two women ever to score a Test match in Australia and, in all likelihood, the world. Slarke and Kelleher are becoming to the score box what Langer and Hayden are becoming to the Australian XI. If the cricket field is a fraternity, the score box is a Lodge.

At the age 16 Merilyn was given her first minor representative match: a colts game, NSW v WA. The following year she was appointed to a Second XI game. She seemed to be on her way. Yet that was as high as she rose in scoring ranks for the next nine years. Although she was given a few more minor representative games, Merilyn was continually excluded from scoring in a first-class match or an interstate one-dayer. And as for a Test match … it seemed as far away as the moon. She felt that a huge glass ceiling hung over her head. Merilyn knew that she was improving every year, adding to her skills and developing her craft, but she began to wonder whether her gender would prevent her from entering the score box at the highest level.

With the benefit of hindsight, Merilyn suspects that she was afflicted with the impatience of youth — and 'youth' was the problem. It was not her gender that held her back in those early days; it was her age. In the main, scoring is a cerebral and subdued occupation, suited to the mature person, and tradition has dictated that those with heads of grey are the folk who perform it. An attractive young blond girl is a rarity in this job and cricket officials don't trust youth or rarities. (Mind you, I must admit, most of the cricket officials that I have come to know don't trust girls either.) So Merilyn had to stay patient and continue to gain the experience the 'powers that be' thought was necessary. Eventually, at the age of 25, Merilyn scored her first interstate limited-overs match and the same year she was appointed to a Sheffield Shield game at the SCG. The glass ceiling was cracking, if not actually falling down.

Later that season Merilyn had her biggest thrill to date when she was notified that she would be scoring in the first international one-day final of the summer. When she first heard the news, she was delighted, but come the day, she was petrified. First, she was required to arrive early and have lunch in the same room as the players and at the same table as the umpires. Then, as she walked onto the top deck of the Noble Stand, she looked out over the arena to the outer. A crowd of 40,000 was pouring into the ground, a seething mass ready to take their fanaticism, frustrations and feelings out on somebody — I hope it's not the scorers, thought Merilyn. Once the game started and Merilyn moved into her familiar ritual, the nerves gradually dissipated. In retrospect, Merilyn realised that big-time cricket was not that much different from a Saturday afternoon at Benson's Lane. Though the players were far more talented and the atmosphere and pressure more intense, the same basics applied: 'Same ice cream, bigger cherry,' Merilyn explains.

The moment for which Merilyn had been yearning came soon after the arrival of the new millennium. In January 2000 Merilyn was appointed to her first Test match; Australia v India at the SCG. At the age of 28 she was the youngest woman to ever score in a Test match in Australia (and, almost certainly, the world.) Merilyn remembers two things about that moment. First, her initial thought — if I pass away the day after the Test ends, I'll die happy — and second, the look of pride in her parents' eyes when she told them. 'I had been blessed,' Merilyn says now.

As the crowd stood for the National Anthems, just before the Test began, perhaps there was a young player standing on the famous arena with moist eyes. He would have been in good company, for up in the scorers' box there was a young woman standing straight as the tears slid down her cheeks. As the umpire called 'play', Merilyn glanced across to her scoring partner for the day. By one of fate's kindly coincidences she had been appointed with Malcolm Gorham, the man who had been with her in her first game at Benson's — Hawkesbury v Wests. This made Merilyn feel a little easier. There were 35,000 spectators, millions watching on television and a press corps ready to besiege her with a host of questions, but at least when tea time came around they wouldn't take her table away from her. What's more, should the Test match turn out to be a tie … well, she and Malcolm had been there before.

*   *   *

Like the game itself, the secret of cricket scoring is in the fundamentals; learn the laws of the game, watch every signal from the umpire and check and crosscheck with your co-scorer. Merilyn says that to be a top-class scorer you must always keep in mind the four 'C's: concentration, communication, consistency, commitment.

Though scoring in interstate or international cricket is 'the same ice cream, bigger cherry', there are some hazards and obstructions in the first-class game that are not there in club cricket. For example, sitting behind you at the SCG is the cricket press corps, who are continually wanting information.

'Merilyn, how many balls has Lehmann faced from Gough?'

'What's Gough's bowling average in this series so far?'

The cricket journalists of Australia are a knowledgeable and hard-headed bunch who understand the difficulties of a scorer's lot. Under the leadership of the 'Father of the Press box', Phil Wilkins from the *Sydney Morning Herald*, they have been nothing but kind and generous to Merilyn. The only minor problem Merilyn has struck so far is sometimes understanding the intonation and articulation of some of the quick-talking journalists from the subcontinent. However, she says that it works both ways — they struggle with her Sydney 'westie' accent too.

There is also the scoreboard to contend with. The grade grounds generally have a scoreboard worked by a couple of the local delinquents; it's nearly always wrong, but the scorers can correct it at their leisure. Not so the electronic board at the SCG, which must always be consistent and correct. Fortunately, nowadays the board is run by Ross Dundas, 'Australia's walking Wisden', so it is usually spot on. However, there is crosschecking to be done and the phone is not always silent. Actually, the phone can be a hindrance to scorers, especially during Shield games that are not broadcast, when the scorers are continually pestered with requests for the scores.

In all first-class matches the home state/country provides the two scorers. (The only exception to this is England, who provide their own travelling scorer. Tradition dies hard with the Poms — they still don't *really* trust us.) The two scorers decide before the match who is in 'the driver's seat' — that is, who broadcasts the information to the press, handles the scoreboard and the like. It will usually be the one with more experience. Also, they must decide who is scoring for the home team and who for the visitors. In her first Test, Merilyn scored for India; in her third Test she scored for Australia. The last fact was of little consequence to the cricket world at large, but it meant an enormous amount to Merilyn.

A third of an over

Let us go for just a moment into the score box for two balls and look over Merilyn's shoulder. Around the scorers, the press corps is doing its usual thing. Greg Baum from *The Age* is relating a story to 'Crash' Craddock from News Limited, Peter Roebuck is writing tomorrow's story in longhand into an exercise book, as Bill O'Reilly used to do. Ignoring the cricket, the young journalist from an English tabloid has his binoculars trained on an attractive lady walking along the Noble Stand concourse. Meanwhile, Merilyn and Ruth are concentrating on the third ball of Gough's seventh over.

Ball 3: Langer facing — leg bye.
- acknowledge umpire's signal by flashing light once
- put 1 in leg-bye column in the 'sundries' section

- cross 1 off progressive tally
- put small L in bowler's analysis (A journalist calls out, 'Hell, there's been a few of those today. How many leg byes is that, Merilyn?')
- put L in linear sheet, under Langer
- put L in notes column on the linear sheet as reminder that there were sundries in the over
- check leg byes. Speak into microphone and announce, 'There have been eight leg byes — six from Gough and two from Caddick.'

Ball 4: Hayden facing — hits four off no-ball.
- acknowledge umpire by flashing light twice — once for no-ball, once for four
- put 4 with circle around it in Hayden's batting line
- cross 5 off progressive tally
- put 1 in no-ball column in sundries section (Phone rings.)
- put 4 with circle around it in the bowler's analysis
- put 4 with circle around it under Hayden's name in the linear sheet
- put N in notes column in linear sheet as a reminder of the no-ball
- answer phone, try to sound polite and say, 'Australia are six more than when you rang two overs ago. Thank you, anytime.' Hang up.
- hear Ruth say, 'The board has missed the no-ball.'
- ring scoreboard.

*　　*　　*

Now a 'veteran' of three Tests and 15 international one-day games, Merilyn can look back on her career and reflect. Whereas she looks at her first Test as 'a blessing', she regards her two Tests since as a bonus and the one-dayers as a great experience. Merilyn is now up at the top of her field, not only in the scoring box but behind the scenes as well. She was recently chairperson of the Scorers' subcommittee, a part of the Umpires & Scorers Association, dealing with scorers' assessments (exams) and has been, along with others, an adjudicator of disputed scorebooks. (If there is an altercation between clubs about the result of a game, both scorebooks are impounded and the adjudicators go through every ball bowled for the whole game. Merilyn, an eagle-eyed sleuth, can pick a mistake, or a deliberate falsification, in a manner that would make Sherlock Holmes seem sloppy.) Merilyn also helped write a manual for scorers and coaches rookie scorers. Cricket has many branches — Merilyn once ran a seminar for scorers from the 'Deaf Cricketers' Association'. All this, and Merilyn continues to hold down a responsible job at an independent school in the Hills District.

Yet more than all this, cricket is a huge part of Merilyn's life — many of her best friends have been made through her cricket connections. One of the nicest things to happen to Merilyn was the positive and genuine outpouring of delight from her peers when it was announced that she was to score in her first Test.

In her cricket career there have been a few negatives but nothing that she couldn't handle. And the glass ceiling was a lot thinner than she'd imagined — if it was there at all! Still, there have been occasions when she has heard of whispered innuendoes of a sexual nature, implying that her popularity with her club and with many in the cricket fraternity was due to things other than her friendly personality and exceptional ability in performing her tasks. There were other moments when innuendo turned to insult, when a few people (of both genders) asked what she had to do to reach the top so quickly — and with whom she did it. Merilyn gave this verbal harassment the response it deserved, but it hurt. She felt comforted by telling herself that those who spoke in such an inane and degrading manner knew little of the game and certainly couldn't play it!

Though appreciated and affirmed by her own club, and many other clubs as well, one thing that quite puzzles Merilyn is the sometimes offhand way scorers are treated by some players and officials in first-class cricket. 'Often it's as if we just aren't there.'

She doesn't see this as a snub; it's more as if scorers are somehow chameleon-like, and blend into the background.

[Merilyn has a point here. Without scorers the game could not be played. Yet in first-class cricket they seem to be like the person who gets you to work in the train — you see the train but you never think about the driver in control. Perhaps the State Associations should make it their business to invite scorers to have a drink with players after training. After all, we are continually being told by those in control that we all work together and we are all 'part of the team'.]

Merilyn is particularly happy with her life in cricket; happy to be with friends and to serve the game she loves in her own way. She will not be drawn into discussion of pay rates for scorers, preferring to leave that to others. Yet even an outsider performing just passing research on the pay and conditions of the game's pencil-wielders could not help but be surprised at their low standing in the cricket world. As a comparison, in a one-day interstate match (ING Cup), scorers get paid less than half the amount of the third umpire. [This fact must cause readers to ponder what exactly the third umpire gets paid for doing. Surely this is the best job in Australian sport! The man dresses in an umpire's uniform, sits in air-conditioned comfort watching cricket on television with a box of balls beside him, on which he places his coffee and raisin toast. Then when Stuey Law hits the stumps from cover point with Michael Bevan scrambling, all he does is turn up the sound, listen to what Tony Greig and Bill Lawry reckon and go along with *them*.] Meanwhile, the scorers are concentrating on every ball without the benefit of refreshment or even a comfort stop.

Notwithstanding these few minor matters, Merilyn wouldn't swap her job with anyone. She is at the top of her field, respected by all who know her. Just recently she was made a life member of the Hawkesbury Cricket Club, a unique and unprecedented honour; making a 29-year-old woman a life member of a male-dominated cricket club must be a first. It is a tribute not only to the lady who received it but also to the club who granted it.

So next time you are sitting at the cricket and Australia is going through one of its mini collapses and there is alarm in the dressing-room, try not to worry. Let your eyes wander up to the scorers in the grandstand and console yourself that all is under control. The press may be screaming for information, the phones ringing ad nauseam, but our scorers remain concentrated and self-possessed — Merilyn is in the 'driver's seat' and calmness pervades the score box.

ELEVEN

A Man of Humours

The journalist Peter Roebuck once wrote: 'At the crease, Michael Slater seems to jump upon a go-cart and ride down a hill. Only halfway down does he pause to reflect upon the likelihood of the brakes working.'

Thereby hangs the conundrum of Michael Slater. He has come a long way, so far, by ignoring the brakes. Still, it is worth asking, would Slater have been able to surpass what he has already achieved if he had not only reflected upon the brakes but also put them in for an occasional service?

At the time of writing, Slater is going through a torrid time. He has been dropped from both the Australian and the NSW teams for lack of form, and there appear to be non-cricket problems as well. Yet within a few months 'Slats' could well rise again, and be seen scoring Test hundreds, kissing the country's coat of arms on his helmet and laughing at what were yesterday's mortifying moments. The cricket world would be a better place for that.

Sometimes good players become lost in their era — hidden by the great players around them. (Bill Johnston and Peter Burge are two examples of this.) In the whole of his international cricket career, Michael Slater has not played with a weak team. Despite this, Slater has never been overshadowed by his contemporaries. The only things that ever overshadowed Slats were his own demons.

Whether Slater could be called a 'great' batsman depends on your definition of the word 'great'. Certainly, 14 Test centuries have seen him travelling along the highway of greatness — even if, at the most inopportune times, he has been known to leave the highway for an unscheduled comfort stop. What cannot be denied is that Slater has flair. He is a player from the Norm O'Neill, Doug Walters school; a batsman who can win his team at least one game per series through his own exceptional deeds. Any player who has the ability to do this, and does it, is worth carrying for the five games.

Nevertheless, an opening batsman doesn't make 14 Test centuries and average in the mid 40s by just having one good match a series. For the last eight years, until the year 2001, Slater has been an integral part of the Australian team. He has been dropped on a couple of occasions but has never been discarded, until now.

The exclusion from the NSW team has hurt Slater particularly deeply. When he was first chosen for the tour of England in 1993, there were many people who were surprised at the selection. John Benaud was then an Australian selector and it was no secret that Benaud was a Slater fan. When Slater was dropped from the NSW team during the 2001–02 season, Benaud was chairman of selectors. Though Slater carries the psychological and financial burden of being dropped from the team, those who know Benaud realised that he too would not be without feelings of irony and regret.

Michael Slater is a good bloke. He is a pleasant person to spend time with. In most situations, Slats seems to be laughing, whether he is the recipient of a dressing-room jibe or the instigator of one. He likes people and goes out of his way for all.

I was managing the NSW Shield side in Melbourne a few years ago. In the city at the same time, there was a schoolboys' cricket carnival. Most of the day I had noticed some 10 and 11-year-old lads in sky blue blazers hanging around the room pestering the players for autographs. When I inquired why these kids were watching the cricket on a school day, they told me that they were representing NSW in the Australian Primary Schools' Championship. In Melbourne, it is vital that inhabitants from climes further north stick together, so I invited the boys and their managers in to have a drink with the team at the end of the day's play. When they arrived at 6.15pm they were genially welcomed by the tired players. Despite the bad publicity often levelled at sporting teams for aloofness and bad manners to fans, it has been my experience that just the opposite is the case. So while the major cricket team in the State of NSW relaxed with a beer, the young members of the NSW Combined Primary Schools' team gorged themselves on soft drinks and hero worship, and cricket's conviviality filled the sweaty air.

Kids love Slats. He's a sort of pied piper, and this particular evening at the MCG, they gravitated to him. I was sitting nearby and watched as two lads approached him. 'Excuse me, Mr Slater,' said the first boy confidently, 'I'm Jason and I'd like to introduce you to Tommy. He's an opening batsman like you and you're his favourite cricketer.'

The Test star shook hands with Jason, tall and robust, and Tommy, small and tubby. 'Come and sit down, blokes,' he said.

As he sat down next to his idol, Tommy kept opening and shutting his mouth, but no words came out. He looked like a novitiate nun who was having an audience with the Pope. So Slats took over. He asked Tommy about the block he took, his approach to various types of opening bowlers and had Tommy show him his stance. Then Jason said, 'Mr Slater, Tommy is too shy to tell you but last week he made a record score for his under 11 team against Rooty Hill.'

'A record score! Gee, that's great, Tommy. As a fellow opener, I'm proud of you,' said Slats, patting Tommy on the shoulder. 'How many did you make?'

Trembling slightly, Tommy managed to stammer, 'I made 387.'

Slats sat up straight and, hiding a smile, said loudly, 'Three hundred and eighty seven! Why did you throw it away, Tommy? What's the matter with you, boy? You had 400 staring you in the face!'

With flair come volatility and vulnerability. Michael Slater has his share of both. From time to time he is called 'Sybil' by his teammates. This nickname came from a movie about a woman called Sybil who, apparently, had major personality changes. Slats certainly has his highs and lows, but whereas others hide their feelings, sometimes the volatile side of his personality takes over, manifesting itself in an occasional bizarre incident. Once, after being dismissed early by playing a poor shot, Slats was seen in the toilet attempting to flush his bat, pads and gloves down the sewer. There was also no justification for his behaviour to the umpire in India in 2001 after Slater was certain that he had caught Rahul Dravid and disputed the decision with an uncalled-for show of histrionics. The lightness of his punishment after such a tantrum should have encouraged him to buy a lottery ticket. (However, without trying to excuse the outburst in any way, I've seen Lleyton Hewitt do far worse and it hardly seems to raise an eyebrow in the tennis community.)

As far as Slater's batting is concerned, once again, Peter Roebuck summed it up perfectly: 'Slater was exciting because he lived on the edge of his competence and our nerves.'

To watch Slater at the crease is an exhilarating experience. What will he do next? Will it be foolish or magnificent? (He receives a short one, he moves back in an instant, swivels on the ball of his foot and dismisses the missile from his proximity with the contempt of a gun shearer discarding a shorn sheep. The ball scorches the grass and dents a hoarding. Next ball is a juicy half-volley, pitched in the slot. Slater hesitates, shuffles across the crease like a 10-year-old having his first tap dancing lesson, plays late with an angled bat and steers the ball to third slip.) Therein lies the excitement! With Slats you just *never* know.

Some of Slater's batting partners tell of the times when he is hit with his personal type of batting affliction — as the Irish would say, 'when the humour is on him'. Nobody knows when this malady will occur but when it does, things happen. First of all, Slats looks very resolute and seems to go into a trance-like state. Then, as the opening bowler comes tearing in, the Slater eyes begin to spin like poker machines (a description a little over the top, perhaps, but so say his fellows). The bat then becomes a lethal weapon. The bowler could be Larwood at his fastest on a greentop, it wouldn't matter. As far as Slats is concerned, the bowler is unimportant; the ball is all that counts and the ball is 'going the journey'. When Michael Slater is in such a frame of mind, his partners give him the strike and stay well out of his way.

There are a number of examples of Slater performing in such a rampantly destructive mood. For instance, the second innings in the fifth Ashes Test in Sydney in 1998–99, where Australia, but for Slater, nearly gave away an impregnable position. Also, Australia's first innings of the first Test of the 2001 Ashes tour, when in scoring 77 Slater shattered England's new-found confidence in about eight overs and set the tone for the rest of the series. When in such a mood, Slater is unstoppable. The ball flies to all parts of the field, and beyond the field as well, with a power and precision that few can match, yet the strokes are vintage. Michael Slater can mishit, 'throw the bat', play the wrong shot at the wrong time — and often does — but he is incapable of slogging. There are no 'cow' shots in the Slater repertoire. Only strokes that make devotees remember.

Those who love to watch great batsmen in action speak of Slater's magnificent footwork. Well, they are partly right. When he is on song, Michael Slater has footwork up there with Neil Harvey's. When the song is off key, the footwork aficionados will be in for a tough day. Yet it is Slater's backlift that causes him the most trouble.

When a batsman is in a slump, there are many things that could have gone awry with his technique. Yet the problem(s) can almost always be found within three areas: head, feet and the position of the bat at the moment of impact. The fault that causes most players problems is a poor head position. (If your head is in the correct position, you can often get away with the fact that your feet are not to the pitch of the ball.) Except for horizontal shots, the bat should be as straight (vertical) as possible at the moment the ball reaches it. How that comes about depends on the batter's personal style. Keith Miller's backlift was high and straight, back towards the middle stump — the perfect technique, some might say. Allan Border had a straight but very short backlift. On the other hand, Don Bradman's backlift went out towards second slip and then came around in a semicircle, but it was vertical as it hit the ball. Michael Slater's backlift is in the Bradman mode. When Slater is hitting them well, his bat goes out towards second slip, then *around* and strikes the ball in an upright position. When Slater is having a horror stretch, the bat comes *across* from second slip, giving him only half of the willow's face with which to hit the ball.

Slater has all the shots, but his signature stroke is his front foot drive/punch off his pads, between midwicket and mid-on. When he's in form, the bat comes down straight, and at the last moment the wrists turn and off hurtles the ball, split seconds away from the fence. The power in the Slater wrists would make an acrobat envious and his timing is a gift from heaven. If this shot is working, Slats is on the way and there is an innings of majesty in the offing. If the bat is slicing across the ball, watch out for snicks, leading edges and just plain old-fashioned misses.

There is very little margin between perfect and ordinary in the Slater technique. I guess that's what Peter Roebuck meant when he spoke of him 'living on the edge of his competence'. Yet one should remember that as his technique can deteriorate in a second, so can it return just as quickly. One shot can bring to a batsman like Slater a feeling of exultation: the demons are exorcised and the clouds of doubt dispersed in an instant. Suddenly, Slats is no longer playing a game in his mind, he is playing the game that his feet, wrists and eye were made to play. Gone is the uncertain cannon fodder of a moment ago, replaced by the confident cavalier. If you are lucky enough to be there at such a time you will realise that the wait has been worth it.

You cannot liken Slater to any of his peers. He is not a Tendulkar, nor even a Langer. The most engaging thing about Slater is that he is Slats. On the surface, a laughing, hot-headed, helpful, brilliant and contradictory man; deep down, where it counts, still the charming and lovable young boy from Wagga. On his day he is a genius; at other times a disappointment. He may sometimes feel that he lets his team down and this will worry him. Yet these worries are unnecessary, because he will make up for it sooner or later and win a game on his own. Often he lets himself down. So be it! Life isn't a problem to be solved, it's a mystery to be lived!

In cricket, as in life, we can give too much credit to the consistent. The 'powers that be' mostly play it safe. They criticise the maverick and congratulate the medium pacer. Yet there are many real lovers of the game who will continue to have a soft spot for the individualist. Give them an opener whose adrenalin pumps as the oval gate slams shut behind him, whose eyes spin as the quickie charges in and they will be happy. These romantics will remain ever loyal to a vulnerable character who sometimes flushes his bat down the toilet when he fails — they actually love him the more for it. We need the Slats of the world. Cricket would be a far poorer game without him, for Michael Slater is a man of humours, a man from a different mould.

What the great Australian cricket writer Ray Robinson once said when describing Keith Miller could apply just as aptly to Michael Slater: 'His qualities are stimulating; his faults are of the kind lesser men can avoid with ease.'

TWELVE

A Wicket Way to Earn a Living

A cricketing mate of mine personified Australia's three greatest grounds in an interesting way. He reckoned, 'Sydney is like your wife. She always has something wrong with her but her diagnosticians keep making excuses and only prescribe bandaids. She has had plastic surgery and she keeps loading on the make-up, but it only makes her look ridiculous. The only reason you don't leave her is because you remember how wonderful she was in her youth — before they ruined her.

'Adelaide Oval, on the other hand, is like your mistress. She is exceptionally beautiful and always perfectly dressed and groomed. The only problem is that all the other blokes are in love with her as well, and keep perving on her.

'The MCG is like a mate. Though he's parochial and ugly, everybody flocks to him. Those who are in his orbit are loud and rude but are also the most knowledgeable cricket followers in the world. Yet deep down, "The G" and his mates are unfaithful to cricket. For even in the middle of an exciting Boxing Day Test you get the feeling that they just can't wait for the footy to start.'

* * *

Perfectly conditioned, every blade of grass the same texture of green and its distinctive dimensions — shaped like an Aussie Rules football — the Adelaide Oval is unique. The ground's unusual contours produce interesting comments from cricket devotees when they see it for the first time: comments about long boundaries straight (difficult fours), and short boundaries square (easy sixes). The wicket itself has been acclaimed throughout the cricket world, though it did go through a time when some said it was 'just too good'. This has been remedied and, while remaining admirable for batting, it is now a 'result' wicket, with games often going into the last hour of the last session, as was always meant to happen in first-class cricket.

The Adelaide Oval is more than just a place where cricket is played. It is an integral part of its city: a green icon surrounded by parks with the backdrop of the beautiful Adelaide Hills stretching away in the distance. All this — and only 10 minutes' walk from the CBD! Adelaide Oval can hold over 30,000 people but it remains a 'cricket ground', never a stadium. The Mound at the northern end is untouched; a green sward, where families lie on the grass, watch the cricket and picnic. At the top of the Mound stands a line of huge Moreton Bay figtrees, which provide shade from the hot South Australian sun and sometimes act as stumps for impromptu cricket matches played by tomorrow's stars, armed with tennis balls and plastic bats.

Along the western side of the oval one grandstand dominates the scene — though in keeping with the Adelaide style of doing things it has been given three names. This stand slopes back up the contours of the land and blends into its surrounds as if it had grown from the soil. It is here that the players' rooms are situated. By modern standards, the rooms are comfortable but basic, and although the wicket is side-on to the players, the

Don Bradman with his wife Jessie in England in 1934, recovering from an attack of appendicitis that nearly cost him his life. Only his closest friends would have known that a few years earlier the world's greatest batsman had suffered another 'near death' experience, after his friend Alec Marks pushed him overboard while the two were out on a boating trip. The Don, it turned out, could not swim.

LEFT: *Alec Marks with his girlfriend (and later wife) Lilian Ward.*
BELOW: *Alec swings a ball to leg in a Sheffield Shield match against Queensland in the 1930s. Don Tallon, legendary wicketkeeper in Bradman's 'Invincibles' side, is behind the stumps.*

NEW ADDRESS:
163 PHILLIP STREET
'Phones: BW2071 (2 Lines).

CITY FORECAST;
Warm and Sultry

DAILY
TELEGRAPH
PICTORIAL

NET SALES EXCEED 141,045 DAILY

No. 15,624   Registered at the General Post Office, Sydney, for transmission by Post as a newspaper.   SYDNEY: TUESDAY, JANUARY 7, 1930—28 PAGES   Agents' supplies between midnight and 2 a.m.: 'PHONE B 1088 or B 4015; after 3, ring BW 2071.   ONE PENNY

DON BRADMAN, BREAKER OF WORLD'S CRICKET RECORDS

HOW DON BRADMAN, CRICKET HERO, WAS ACCLAIMED by Queenslanders and the Cricket Ground crowd yesterday after his amazing innings of 452, not out. It broke the world's record highest score of 437, made by Ponsford against Queensland in December, 1927. Curiously enough it was in December, 1927 that Bradman, the Bowral youth, played his first Sheffield Shield match. He scored 118 in his initial appearance in first-class cricket, and has since become Australia's most prolific and forceful run-getter. Thirteen centuries is his record in first-class cricket, and there is no saying what new records he will create before 1930 draws to a close.

Don Bradman is chaired from the SCG by his weary Queensland opponents after hitting a world record 452 not out for NSW in January 1930. A few hours later, he and his good mate Alec Marks were at the Mick Simmons sports store in the city, organising for the bat that hit the record score to be prominently displayed.

Bradman goes out to bat with Bill Brown. The pair made three tours of England together — in 1934, 1938 and 1948. 'He was dynamic,' says Bill of The Don. 'He hit fours off balls that others couldn't snick.'

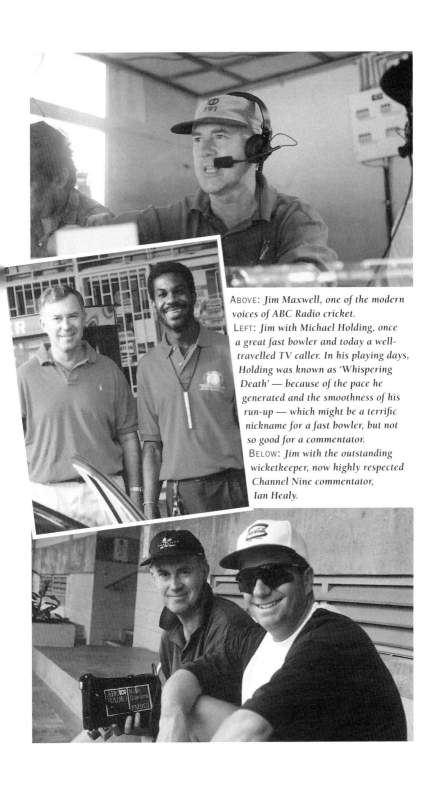

ABOVE: *Jim Maxwell, one of the modern voices of ABC Radio cricket.*

LEFT: *Jim with Michael Holding, once a great fast bowler and today a well-travelled TV caller. In his playing days, Holding was known as 'Whispering Death' — because of the pace he generated and the smoothness of his run-up — which might be a terrific nickname for a fast bowler, but not so good for a commentator.*

BELOW: *Jim with the outstanding wicketkeeper, now highly respected Channel Nine commentator, Ian Healy.*

LEFT: *Lindsay Hassett (left), a superb batsman and captain, and later a brilliant analyst for ABC Radio, and Alan McGilvray, without doubt the greatest ball-by-ball cricket commentator Australia has produced.*

RIGHT: *West Indies captain Clive Lloyd (left) and ace reporter Mike Coward in animated discussion.*

Mike in New Zealand in early 1986, at an Allan Border press conference with New Zealand cricket writer Don Cameron (far left) and News Limited's Mike Horan (centre).

ABOVE: *Merilyn Slarke (right) at the SCG with fellow scorer Ruth Kelleher and ICC match referee Ranjan Madugalle during the third Australia v South Africa Test of 2001–02.*
BELOW: *Adelaide Oval Manager Les Burdett (left) with his great mate Ross Bennett before the third day's play of the first Test of the same series. For 25 years until his retirement during this season, Ross was Les' second-in-command and close confidant.*

Michael Slater blazes away in England in 1993 — 'living on the edge of his competence and our nerves'.

Richie Benaud, king of the Channel Nine team and master of the art of TV cricket commentary. Acknowledged as one of the great captains, he always checked with the scorers before declaring ... unlike Jimmy Burke!

LEFT: *Arthur Morris and Len Hutton toss the coin before the start of the second Test of the 1954–55 Ashes series. A few years earlier, a selector had questioned Arthur's ability to even captain NSW … because away from the cricket field the champion left-hander sometimes wore suede shoes. Typical selectors' logic!*

BELOW: *Arthur with Sir Donald Bradman. Arthur considers his 196 in the fifth Test of the 1948 Ashes tour to be his finest innings, but nobody remembers it because up the other end The Don was bowled for a second-ball duck in his final Test.*

Arthur Morris in New York with the legendary Yankees baseballer Mickey Mantle. Here's a hypothetical for readers: what would be some possible occurrences if Mickey used Arthur's cricket bat at Yankee Stadium in the first game of a World Series, and Arthur used Mickey's baseball bat in an Ashes Test at Lord's?

Merv Seres' official title is 'Room Attendant', but to all in the world of cricket he is known as 'the roomy'. During years of loyal and faithful service working in the home dressing room at the SCG, Merv has won himself a legion of admirers, including Mike Whitney (left) and Merv Hughes (below). When the two Mervs swap stories, the laughs are many and time is irrelevant.

aspect towards the Adelaide Hills is superb. Hanging on the walls of both locker rooms are boards showing names of those who performed mighty deeds at the Adelaide Oval. Just the sight of these names must have caused many a novice's neck to tingle, and merely to sit in the viewing room, where once sat the gods of the game, would be a day well spent for most. It is here that for nearly 40 years has sat Australian cricket's most lovable character, Barry 'Nugget' Rees — mentor, mascot and motivator of South Australian and Australian teams — a tradition in his own lifetime. Adelaide Oval is big on tradition!

At the River Torrens end of the ground is the new 'Bradman Stand'. Blending perfectly with the old, this structure brings all the modern conveniences to sports watching, while also giving the impression that it was built a century ago. This building is in direct contrast with the Adelaide Oval lights, the most inappropriate structures erected in this country since the Australian government approved the multi-storeyed phallic symbol on top of Parliament House. When these lights were built, the public was told that the towers were retractable — they would sit unnoticed in their burrows and, like the platypus, remain nocturnal. However, soon after construction, one of these electric atrocities fell over. This led to the belief that, should such a disaster occur during a game, some paying customers could be injured — not to mention the program seller, ice cream boys, and the fieldsman at deep midwicket, waiting for a catch from a skied hook shot So now they stand there in their ugliness, far sturdier than originally planned but no longer retractable; four ugly towers rising up into the clouds above this lovely oval. They are now completely safe and functional, but remain a stark reminder of man's ability to spoil what is beautiful, a drastic example of visual pollution — as incongruous as the sight of a nun wearing stiletto heels.

Outside the oval, towering over even the Moreton Bay figtrees, stand two symbols of Adelaide: the statue of Colonel William Light and St Peter's Cathedral. Colonel Light, explorer and founder of Adelaide, stands proudly on Montefiore Hill, gazing over deep third man, out towards his city. He has a determined look on his face, his arm is outstretched and his index finger is pointing towards the dressing-room, as if he is saying, 'You're out, mate. Don't argue with me, you were plumb!' (The sculptor of the statue was obviously a bowler.) Around from Colonel Light, behind the beautiful old-fashioned scoreboard, stands St Peter's Anglican Cathedral, an impressive edifice of stone and spires looking down admonishingly on the flannelled figures below. To sit in the viewing room and look across the green oval towards St Peter's is a vista of which you could never tire, and it is without doubt the best place from which to view the Cathedral. Strangely, the closer you get to St Peter's the less impressive it becomes — a description that could also apply to Australia's faction-ridden Anglican hierarchy. Nevertheless, with Colonel Light at deep third man and St Peter's at backward square, Adelaide Oval is well guarded by both history and heaven.

I guess by now most readers would have gained the impression that by good fortune or divine intervention, Adelaide Oval has everything that a great cricket ground would ever need. Well, most readers would be right! Except that this great ground has one other asset that puts it even further ahead of the pack. The Adelaide Oval has Les Burdett!

*   *   *

There is an old story in cricket that concerns a young lad playing in his initial first-grade match. Under difficult conditions, he made a big score and won the game for his team. In the room afterwards, his captain patted him on the back and said, 'Well played, son, you batted with great maturity.' The lad thanked his skipper and the older man went on, 'And how did you find the wicket?'

'Oh, it wasn't difficult,' replied the young batsman. 'I just walked out to the centre of the ground and there it was.'

Les Burdett's title at the South Australian Cricket Association (SACA) is 'Oval Manager'. His brief covers a multitude of responsibilities, from presenting the ground, to lining the tennis courts, to repairing the pavilion roof. All these tasks and dozens of others, Les and his staff of 13 perform with utmost efficiency and maximum dedication. Yet if those cricketers who know the Oval Manager were asked to give a concise description of his duties, they would have no difficulty being succinct: 'Les Burdett is a maker of cricket pitches.'

Not only is Les 'a maker'; he is an artist. Les is the Picasso of pitches, the Rembrandt of the roller, a genius over 22 yards of rolled grass.

As the sixth in a family of seven boys, Les was imbued with the work ethic of his father, who was a fencing contractor. When he was growing up, hard work was as natural to Les as kicking a football and it became a way of life that remains with him to this day. In a way, it has been one of Les's few drawbacks, because his tendency to toil and his passion for his job have made him, in his own words, 'a workaholic'. In the summer season Les always intends to have one day off a week, but there are many weeks in which he doesn't. (The outfield at the Torrens End has a problem with a fungus or the wicket on the No. 2 ground is keeping low or there are only 10 days before the Test against the West Indies or … well, there's always something!) The drive for perfection keeps Les away from his family more than he'd like and often makes him feel guilty. Fortunately, his wife Jane (a university lecturer) and his two daughters (Zoe and Emma) are understanding.

As a boy, Les was besotted with cricket and football. He represented at under 12 cricket and tried out for the Norwood Football Club at the age of 17. He once slept all night outside the gates of the Adelaide Oval so he could get a good seat for the Sturt v Port Adelaide grand final. A couple of years later Les played at the Adelaide Oval in the grand final of the South Australian Amateur Football League, where his team, Adelaide Teacher's College, won the flag. Little did Les know then that he would later become one of his town's most influential figures. The reason for this was Australia's most beautiful oval — the ground on which Les once triumphantly kicked a ball and outside whose gates he'd unrolled his sleeping bag and braved the cold Adelaide night.

In 1969, Les applied for a job at Adelaide Oval and he was appointed as an apprentice groundsman. However, National Service ('nashos') interrupted the early part of Les' career and for the next 18 months he was trained to defend democracy.

To most young men of those days, 'nashos' was an unwanted interruption to growing up, the gatecrashing of young lives by pompous uniformed men who barked orders and hated underlings. To the young Les Burdett it was different. The army taught Les to understand and respect authority. It reinforced the values of teamwork and self-discipline that had been instilled in him at home and that he'd witnessed on the sporting fields.

In 1972, after coming out of the army, Les rejoined the ground staff of the SACA at the Adelaide Oval. It was here that he came under the guidance of one of the greatest cricket curators of them all — Arthur Lance. Les came to view Arthur Lance first as a father figure, then as a mentor and finally as a friend. On the foundation of Arthur's example, Les built his career and to this day Les remains thankful.

Les had been working for a time as a young groundsman, doing the menial work and watching Arthur Lance weave his magic on turf and grass, when one day the older man called him over to the middle of the Adelaide Oval and said, 'Okay son, make a wicket.' Then Arthur walked away and left the youngster on his own. Suddenly Les was in the deep end and his 'floaties' were home in the cupboard! Somehow Les prepared the wicket, but he admits now that he was very glad that *he* didn't have to bat on it.

Arthur Lance taught Les many things, but the piece of advice that remains in his memory, and the maxim by which he's worked for nearly 40 years, is this: 'Back yourself, son, and don't go getting upset if you make a mistake. But don't *ever* make that mistake again.'

Sitting with Les Burdett over a cup of tea or a beer, you get the impression that there is nothing he would rather do than tell Arthur Lance stories. For Arthur was not only a great groundsman but a character in his own right.

Arthur had fought a war so, like most ex-diggers, he didn't worry much about little things. Yet even the greats make simple mistakes. One particular blunder was so unbelievable that Les still shakes his head when he thinks of it. Now, when things seem to be going easily and falling into place, Les remembers it and he forces himself to concentrate.

During a Test against England, the players had come off the field at 3.40pm, when suddenly Les looked up and saw Arthur Lance in the centre directing the heavy roller onto the wicket. Just as the roller purred into motion, Les raced out to the middle and yelled, 'Arthur, why the hell are you rolling the wicket?'

'Australia has closed,' answered Arthur Lance

Les looked at the scoreboard. 'Closed! But they're only 3 for 130.'

Arthur looked surprised, 'Then why have they come off?'

'Because it's tea time,' Les shouted.

Arthur's face didn't change. He walked over to the roller, which had moved about three yards up the pitch, and called to the man driving, 'That's enough!'

As Arthur Lance got older, his health began to fail and he had to have his leg amputated. Arthur, being the man he was, refused to have a full anaesthetic because he wanted to see what was happening. After all, Arthur and his leg had been together a long time and the least he could do was say goodbye. Just before the operation began, the surgeon asked Arthur if he would like to listen to some music. Arthur asked what there was in the way of tapes, but when they went through the list there was really no music that he fancied. So the surgeon suggested some Elvis Presley. Reluctantly, Arthur agreed and put on the earpieces. Halfway through the operation the surgical team was amazed to hear the patient crooning a song:

I love you, I love you,
Please don't break my heart in two,
'Cause I don't have a wooden heart.

Arthur Lance didn't have a wooden heart, but he had a brave one!

At age 25, Les was promoted to the position of Assistant Curator to Arthur Lance. Two years later, Arthur retired and Les was given the top job. At 27, Les Burdett became Australian Test cricket's youngest ever curator — a record that will be broken at around the same time as some batsman averages more than 99.94. Now, aged 51, though looking a lot younger, Les is 'Oval Manager', virtually running his own race. He has under him a loyal and proficient team, all of whom love the game of cricket.

Within a couple of seasons of taking over, Les made his mark. He silenced the doubters who had whispered that nobody could be as good as Arthur Lance and soon other curators were asking his advice. In the years to come, he would be appointed as 'Neutral Groundsman' for the World Cup in India and invited to South Africa, early in 1991, when the Proteas were readmitted to the ranks of world cricket, to advise the South African Cricket Association and curators on wicket preparation.

Thirty-three years after coming under Arthur Lance's wise old eye, Les is the doyen of his craft; a man who is listened to by those in his trade in the same manner as Dennis Lillee is heard by young fast bowlers. The SACA now controls three grounds. Les oversees these grounds and the five turf wicket tables (the pitch area in the middle), which contain a total of 32 wickets. There are also 62 turf practice wickets which require close attention from Les and his men. It should not be forgotten that on the Adelaide Oval they also play Aussie Rules football in the winter (rugby league had a few seasons there during the Super League era) and there is talk that some matches will be played at this venue during the coming Rugby World Cup.

Despite his enormous responsibilities, the SACA doesn't keep Les locked up in a cell at the Cathedral End for its own selfish purposes. If other cricket grounds need help and those in charge request Les's expertise, the SACA lends him out. (Recently Les was in charge of preparing the wicket for a series of one-day games at Docklands Stadium in Melbourne, the first international cricket matches ever played under a roof.) Now speaking engagements from cricket associations pour in and Les does the best he can to spread the word. Les is fortunate, and grateful that when he is away he has a reliable staff who know their stuff.

'Make a wicket,' Arthur Lance once said to the young Les Burdett and he did, and it was a labour of love. Little did Les realise that one day he would be making nearly a hundred of them in Adelaide alone and then hopping on a plane and helping prepare cricket pitches in places far away.

*   *   *

If you reckon that an opening batsman is nervous a few minutes before a Test match, let me tell you, compared to the curator, the opener is a cockeyed optimist on uppers. Even after a quarter of a century in the job, Les is still strained and apprehensive. In the early days he couldn't sleep, he would write himself notes and prowl around, imagining scenarios so awful that a poisoned chalice looked inviting. For no matter how well a curator may perform as the seasons come and go, his whole career is judged on the type of Test match wicket he makes.

A Test match

Les watches out of the corner of his eye as one of his men gives the wicket its last 'polish' with the heavy roller. He marks the creases, nods to the Channel 9 cameraman and endeavours to ignore the butterflies playing chasings inside his tummy yet again. Actually, there is nothing that can be done now to improve this 22 yards of turf that all Australia and a couple of hundred million others worldwide will be watching over the next five days. All the hard work has been done weeks before. There are no short cuts, no secret recipes in preparing a Test strip. Just elbow grease, experience and instinct. So he completes the cosmetic touches and awaits the approach by the home captain and then the visiting leader, which he knows will come. 'What do you reckon, Les?'

'I'd bat.' Les tells it as he sees it and gives his opinion without fear or favour. It matters naught who asks the question; they are all cricketers. Captains and media want Les' opinion about his creation, the wicket on which the game will be played. He gives the same answer to all.

It's nearly time to start. Soon the umpires will appear, so Les takes up his position: alone, behind the opening bowler's arm at the Torrens end, on the south-east side of the sightboard, and awaits the first over of the Test. As the bowler measures out his run, the tummy butterflies form a conga line.

Deep down, Les is confident that the wicket will play as he expects but a curator's demons are never far away. Did the rain that interrupted preparation last Wednesday affect the grass cover in any way? Did he hose on half a litre too much before breakfast this morning? The batsman takes guard and looks around the field. The crowd becomes quiet ... 'Play!'

The opening bowler charges in and lets it go at reasonable pace but the ball angles down wide outside leg stump. This shows Les nothing — nobody can judge a pitch from a ball that's almost a wide. Then on the third ball of the game, the opening bowler drops one short, the batsman ducks and the keeper takes the ball in front of his eyes — good bounce but not flying. Les breathes a little easier.

Five overs have now gone by. There has been a little lateral movement but no swing. Australia is 0 for 15, although if third slip hadn't missed a sitter they would have been 1 for 4 in the second over. The pitch is playing as Les wants. Now, feeling much more comfortable, he can sit back and reflect on the future of the match. If it goes according to Les's forecast, Australia will be about 2 for 95 at lunch. The wicket will become easier as the day progresses and at its best after lunch on the second day. It will begin to spin on the fourth day. The media will then predict that the side batting last on the fifth day will struggle against the large amount of turn. Les knows this will be so, although it will turn not so much from a good length as from the foot marks. What *will* cause the batsmen problems on day five is the slightly uneven bounce that will occur after lunch from the quicker bowlers.

Thus, as Les sits watching the first hour of play and pondering on precedent, he wonders why the Aussie selectors picked two spinners. In Adelaide, in Test (or Shield) cricket, if Les was captain and was given four specialist bowlers, he would always take three quickies and one wrist spinner. Early and late in a game in Adelaide, the quickies are the danger. Perhaps if you had Grimmett and O'Reilly or Warne and MacGill it would be different, but he has sat in this very spot and seen it happen time and time again.

Throughout the five days the game ebbs and flows. Then in the last session, while around the nation people are glued to their televisions and radios, Australia snatch victory with one over and three balls to spare. Les is happy that the game was exciting right to the end, but the Test is over and there is a Shield game starting Friday and he's concerned that the wicket will be drier than usual. After the umpires have left the ground and the seagulls have landed, he walks out to the centre. A wit having a celebration drink in the Scoreboard Bar calls out, 'Hey Les, they shoulda made *you* "man of the match".' There's many a true word spoken in jest!

*   *   *

The feature of Australian Test wickets is their diversity. Perth bounces, Sydney spins, Brisbane seams and so on. Each game is a 'Test' in the original meaning of the word. Yet economics and the multi-use of grounds are changing the way turf wickets are made. Within a decade all major grounds will have wickets of the 'drop-in' variety. (These portable pitches are grown in hot houses and physically placed into the middle of the ground by machines when the cricket season begins.) Les does not feel uncomfortable about this; indeed he sees it as an advantage. For example, there could be a buffer zone between wickets, which would mean that individual pitches would be less damaged during a game. One of the problems of modern-day cricket has been the advent of the 'bat pad' position and the return of 'silly point' to field placing. These fielders jump up and down, swivel around, dive, kick the ground and perform 'victory' leaps when they take a catch. By the time the game is over, the strip next to the one being used, looks like 'no-man's land' on the Somme and can't be used for weeks. Producing portable pitches could well become Australia's next growth industry

To those not conversant with wicket preparation (which is just about all of us), it is a mystery how Les and his cohorts understand what is going to happen four days on. How *does* Les know that there will be uneven bounce occurring on the fifth day? Well, to begin with, Les has eyes but in this case, to back up his eyes and experience, he has a simple piece of equipment — which for want of another name let's call a 'bounceometer'.

The bounceometer is a pole 15 feet in height with a piece jutting out. It looks like a sort of skinny diving board. Les places the bounceometer over an area of the wicket, then puts a cricket ball on top and drops it. The results vary a little but over a number of Tests they have come up with pretty much the same sort of results. On the first morning of the Test, the ball bounces consistently to a height between 36 and 40 inches. Gradually, as the game progresses, cracks occur on the wicket's surface and platelets form between these cracks. Some of these platelets remain solid, others become softer and are inclined to move when pressure is put on them. Thus, on the fifth day, when Les drops the ball from 15 feet, the bounce varies from between 30 and 48 inches. Consequently, the ball can come through at unpredictable heights and batsmen once again wish that, as kids, they hadn't swapped their surfboard for a cricket bat. Yet this is part of the unpredictable ebb and flow of a cricket match, for it is when times are not easy that those with the technique, temperament and 'ticker' come through. Those players who do not possess these attributes won't. On the last two sessions on the last day of a game in Adelaide, the term *Test cricket* takes on its true meaning!

A curator's equipment can be fancy or sophisticated but since Victor Trumper was in the under 11s, the groundsman's greatest asset is the heavy roller. In the old days the roller was not driven but pulled by a large horse in slippers. Now all first-class wickets are covered (a law that has allowed the game to become more predictable, but caused 'the glorious uncertainty of cricket' to be far less uncertain). Therefore the heavy roller has become almost the only roller. Between innings the batting captain has the choice of rollers to use — the light or the heavy. Under almost all circumstances, Les would use the heavy roller. The utilisation of the light roller goes back to the days of uncovered wickets and also to a belief in the ill-informed dictum that 'a heavy roller breaks up the wicket'. On the fourth and fifth day, the wicket will break up eventually but the use of the heavy roller will bind it together for a longer period, stalling its eventual disintegration.

When a captain says he wants the light roller, Les just shrugs his shoulders and says, 'Okay, mate, if that's what you want.' If the captain asks Les's advice he will give it. Though there was one occasion when Les deviated from his usual practice. Australia were playing India and Sachin Tendulkar was captaining the visitors. He requested the light roller. As Tendulkar walked away, Les said, 'Sachin, are you sure?'

The great little Indian batsman turned and came back. 'Yes I'm sure,' he answered, and then, hesistantly, he went on, 'but, Les, if you were me, what would you do?'

'I'd use the heavy roller.'

Tendulkar grinned and said, 'Give me the heavy roller will you please, Les.'

In the cricket season Les sleeps with one eye open. If it is windy during the night, he starts to worry if the covers are staying down. If it's raining as well, Les often gets in his car and goes to the ground to check that water hasn't blown under the covers. Over all his years on duty his wickets have remained dry, although Les himself always comes home sopping wet.

Les treats people with respect and is given respect in return. He is admired for his ability and his dedication and has been praised by the famous. While preparing the wicket for the indoor series at Docklands Stadium, Steve Waugh was interviewed about the pending matches. When asked about the wicket preparation, Waugh replied in words that implied that this was the least of his worries because Les Burdett was on the job, and when Burdett is in charge the wicket is always good for cricket.

Over the years, Les and Sir Donald Bradman had spoken on many occasions and though he had always been encouraging, Bradman had never actually praised Les. One day Les was talking to the Chief Executive of the NSWCA, Bob Radford, who recounted a conversation he had with Bradman. Radford said, 'Sir Don reckons you're the best [curator] in the country.' If Les Burdett had fallen under the roller that morning he would have died a happy man.

On another occasion, the SACA had decided to spruce up the old ground by painting the seats in different colours. Les arranged for the job to be started and the men set about their task. A few days later, Don Bradman was walking along the concourse on his way to the SACA offices. As he strolled past the newly painted seats, one of the men called out, 'Hey, Sir Don, what do you think of the colours?'

Bradman, stopped and took a closer look. 'I like the yellow, blue and green but I'm not too keen on the red.' Ever the cricketer, Don Bradman was obviously thinking of the fielders trying to pick out a ball against a red painted seat.

The worker was a bit of a stirrer and pursued the matter. 'Oh come on, Sir Don, a group of colours without red would be like a salad without tomatoes.'

As he walked away The Don replied, 'I'm not too keen on tomatoes either.'

Some years ago Les was helping his youngest daughter, Emma, prepare for a pool party to celebrate her birthday, when his daughter came up with a request. She explained that Greg Blewett was the favourite cricketer of herself and her friends and asked if it would be possible for Les to invite Blewett to her party. 'Dad' replied that he was sure 'Blewy' would love to come to the party, splash around the pool with Emma and all her mates and then take a piece of cake home, but unfortunately, Blewy would be otherwise occupied in Perth, playing a Sheffield Shield game against Western Australia.

However, Emma is a quick thinker. 'Oh in that case,' she said, 'you can invite Sir Donald Bradman.'

The amazing thing about Les's career as a curator is that his employer has always been the SACA and 95 per cent of his time has been spent at the Adelaide Oval. Surely there must have been other grounds who wanted to recruit 'the best in the country'?

Les has had other offers but has never really considered them. As the Aboriginal people are tied to the earth of Australia, so is Les Burdett tied to the Adelaide Oval. It is a partnership that will not be broken by man, only by time. After all, if a bloke likes to work in a beautiful environment, if he yearns to be close to the soil and if he loves watching cricket, where else would he want to be?

*   *   *

The game is nearing its end — there's just one more wicket to win. You look across the ground as the shadows from the old stand lengthen onto the oval and the seagulls feed down at the Torrens end. It's like being in a time warp. Is that batsman George Giffen? Could the spinner be old Clarrie Grimmett? You let your eyes wander from the Cathedral up to the distant hills. They are very dry — there will be bushfires this summer. Behind the bowler's arm sits Les Burdett, in the spot where Arthur Lance used to sit, southeast of the sightboard. Opposite, under the Moreton Bays, kids chase a ball and a man lies bare-chested, fast asleep. There is a raucous appeal from the middle. The umpire doesn't move for a moment, weighing up the options. Could it be Mel McInnes? 'Out,' he says. And gazing down from Montefiore Hill, Colonel Light's finger points the way.

THIRTEEN

Back to you, Richie

In the days before colour and pay television, when the print media dominated, sport needed the press only for publicity and to give the results. The newspapers, on the other hand, saw themselves as instruments for comment and influence and only grudgingly as a provider of public information. Nowadays, sport and the media need each other as pubs need beer. The coming together of these two highly influential forces has, in many ways, benefited both, and certainly the public at large has been the big winner.

This publication, though, is about one sport only. Cricket is an entertainment around which swirls a specialist sub-branch of all the media parts. Those involved describe, write about, photograph, record, criticise, paint and live off a pastime that is part sport, part culture and part industry. Once it was just a game.

Back in the days before World Series Cricket, Kerry Packer saw an opportunity with the game of cricket. Cricket was a game invented for television, though at the time this fact was not apparent to those who ran the game. Packer saw and understood this and World Series Cricket was born. Channel Nine moved in and by cleverly combining show business with tradition brought cricket to a larger and less discriminating audience. With the top television station in its corner, cricket was given a life-saving transfusion and, with renewed strength, bounded ahead to a future undreamt of just a few years before. Yet there were those at the time who believed that in saving its body, cricket lost its soul. Be that as it may, from then on, the game of cricket would never be the same again.

Having lived through both periods of the game, I do not espouse the theory that cricket emulated Faust. In the days before Packer's intervention, the game of cricket was run by part-time volunteers. In NSW these officials, called 'delegates', were elected by the clubs and were well-meaning lovers of the game. From these delegates, three members were appointed to the Board of Control, which ran the game throughout the country. As so often happens in sporting and political organisations, the cream often fails to leave the bottom. To observers on the outside looking in, it seemed that control fell mostly into the hands of autocratic, inflexible men who grabbed the reins of power and hung on until they were forced into nursing homes or died. These administrators held the conservative line, regarded initiative with suspicion, 'change' as a euphemism for 'revolution' and players as a necessary evil. Those in control encouraged men of like mind — and on more than a few occasions, of like religion.

[Though by no means an everyday illustration, the story of Bill O'Reilly standing for a position as a delegate from the St George Cricket Club is an example of the thinking of the time.

In his era, Bill 'Tiger' O'Reilly was the next most famous cricketer to Bradman and arguably the greatest bowler in the history of the game. Bill O'Reilly was also a very good judge of players, an astute cricket thinker and a hard-hitting and literate sporting journalist of immense reputation. Added to that, O'Reilly had a university degree and at one stage worked as a high school English teacher. He was extremely well read, a lover of history, liked a drink and was a passionate Australian who had once met Henry Lawson (the bush balladist — not Geoff 'Henry' Lawson, the fast bowler). Mind you, Bill O'Reilly was a tough character. He could also be obstinate, didn't tolerate fools gladly and spoke his mind without fear or favour.

I'll bet readers are now saying to themselves, 'With a CV like this, why would Tiger O'Reilly bother standing for a small-time position as club delegate? With those credentials he could be Prime Minister! A sort of top-spinning Ben Chifley!'

Well guess what? In the ballot for the St George Cricket Club committee, Bill O'Reilly was beaten by a second-grade player!]

Now cricket is televised worldwide by a number of organisations, but Channel Nine is still the dominating player in Australia.

Whether it was a fluke or not, someone in Channel Nine got it right when, a quarter of a century ago, they chose their commentators for World Series Cricket and beyond. A few of the originals have slipped by the wayside, but the 'Big Four' (Richie Benaud, Ian Chappell, Tony Greig and Bill Lawry) are still there, performing as well as ever. Originally, I suppose, these four were chosen because they were high-profile cricketers and high-profile international captains. But over the last two and a half decades they have moved from being former cricketers broadcasting the cricket to being symbols of the very game from which they make their living. As Dame Edna is now a mega-star, not Barry Humphries' creation (or even a Moonie Ponds housewife), so have these four become as big as cricket itself. It would not be going too far to say that they are more recognisable than the players they talk about. Furthermore, they have introduced words and phrases into the language of their country, their props and clothing are known throughout the land and others make money by imitating them.

Thousands of words have been written about the Channel Nine commentary team, so I guess a few more won't hurt, for they are the lead riders in cricket's media merry-go-round.

The Master

Richie Benaud has spanned cricket's spectrum. He was the commanding leg spinner between Grimmett and Warne, a captain in the class of Armstrong and Bradman, a fine journalist, a cricket broadcaster who possibly exceeds even McGilvray, and a personality whose contribution to the game has been innovative and beneficial.

As a player, Richie Benaud began his career as a batting allrounder. Later, when bowling became his strength, his batting slipped a little. It seems now that commentators and historians speak of him only as bowler. Yet Benaud was always a dangerous and forceful bat, able to adapt his method to the situation of the game. (In a club game, at Waitara Oval, I once saw him play on a very difficult sticky wicket, 'gluepots' they used to be called. With a combination of technique and guts, Benaud hit the ball as little as possible, took the knocks, got through the tough part and when the wicket dried out thrashed a strong Northern District attack into submission.) Benaud had all the shots but was more a powerful clubber of the ball than a stylist. As a captain, his ambition was to win and his watchword was 'attack'. A draw was tantamount to a loss to Richie Benaud.

Good captains make their own luck and Richie Benaud made more luck than most, but in the cut and thrust of post-match dressing-room celebrations, one would have to be an optimist to expect a compliment from your teammates. In the early 1960s, there was a Shield match against Queensland which, for most of the last day, NSW looked like losing. At a vital moment, Benaud pulled a rabbit out of his baggy blue cap and NSW claimed a most unlikely victory. In the Blues' room soon after the post-match celebration had begun, one of the team was heard to shout to his captain, 'You know, B'nord, you're so lucky that if you lived at Manly you'd walk to work.'

*   *   *

In my early years of playing grade cricket, one of the funniest incidents I ever saw on the field occurred at Cumberland Oval and concerned Richie Benaud (then captain of Cumberland, NSW and Australia) and my Northern District captain, Jim Burke. It was here I saw the slightly cynical Benaud sense of humour for the first time — and at its best. Northern District had knocked Cumberland over for the paltry total of 73. (In those days a first innings win was worth six competition points, while an outright win was worth 10.) In reply, the scoreboard showed Northern District 2 for 73 with Burke 41 and Marks 6. Benaud bowled to Burke, who jumped down the wicket and forced it to the right of the midwicket fieldsman. We scampered through for a run — 2 for 74, read the board — Northern District now led on the first innings. (Burke knew he had gained the six points and wanted to close and shoot for the outright.) On reaching the bowler's end Burke turned to his opposing captain and said, 'That'll do us, B'nord, you have another go.' But as we were walking off the field, there was a commotion from the scorers' area.

Each team had experienced scorers: Ernie Gould from Cumberland and Bob Fraser from Northern District. 'Go back, Burkey,' called Bob, ' the scoreboard is wrong, we are only 73.'

'Richie, it's a tie,' yelled Ernie. 'We've played a tie.'

Suddenly, Burkey realised he'd made the most fundamental mistake in grade cricket — that is, he'd taken notice of the kids working the scoreboard, when the only thing that actually matters is what the official scorers say. And the official scorers said that Northern District and Cumberland had tied on the first innings! As we walked towards the gate, Burkey suddenly stopped and looked around. Coming up behind us was the captain of the Cumberland team, wearing a grin on his face so wide it made the Cheshire Cat look like an income-tax investigator suffering from piles.

'Er, B'nord,' stammered Burkey, 'we've, er, stuffed up.'

Richie Benaud, smile spreading wider, replied, 'No you haven't, Burkey, you have made a most positive decision. The game is a tie, each team gets three competition points and now we go on and play for an outright. It will be a great game of cricket.'

I was still in my teens, yearning for the big time, and I, also, had a cynical sense of humour, but in this situation I kept it well in check. So there I was, in the midst of a confrontation between the captain of Australia, a man I had admired only from afar, and Jimmy Burke, my captain, mentor and close mate, who had just messed up, big time. I listened as the conversation ebbed and flowed, but I knew that the captain of Cumberland had the whip hand. And he knew it too. 'You know, Burkey, I really admire you,' said Benaud happily. 'A lot of captains I've come up against would have merely taken the first-innings points and batted on. Instead, you settled on a tie and opened the game right up.'

'But B'nord, it was *your* scoreboard that was wrong! It wasn't my fault!' (Jimmy Burke was taking the high ground.)

Wilf Ewens, one of the Cumberland players, interrupted. 'Richie's got nothing to do with the scoreboard. It's owned by the Parramatta City Council.'

'Well it was a genuine mistake. Let's go back, get one more run and I'll close.' (Jimmy Burke was taking the middle ground.)

Richie Benaud's face was now deadly serious as he replied, 'But, Burkey, you've already closed, it would be illegal for us to go back on again.' Ron Mulock, the Cumberland opening bowler, was a lawyer by profession, and later rose to the position of Deputy Premier of NSW, and I remember thinking that perhaps the scorers could try the case in the middle of Cumberland Oval and Ronnie could be the prosecutor.

Actually, Richie was correct. The declaration had been made and that was that. In reality, the umpires should have walked off saying nothing except, 'Cumberland to bat.' The umpires, however, were as fascinated as the rest of us by this wonderful piece of cricketing theatre featuring Australia's opening bat and Australia's captain.

'Please, B'nord, please! I should have checked with the scorers, but these things happen … c'mon, mate!' I had the impression

Burke was about to fall to his pads and beg for mercy. (Jimmy Burke was heading for the low ground.)

The serious look left Benaud's face and he laughed as he called to his troops, 'Okay, fellas, let's go back,' and he walked away to the middle to measure out his run again. I had strike and managed to thick-edge a short ball behind point for a single. It was an ordinary shot off a poor ball, which is quite understandable, I guess, as both the bowler and batsman were still laughing. Anyway, Northern District were *now* 2 for 74. The captain could close if he wished.

Angry at himself and at those in the middle who couldn't hold back a laugh, Jimmy Burke turned and stormed from the field. 'Where are you going, Burkey?' Richie Benaud called.

Without looking around, Burke shouted, 'We're closing.'

Richie shouted back, 'Have you checked with the scorers?'

*　　*　　*

The great race broadcaster, Ken Howard, must have had hundreds of ambitious young men copy his wonderful style and his brilliant broadcasting rhythms, (those rhythms which Australian race calling has made its own). Conversely, the precise, clipped-speech style of Benaud is so distinctive, so Benaud, that for a professional broadcaster to use it would border on plagiarism. Such an artificial version would be un-Australian. It is a style patented by nature.

Richie Benaud's broadcast technique is the mode of the man in his ordinary life. That is, if anyone wants to call the life of a man who jets around the world watching cricket and who resides spasmodically in London, the French Riviera and Coogee, *ordinary*!

To begin with, Richie Benaud knows the game of cricket thoroughly. And so he should! For six decades he has been more closely attached to it than anybody living. Looking at the game through the eyes of experience and with an attitude of gentle awareness, he doesn't live in the past, yet he still holds to the original traditions for which cricket is noted: fair play, sportsmanship and respect for your opponent.

If Richie Benaud has a blind spot, it is with cricket's administrators. Not that Benaud is exactly agin the government, it's just that he has never actually trusted it. Back in the 1970s, his brother John was symbolically crucified for the minor misdemeanour of wearing cricket boots to which certain powerful NSW delegates objected. Richie immediately handed in his life membership of the New South Wales Cricket Association, over issues relating to the ban. Then came World Series Cricket and Richie Benaud was one of the main instigators in the formation of the rebel group. This caused him to be regarded, by many in the cricket establishment, as a sort of flannelled Quisling. Sadder still, friendships between great cricketers were wrenched apart. The wheel has now turned, World Series Cricket is but a memory and the cricket administrators now claim that their relationship with the media is open and harmonious. Furthermore, Richie Benaud is now back with the Establishment — or so the Establishment believes! Those of us who lived through this sporting cold war should be excused if sometimes, over a stimulating drink, we sit back, reflect on those days and smile a bemused smile at the vicissitudes of life.

Richie Benaud broadcasts as he used to bowl, with a studied precision and the ability to improvise. He is always composed, a man completely at home in his camera-regulated environment, treating the viewer as an equal and allowing his verve for the game to come across through the small screen. This enthusiasm is controlled, but it is always there. For Richie Benaud is a cricket enthusiast. Year after year he follows the sun, watching cricket matches on different continents, on different pitches, often witnessing sub-standard performances (remember, he sees a lot of cricket in England), but to Benaud the game is always full of highlights. Mel Gibson must surely tire of acting and Brian Henderson of reading the news, but Richie Benaud's job is an ever-moving labour of love.

'Good morning and welcome to the MCG [or wherever].' These are the first words of every cricket day. They come from Richie Benaud and are the cue for the Test to begin. Players ready? Umpires ready? Groundsmen ready for Tony's pitch report? Yet the day for Benaud has begun long before this. Scores from other Tests around the world must be checked, overnight comments from the press read and scuttlebutt noted — if not always absorbed. Benaud knows that there may well be a reason to mention a morsel from such information later in the day. Many people are employed behind the scenes to assist the commentators, but nothing has ever replaced a commentator's own homework.

As a trained journalist Richie Benaud is a fine wordsmith, but it is not so much his phrases (knowledgeable and lucid though they are) that make listeners sit up; it is the Benaud silences and understatement that mark him as the master of his trade. For instance, when the opening bowler is delivering a tirade of lip-readable expletives to a batsman who has played at and missed three balls in a row, some of the Channel Nine team would say, 'Boy, McGrath is giving Lara a gobful.' Benaud's response would be, 'McGrath is now conveying to Lara a quick lesson on the art of footwork.' However, my favourite Benaud responses occur when one of Benaud's co-commentators makes a remark that is clever but contentious. *Silence*, comes the stern reply from Benaud. This silence couldn't be described, in the contemporary vernacular, as 'going through to the keeper'. It sort of hangs there, like a wisp of smoke coming from a chimney in winter, slowly moving out into the ether. Then the subject is changed as Richie Benaud says, 'Gough bowling to Martyn.'

I know as much about fashion as I know about art. As a matter of fact, I recently had an old cricket mate of mine come up to me and say, 'Hey, Harpo, don't you reckon it's time you stopped wearing those tracksuits?' I was inclined to agree, but I wasn't quite sure what else I had. Therefore I feel a little awkward disapproving of Richie's cream coordinates. Yet if I was looking for something to criticise in his television performance, without wishing to appear obsequious, this would be the only thing I could find. It may be a trademark but, let me tell you, it's the wrong colour. I mean, with the attractive grey hair and still adequate features, why wouldn't Richie wear blue? (I'm not going so far as to suggest a navy tracksuit, white shirt and red tie with a Windsor knot, but … um … I dunno?)

There was a painting which once hung in the entrance of the revered old Cricketers' Club in George Street, Sydney. This original, by Arthur Mailey, showed cricketers at the end of a day's play, hot and thirsty, trooping off an oval somewhere in a suburban park or a field in the outback (it was hard to tell which). Underneath the painting was the caption, *There Is No Summer In This Land Without Cricket.* The Cricketers' Club has now gone and so, to the best of my knowledge, has the painting. Yet seven decades since Arthur finished his painting, things haven't changed much. It is not the first bloom of the jacaranda, the 30+ sunscreen coming out of the closet or the initial rendition of *Jingle Bells* in the local shopping mall that proclaims the beginning of our hot holiday season. The words come from Richie Benaud, 'Good morning and welcome to the Gabba, for the first Test of the series.' A metaphorical curtain opens and the Australian summer, in all 'its beauty and its terror', is with us again.

Runs in the family

There was no affectation in Ian Chappell's demeanour on or off the cricket field. On the field, he was out there to win, the ball was to be hit hard and often, batsmen were to be dismissed as quickly as possible, officials were freeloaders and the beer was to be cold at the end of the day's play. His broadcasting style is a bit the same. Chappell looks at the scene out in the middle and speaks about what is happening in a straight-from-the-shoulder manner because he *knows* what is going on. He does not need catchphrases or gimmicks. All Ian Chappell needs is a game of cricket and he'll tell those watching exactly what is happening.

In his playing days, Chappell, like Richie Benaud, distrusted officialdom. In many cases, the feeling was reciprocated. Yet although some cricket administrators viewed Ian Chappell, captain of Australia, as they would regard their son's pet funnel-web spider, they were muted in their criticism because of the results Chappell achieved and the immense loyalty given to him by his team. Added to this was his huge popularity with the Australian sporting public. As a broadcaster, Chappell is far less controversial. His manner is quiet and controlled and his pleasant, well-modulated Australian accent is most pleasing on the ear — despite the occasional pronunciation which shows his Adelaide background. (For example, in such words as 'fool', 'school' and 'pool', the dropping of the L and the replacing of it with a W — foow, schoow, poow.)

The other commentators (with the exception of Benaud) have their share of knockers. Chappell has fewer than most. Viewers appreciate his insight and remember that in his playing days he was the one who led from the front. If you were down in the trenches and ready to go 'over the top', Ian Chappell is the type of bloke you'd want next to you. The only minor criticism of Chappell's broadcasting style comes from those who say that he is inclined to reflect back too often to his own era (Doug Walters, Dennis Lillee and so on). If this is so, it is not just a shortcoming of television commentators. It is also a failing of, among others, old soldiers, thespians and authors. As a matter of fact, about 50 per cent of the book you are now reading concerns people from the writer's era.

Nobody, however, has ever challenged Chappell's impartiality. The driving passion of Chappell's cricket life was 'to beat the Poms', but, paradoxically, there has never been a hint of parochialism in his commentary. His criticism is incisive and based on experience, intelligence and a knowledge of the game up there with Benaud's. Chappell's broadcasting of cricket has nothing to do with allegiance or showmanship.

If Ian Chappell wasn't on television he could probably buy a small tent and a crystal ball, and travel around the show circuits of Australia as a fortune teller. For not only does he seem, tactically, a step ahead of both the captains on the field; more often than not he can predict what is going to happen. Just as an old salt sniffs the breeze and knows the wind is about to change, so Chappell can sense a shift about to occur in the game he is calling. In a match that may seem to others to have developed an orthodox pattern, you may hear Chappell say, 'The ball is now starting to "reverse swing", and though Ponting is middling them beautifully, he is playing his drives a little away from his foot. If England can make a break here, a couple of wickets could fall quickly and Australia will be in trouble, batting last.' Sure enough, Ponting will nick one onto his stumps, Australia will lose another wicket soon after and suddenly the game has turned. This type of prognostication comes not just from observation, but from instinct as well. It is an instinct that is inherent in only the great captains. Ian Chappell has taken this instinct into his commentary. He has the ability to know what should happen, anticipate it and then effectively explain it all.

Ian Chappell is a cricketer's cricketer. He brings the same focus and dedication to his broadcasts that he brought to his playing. Those who love the game listen to Chappell in the hope of affirmation of their opinions; those who are not so conversant with cricket's peculiar dialogue and plots listen to him and learn. But above all, 'Chappelli' is the caller for the connoisseur.

Broadcasting from Bay 13

In some of his after-dinner speeches, Bill Lawry uses the line, 'It's hard to be humble when you're a Victorian.' That Bill 'Phanto' Lawry hails from Melbourne there is no doubt. Like all Victorians, he played his sport hard and tough, gave no quarter and asked for none. As a batsman he was well balanced, with a great defence but although he had every shot in the book, he often seemed hesitant to use most of them. Between the wickets his loping stride took him to the other end and back again, with the judgement and assurance of a top jockey in the straight at

Flemington. Lawry is also another example of the critics overlooking the fielding of a world-renowned batsman, just because he doesn't stand in the glamour positions. With a strong arm and sure hands, Bill Lawry was one of the best fielders of his era. If you had to pick a team to play for your life and you were sent in to bat on a bumping pitch with a blinding light, you'd pick Bill Lawry to open the innings. (If for no other reason than Bill would immediately appeal against the blinding light.)

As a captain he led from the front, although not even his most fervent fans would place him in the ranks of the great strategists. His outlook was conservative, lacking the flair of Mark Taylor, the instincts of Ian Chappell and the audacity of Benaud. Bill Lawry was a scrapper who believed in getting on top and once there he was not going to relinquish the advantage to anybody. Though the mob may bray, the press carp and the Australian Cricket Board give lip service to 'brighter cricket', it wouldn't worry 'Phanto'. (A *Victorian's* crease is his castle, and he'd stay there as long as he pleased!) Therefore, as a captain, Bill Lawry wouldn't take a gamble to win, but he wasn't going to lose either. I hesitate to imagine how Lawry felt when Adam Gilchrist closed at Headingley during the 2001 Ashes series and left England 315 to get in 110 overs on a good wicket. (No doubt Bill felt calmer after he was released from the Intensive Care Unit and spent a few days back at his hotel recovering.)

Bill Lawry's commentaries are nothing like his game. His broadcasts are filled with excitement and bubbling enthusiasm. The accent, broad and high pitched, identifies with the throng in the outer. 'The crowd is building, there should be six'y five to sev'n'y thous'nd here today. Bay 13 is full already. There is a wun'erful atmosphere at the great Melb'n Crik't Grownd.' This is not the accent of the Melbourne Establishment, not the accent of the Members' Stand. It is the voice of the people who love and understand this game, which is second only to their beloved footy — a fair way behind, I'll admit, but second nonetheless!

Despite his normal ebullient mode, on occasions Bill Lawry cannot prevent his disappointment showing through. During a day–night game recently, the Australian side was bowling the 48th over and the opposition hadn't made as many runs as they had expected. The batsman, in desperation, threw his head back and had a wild slog at the ball, which went high in the air and was easily caught by the keeper. 'Oh, that was a poor shot. He didn't need to do that at this stage of the game,' called Bill. (This statement must have caused many viewers to ponder. If the batsman didn't need to have a slog in the 48th over, when the hell should he start?) Though such an attitude may ignore the ground rules in the sports broadcasting textbooks, it shows Lawry's individuality and his need to tell it how he sees it. For those who saw Bill Lawry batting in defensive mood, the kindest description of it would be 'bland'. There is nothing bland about his commentaries.

Of all the on-air combinations, the one I find the most entertaining is Richie Benaud and Bill Lawry. It is a compound of contrasts. Benaud, controlled and laid-back, Lawry wordy and excitable. Take, for instance, a batsman who is struggling against the fast bowler. Suddenly he gets beaten for pace and stumps fall backward and bails fly high.

If Benaud is on air you will hear, 'Bowled!' (Pause.) 'A wonderful inswinger.' (Pause) 'England 3 for 42.'

If Lawry is at the microphone, hold onto to your beer, lock the dog away and shove your head under a pillow. 'GOT HIM — KNOCKED HIM OVER, THROUGH THE GATE, STUMPS EVERYWHERE, BOWLED HIM NECK AND CROP, LOOK AT LEE CELEBRATING, WHAT A BALL, ENGLAND IN BIG TROUBLE.'

Or take the time Warne bowls his flipper, the ball zips through, the batsman plays for the leg break and is hit on the back pad. 'GOT HIM, LBW!' calls Bill. WHAT? "NOT OUT", SAYS THE UMPIRE?'

Bill growls, 'I'd like to see that on replay.' We go to the replay, which shows that the middle stump would not only have been knocked out of the ground but would have impaled Adam Gilchrist somewhere between the navel and the protector. 'Oh, that's a disgrace,' cries Bill. 'When are the cricket authorities going to improve the standard of world umpires? Umpire Cheetham from New Zealand has had an absolute shocker! There's the replay again from a different angle. Bad decision Richie!'

'Hmm,' Richie murmurs, 'very close. Warne moves in again to bowl to Crawley.'

The fact that Bill Lawry wears his heart on his sleeve is the major reason for his popularity. He stated that Umpire Cheetham was having a bad match because Umpire Cheetham was having *a horror*. That's what the paying customers in Bay 13 thought and that's what the 'rating' customers in their lounge rooms reckoned as well. It is a fact of human nature that people want to mix with those who agree with them. The same goes for the media. Viewers want someone who says what they feel, so that they can turn to their wives and announce wisely, 'See, Love, Bill said what I was just telling you — this umpire is hopeless!'

This contrast in broadcasting styles is one of the reasons for the Big Four still being on air after a quarter of a century.

When you're sitting back at home watching the cricket and you suddenly hear a high-pitched voice call, 'It's all happening at the Melb'n Crik't Grownd', you can rest assured that it is — because Bill Lawry is there and he's telling you about it.

The key to success

Tony Greig is a man of many parts. Part South African, part Englishman, part Australian — and loyal to them all. Although, sometimes, when these countries are playing cricket against one another, Tony struggles with his allegiances. The one thing Tony Greig has no difficulty with is his fidelity to the game of cricket. He is passionate about the game and these feelings come through to the viewer. Yet this passion is not so muted by respect for the game that Greig refrains from criticising when the occasion demands. In this regard he tends to be a commentator in the Lawry style rather than in the ilk of Benaud or Chappell.

'We cross now for Tony Greig's pitch report,' says Richie Benaud. How many times have viewers heard those words? There stands Tony, microphone in hand, cord trailing off beyond the eye of the camera, large hat protecting his nearly hairless dome from damage by Australians' greatest enemy, the sun. Tony Greig's dress is immaculate, and though the accent is a mixture of his three countries, the voice is resonant and manly. His shoes sparkle, the trousers are just the right length and his fingernails are manicured to perfection. For, surely, there is nobody else on Australian television whose trouser cuffs, shoes and fingers receive as much camera exposure as do those of Tony Greig.

Of all the Channel Nine commentary crew, Tony Greig is the one with the most imposing camera presence. He stands tall and in command, and even when he squats down to penetrate the wicket with his car key his bearing permeates the small screen. The car keys themselves have a place in the realms of television history. I wonder, over the years, how many of these implements have ravished parts of the most holy turf in Australia? What would they bring at an auction of cricket memorabilia?

('How much am I bid for the key Tony Greig broke trying to force it into the WACA wicket on the first day of a West Indies Test?' — 'Next item is the key that slipped through the four-inch crack on the fifth day of a Test at the MCG. Slightly rusted, it was recently dug up by the groundsman's three-year-old son while he was building sand castles in the area of the centre bounce at the conclusion of the Hawthorn–Essendon game.')

Doctors learn more about disease as they get older. The same applies to cricketers in regard to cricket. Even when they stop playing, cricketers can still watch and keep learning. In other words, as knowledgeable as he is now, Steve Waugh will know even more about the game when he is 50. There is, however, one exception to this rule: a cricketer's knowledge of turf wickets. No matter how long a cricketer lives he will consistently read pitches wrongly. I do not know why this is so. Perhaps it's another example of Mother Nature keeping humans in their place.

This brings us back to Tony Greig's pitch report. There he is, fingernails immaculate etc, rubbing his hand over a fine mat of grass before the much-awaited key insertion. Then he rises to his full height and predicts the future. 'This wicket will have a bit of life in the first session, then flatten out to a perfect batting strip for three days. By day four it will start to turn and then keep low on the last day. Back to you, Richie.' It's possible that Tony Greig could be correct. It is also possible that he could pick the quadrella in the Caulfield Cup — but he won't!

There are occasions when the captains, selectors and broadcasters are even more uncertain about a pitch than usual, so they go to another source for advice.

Once more, Tony has the mike: 'This is an unusual wicket, mottled in colour and a little patchy on a good length. I've never before seen a Gabba wicket with this type of look. So I spoke to the groundsman, Jock Quagmire, and asked him what he thought.' Oh, Tony! Tony! Will you never learn? In this life there are three things a sportsman must never do. He ought never ask a doting father if the man's son is a good player, he should never wear his best suit to a football club reunion and he must never, never seek a groundsman's advice about a wicket that the groundsman has prepared himself. (The one exception, as I explained in the previous chapter 'A Wicket Way to Earn a Living', is Les Burdett, the groundsman at the Adelaide Oval.)

[I learned a personal lesson many years ago when I was a NSW state selector and was delegated to choose the 12th man on the morning of a Shield match. I was faced with the usual options: play two spinners, play a third quickie or play it safe and pick an extra bat.

I strutted out onto the Sydney Cricket Ground in the self-important manner of all selectors, looked at the wicket, prodded it with my finger and searched for my car key. At the Randwick end the groundsman (chief curator) was hammering the stumps in. 'How's it going to play, mate?' I asked, not really wanting an answer but wishing to appear polite to a man with whom I'd become acquainted over the years.

He stopped his hammering, walked over to me and in all earnestness replied, 'The usual. A lot of bounce and cut in the first few hours, then it will start to spin sharply.'

'So you'd put 'em in?' I said.

'Oh no,' he replied, 'it will be great for batting.'

I walked slowly back to the pavilion as the captain strolled over from his fielding drill to meet me. 'Who's 12th man, Harpo?' he asked.

'The wicketkeeper,' I replied.

'The *wicketkeeper*!!??'

'Yeah,' I answered, 'we can't possibly do without any of the others.']

Tony Greig is also a polished interviewer. I imagine it is not easy to conduct the post-match captains' interviews — there is usually little time available and the players are likely to be speaking only in platitudes. ('We'll have to regroup', … 'It was a team effort', etc.) It must be even harder to stand in the middle of the SCG at the end of a series and present the trophy to the winning team, which is awash with champagne, and a meagre cheque to the losing team, which is aghast at the umpiring decisions. Huddled around the makeshift stage are 10,000 people wanting to be heard, and next to Tony is the Managing Director of Australian cricket's major sponsor; such a person often hails from such places as Okinawa, Japan or Chicago, Illinois, and doesn't know cricket from a cicada.

Whatever happens, Tony Greig handles this off-the-cuff situation with confidence and aplomb. He has no cue cards, he can't stop the camera, he can't start again. He flies by the seat of his pants, and in doing so brings the players closer to the fans at the ground and those watching on the television, too.

Tony Greig is a television performer of proficiency and professionalism, prepared to say what needs to be said. As a cricketer, Tony Greig never flinched. As a broadcaster, he shows the same trait.

* * *

The four commentators perform different roles:

- Benaud, the benevolent sage who is a master of the broadcasting craft, the anchor that keeps the ship from drifting.
- Chappell, the hard-nosed cricketer whose instincts and knowledge put him up there with his leader.
- Lawry, whose enthusiasm and Ocker background make him the working people's broadcaster.
- Greig, the man on the ground with the mike, who is not afraid to tell it how it is.

With them now are the young guns. Just as knowledgeable in the game of cricket, but learning the art of broadcasting.

Tayls and Heals

Mark Taylor followed Allan Border as Australian captain. This in itself was not an easy thing to do. Border had taken over the cricket leadership of his country when Australia was desperately in need of a leader. He brought Australian cricket from the shadows of humiliation back into the sunlight of success. 'The Little Aussie Battler' resurrected the honour of 'playing for your country' and brought back pride in the baggy green cap. Thus Taylor was not succeeding just another act: he was following the 'top of the bill'. That Mark Taylor moved into the position with such ease and imparted his own style so quickly says much for the strength of the man and even more for his understanding of the traditions and nuances of the game he now controlled.

Whereas Border led Australian cricket into the sun, Taylor took it marching into the Promised Land. For under Mark Taylor, Australia once again became the greatest cricketing nation on Earth — the position most Australians, indoctrinated from birth, expect to be in. Steve Waugh built on Taylor's legacy and raised the stakes and expectations even higher. Now the end is in sight for Waugh (perhaps further in the distance than some believe, but in sight, nevertheless). The captain of the Australian XI controls the destiny of the team more than any other on-field leader in any other sport. The possibility that the next captain of Australia will have the attributes of his three predecessors is extremely unlikely. The chances of the next *three* being in the same league are about the same odds as winning Lotto.

The high standing of Mark Taylor in the cricket world is undisputed. His attributes are many. He is a man of Australian values; confident but not cocky, a thinker (although he never appears to be ruminating), a person who loves a drink with mates, golf, a barbecue and a swim. Above all, he is a man whose greatest joy is being with his family. When he was chosen as Australian of the Year, many people probably thought — fair enough, he's captain of Australia, so why not? Those who knew Mark Taylor said, 'At last they've got it right!' The people of Australia regard Mark Taylor with respect. Respect. Wouldn't we all settle for that word on our tombstone?

As a broadcaster, Taylor is fitting into his role well. He too, has a convincing on-screen presence, and his strong, honest face looks at the camera with ease and friendliness. Whereas Bill Lawry has the accent of the suburbs, Mark Taylor has an inflection from the bush. Though he was born and bred in the country, Taylor has lived in the suburbs of Sydney for the last 22 years. The boy has long left the bush and travelled the world, hobnobbing with some very sophisticated and intelligent people (and cricketers as well), but those 15 years in country NSW will be ever part of the man's personality and attitude. In the easygoing gait and the pleasant twang in his speech there remains a little bit of Leeton and Wagga Wagga.

Strangely enough, despite his bush inflection, Mark Taylor speaks quite quickly. In his early days on the commentary team this led to some criticism from viewers. After a couple of seasons of continuous broadcasting he seems to have overcome this minor fault and is developing his own natural style. It is a true Taylor style: the relaxed manner of the good bloke next door combined with the steel-trap mind of a great Field Marshal.

Listen closely and you will hear Mark Taylor playing the part of captain — placing the field, plugging the gaps. 'The slip cordon is a little wide, perhaps the captain should move the floating slip into a more orthodox fourth slip or finer gully.'

Mark Taylor is a younger Ian Chappell, predicting, anticipating, ahead of the game. He is learning the art of broadcasting as he learnt the art of cricket, with thoroughness and by understanding himself. So far as his broad range and knowledge of cricket is concerned, only the gods are in front of him, and Tubby Taylor has plenty of time to catch up.

*   *   *

Wicketkeepers are a feral breed. They're neither one thing nor the other. They lack the stylish polish of a graceful batsman, the inbred cruelty and foul mouth of a 'quickie' and the finesse but deep-rooted insecurity of a class spinner. Keepers are the scrum halfs and ruck rovers of the cricket team. They are always in the game. There is no place for them to hide and they will never know the feeling of being able to walk onto a cricket ground free and unencumbered, instead of wearing more protection than a jousting knight. (I once had a mate who retired from keeping and became an umpire. He continued to wear his protector while out on the field — he said he would feel naked without it. There's an opportunity for a clever one-liner here, but I reckon I'll just let it go through to the keeper!)

Over many years of watching cricket I've seen batsmen back away when the ball was flying and bowlers give up the ghost when the sun was blazing down and the wicket dead. Yet though I have played with and against keepers who would sledge their three-year-old daughter in a backyard game and laugh at a batsman who has just been hit in the throat, I have never met a keeper who 'dogged it'. Keepers may whine and complain, they have names for umpires that an expert in graffiti has never seen on a wall, they blame bowlers for wides, fieldsmen for returns and captains for everything, but they never, ever, throw in the towel. Come to think of it, I can't recall ever seeing a keeper who *owned* a towel. When they have a shower, which is rarely, they usually pick up a dirty one from the floor.

There is only one keeper in a team, and he always hates the opposition with a passion — but not half as much as he hates the reserve keeper. 'Never give a sucker an even break' is the credo of the wicketkeeping religion. This is the reason keepers play with broken hands, busted thumbs and with vertebrae that take unnecessary detours around the back before reaching the spinal column. For a keeper to walk onto a field with only *one* broken finger means he is 100 per cent fit. Keepers are to painkillers what alcoholics are to the liquor industry.

Ian Healy was the quintessential keeper. He came quickly from obscurity to fame and ended his career by being chosen in the Greatest Australian Team of the 20th Century. Despite the somewhat derogatory comments made previously, most keepers are intelligent and can read a game with understanding. So they should! After all, they have the best view on the ground. A knowledgeable keeper can be invaluable to a captain — Ian Healy was certainly invaluable to the captains he played under. He had the ability to quickly pick opposition players' faults and, just as importantly, to notice an error creeping into the action of his own bowlers. For the leader, on the field, having access to such on-the-spot data is worth three coaches and a dozen computers in the grandstand.

After leaving school, Ian Healy trained as a teacher, but it is as a student of the game of cricket that he has made his living. As a commentator, he keeps viewers up to date with the theories of coaching and developments in the training of cricketers. At Teachers' College, whether Healy majored in psychology or biomechanics I'm not sure, but he seems to know as much about these sciences as he does about the art of whipping off the bails. Healy can sum up more quickly than most what a player is doing wrong and can suggest a solution, which could be anything from changing the player's mental attitude to altering his body rotation. Whereas Taylor is the tactician and strategist (looking at the team situation), Healy seems to be the expert on the mechanics of the game and the disposition of those playing it. Ian Healy could be described as a 'snick-doctor' of cricket.

Confidence was one of Ian Healy's greatest strengths on the field. He is the same in the broadcast box. The former keeper is now as familiar with his Channel Nine cohorts as he once was with his Queensland Shield teammates. His penchant for nicknames is an interesting sidelight of his commentaries. 'Good afternoon, "Tubs", "Chappelli", etc' is now part of his casual but eloquent style. Of course he hasn't reached the 'G'day, B'nord,' stage yet — a freshman can only go so far!

As they did 25 years ago, Channel Nine seems to have got it right again with Taylor and Healy.

Guests

And there are others, who usually appear when the countries they used to represent are touring. Some annoy me, such as the former England fast bowler who sounds as if he has come to the microphone direct from the cremation of his faithful, much-loved family dog. To me, Geoff Boycott's commentaries sound like the Leader of the Opposition replying to the Treasurer's Budget speech. (If Florence Nightingale and Mother Teresa put on a 200-run second-wicket partnership, in even time, I reckon 'Boycs' would still be struggling to find something to praise.) On the other hand, David Gower broadcasts as he batted and fielded. He is a class act. Ian Smith is not like Gower in style — his rough New Zealand accent sounds as if it is coming from the bottom of a ruck at Carisbrook Park — but he is a tough and knowledgeable commentator. He respects Australian cricket but won't tolerate patronising or gloating, especially if they come with an Australian intonation. What's more, if you want an argument, Smithy won't step back. Good on him! Maybe the one thing that has been missing over Channel Nine's excellent 25 years has been a good old-fashioned stoush!

FOURTEEN

Bowlers Have to Laugh

ustralia is now a multicultural society, but in our midst there
will always remain many Aussies whose forebears originally
came from the Emerald Isle. Although these folk have lived
away from the Shannon and the turf fires for many generations,
in their genes there exists a seed of the shamrock, in their eyes a
glint of humour from 'the little people' and, when the time is
appropriate, from their mouths is heard a touch of the blarney.

The Irish are also the most effective people in the world at stating
the obvious. Let me give you an example. Some years ago my wife
and I were travelling around Ireland, and while in the little town of
Cashell we stopped at a little tea shoppe for a cuppa and a
sandwich. At the next table was a beautiful young Irish girl sipping
coffee. On her lap was a cute little baby of, I guess, about 12
months. Now, like most women, Herself is besotted with babies. So
within seconds she had struck up a conversation with the young
Irish lass by commenting on how cute and well behaved was her

little baby girl. One thing led to another and soon the young girl said, 'Would you like to nurse her?' Would Herself like to nurse the baby!!! Does Shane Warne like beating batsmen through the air, dragging them forward and having them stumped? Herself took the babe, gooed and gahed over her for a while and then turned to the young mother and asked, 'What's the baby's name?'

'Lisa,' replied the lass.

'Lisa,' Herself repeated, 'what a lovely name. Do you spell it with an "S" or a "Z"?'

The girl shook her head. 'With an "L",' she answered.

* * *

I don't know how far back my old friend Greg Lynch's Irish ancestry goes, but every time he tells one of his lovely cricket yarns there is a glint in his eye, a modicum of self-deprecation, a touch of soft cynicism and perhaps just a tad of the blarney as well. Greg played for the Northern District Cricket Club as a spin bowler for over 25 years and in this period he accounted for 534 batsmen. However, despite his deeds with the ball, Greg is remembered mainly for the embarrassing fact that he captured more wickets than he scored runs. In a quarter of a century of sterling service to his beloved club, Greg snared 534 wickets but could compile only 323 runs. So this is the reason that when old-timers get together at the club's reunion dinners to talk about the past and discuss who was the greatest batsman ever to play for the club, the names of Mark Taylor, Jimmy Burke and Neil Harvey dominate the conversation but Greg Lynch is never mentioned.

As well as being a fine club spin bowler, Greg was a leading executive with the Esso oil company in the late 1960s and 1970s, at which time Esso was the sponsor of the Australian Davis Cup team. The team was touring the world trying to recapture tennis' holy grail, which had been ours for so many years previously. Greg's great friend and clubmate at Northern District was a man named Tim Caldwell, who was then a member of the Australian Cricket Board (as it is now titled) and the chairman of the

Executive Committee of the New South Wales Cricket Association. Around this time 'The Blues' had unearthed a young player whom the pundits believed was the fastest bowler in the country — and the pundits proved to be right. His name was Jeff Thomson. There was one problem, however. Just when Thomson had begun to feel comfortable in first-class cricket and was ready to be unleashed against all the Blues' traditional cricket enemies, one of these enemies offered the young bowler lucrative inducements to leave the Harbour City and journey north where the wickets are bouncy one day and bouncier the next. This was a body blow to NSW cricket, so Caldwell marched to the Esso building in the city to have a serious talk with his old mate.

'Listen, Lynchy,' began the sagacious Caldwell, as the two men sat opposite each other drinking tea in Greg Lynch's office, 'we have a young bloke named Thomson who is the fastest bowler in the world and Queensland is pinching him off us with an offer we are finding hard to match. Now I hear that Esso sponsors the Davis Cup team, so what about digging deeper and helping out your *real* love — NSW cricket?'

Greg Lynch nodded and replied, 'Crikey, Tim, we have enough blokes around this organisation who *act* like fast bowlers, now you want to saddle me with a real one.' Nonetheless, Greg Lynch began to ask questions, as is normal when a business executive is confronted with a 'job application'. 'What work could he do for us?' he asked.

'None,' replied Caldwell, 'he's a fast bowler.'

'I see. On what terms would you want us to employ him?'

Caldwell gazed out the window for a moment, then replied emphatically, 'Executive salary, company car, accommodation, full benefits and nobody telling him what to do.'

'When would he be able to come to work?'

'He wouldn't. When he's not playing cricket he would be *training* for cricket. He certainly couldn't be expected to be given time off cricket for work,' Caldwell replied, in a tone that stated the obvious. 'Mind you, he'd be a popular employee. Everyone likes Thommo — except batsmen.'

'Then what benefit would he be to the Esso organisation?'

'None whatsoever.'

'I see. *How* fast did you say this young bloke is?'

'The fastest bowler in the world!'

Greg Lynch nodded and said in his most businesslike manner, 'He seems to be just the man we're looking for.'

[Unfortunately for NSW, Esso couldn't match Queensland's offer. So Thommo went north to enjoy the perfect weather and bowl at a speed somewhere between sound and invisible … and the rest is cricket folklore.]

*   *   *

Over a drink once, Greg related this story. 'I was playing a game at Hurstville Oval many years ago, and Herb Elphinstone was umpiring. In my first over, I hit the batsman on the pad and yelled, "Howzat?" Herb shook his head and said, "Not out." The next over I did it again and, let me tell you, the batsman was plumb. "Not out," said Herb emphatically.

'At the end of the over Herb handed me my cap and I asked him why he had denied my two appeals.

'Herb smiled at me and explained, "I wasn't sure the ball would have hit the stumps."

'I then asked him how many times in an innings he really *was* sure and he replied, "Greg, I'm never sure."

'I took my cap and said, "Thanks, Herb, but I hope you won't regard me as impolite if for the rest of the game I bowl down at the other end."'

*   *   *

Like many others of the spin brotherhood, when Greg Lynch retired from bowling he took up bowling — not 'spin' this time, but lawn. He soon became most proficient at the game and was elected president of his local bowling club.

A few years ago I ran into him at a cricket match at Waitara Oval and commented that I had not seen him for a while. He explained that he had been laid up with a nasty injury. 'I was playing bowls recently,' he explained, 'and I stepped backwards into the ditch and fell over. I blacked out and when I woke up I was in hospital with concussion and a couple of busted ribs.'

I was quick to give my sympathy to an old mate who was obviously inconvenienced and appeared to be still in pain from the accident.

Greg shrugged his shoulders, grinned and replied, 'Well, Marksy, I guess a bloke has got to expect such injuries when at the age of 78 he continues to play contact sports.'

[Greg is now over 80, still smiling and quick with a quip. He is not as mobile as of yore but he's still going well for a bloke who spent most of his life politely bowling down the other end.]

FIFTEEN

The Bloke from the Board

As a boy of 14 I attended my first of many annual general meetings (AGMs) of the Northern District Cricket Club. It was my second season with the club and my father felt it only right and proper that I get to learn about my club and what made it function from the inside. This began my intense loathing of AGMs — a malady that remains with me to this day.

[Later in life, I used to have a recurring dream. I dreamt that I had died and was standing at the gates of Heaven. As I looked around wondering where to go, St Peter suddenly appeared and said, 'You're not coming in here, Marksy.'

I replied, 'I'm being sent to hell?'

'No,' he answered. 'For your sins you are condemned to spend the rest of eternity attending annual general meetings of cricket clubs.']

This first meeting was held at a cold dank hall in the northern Sydney suburb of Hornsby, a structure which would have been condemned as uninhabitable by a greedy Dickensian landlord. The local Member of Parliament had been president of the Northern District club for as long as most of the old-timers could remember. He was a decent enough old bloke, for a politician, but well past his 'use-by date' as the person elected to preside over a cricket club of few past triumphs but with enormous potential. Our president's performance, chairing the AGM, was one example of his anachronistic style and fading memory. He went through the motions in a parliamentary manner but in doing so dropped his papers, called each speaker by the wrong name and declared the meeting closed in the middle of a critical harangue from the third-grade captain on the controversial subject of selection policy.

Sitting at the front table with the president were the club secretary, the club treasurer, and a representative from the New South Wales Cricket Association (NSWCA) — the guest of honour for the night. If our club had won the Club Championship or the First Grade Premiership, we would have been graced by the presence of the president of the NSWCA or the chairman of the executive committee of that august body. However, in those days the 'Districts' were lucky to win a couple of games a season; the chance of a premiership was about as far away as Hornsby is from Honolulu.

The main table looked down from a dais towards the body of the hall and those in the hall looked back up at the table, like a congregation of sinners gazing up at a priest who was about to discharge a drastic dose of damnation. After the president's dropped papers had been replaced in front of his fading eyes, we went through the usual boring proceedings and then our guest of honour was called upon 'to say a few words'. This was the time of the meeting when the NSWCA's representatives unleashed their version of administrative fire and brimstone. This particular representative happened to be the delegate from the Western Suburbs club — a 'minor league' rep, as was befitting our status of a club sitting near the bottom of the ladder. He was dressed in a dark suit with a black tie stuck in between a winged collar, which looked as if the starch had run amok or he was wearing a neck brace. As he waved his written speech in the air, he reminded me of Neville Chamberlain returning from Munich after meeting Hitler.

He started in the time-honoured manner of emissaries from the head office of cricket in George Street. Over the years, in the dozens of AGMs I have attended, these words of the representative from town have never varied — only the number on the report has changed. 'Mr Chairman, I bring you greetings from the NSWCA and congratulate your club on the compilation of your 41st annual report.'

[Now let me tell you, I have seen some cricket club annual reports containing fewer than seven pages and held together by paper clips; I have seen annual reports which have had their typographical errors corrected by 'a thumb nail dipped in tar', on a gauge of paper that toilet roll manufacturers would reject. Yet with an aura of sincerity and a straight face, the representative from 'head office' would stare at the top table, hold the tattered document in the air and congratulate the club on 'the compilation of your report'.]

Let me return to my first ever AGM. While congratulations continued to hang in the tepid air of the Hornsby hall, the NSWCA official then turned to far less benign matters. 'Now let me say a few words about the press,' he began, and his upper lip curled above his top row of teeth. 'You may have read recently that certain ex-players, who now call themselves journalists, have been writing scurrilous remarks about the members of the NSWCA. Let me say, on behalf of my fellow delegates, that this sort of criticism not only denigrates the writers, who have made their fame from this great game, but also places the game itself in disrepute. *And* also let me remind you that I and my fellow delegates are not being paid one penny for the endless hours that we put into the game. We are people who work for the game because we love it. We are here to be of help, not to be criticised.' On he went for about 20 minutes. Eventually he sat down, to a smattering of applause from those of us in the hall and the nodding acquiescence of those at the top table.

When I returned home, my dad was sitting up in a lounge chair, reading. 'How did the meeting go, mate, and who was the rep from the Association?' he asked. I recounted the diatribe from the delegate from Western Suburbs. He laughed and said, 'Oh *that* old blowhard.' Then he placed his book on the arm of his chair and gave me some very sound advice that has stayed with me to this day.

He said, 'Son, take no notice of anybody who, when criticised, responds by saying "You can't criticise me, because I do it for nothing." Nobody does anything for nothing! In the case of cricket officials, they do it as a hobby or because they are looking for a way to fill in their time or because they get free lunches. They stand for office because they see it as prestigious or they like the power or they can tell their mates down the pub how they sat next to the Premier, the Governor or Bertie Oldfield. There are even a few who do it because they love the game deeply and want to make sure that they repay cricket for the joy that they received from it. But, mate, none of them do it for nothing and none is exempt from criticism.'

Since those early days I have come to know most of cricket's top administrators and on many occasions I have pondered my father's advice. As it happens, I also spent many years as a cricket official (I hesitate to refer to myself as an 'administrator') and there were moments when I asked my subconscious, 'What are your motives, Marksy? Do you know something?' I don't believe I ever received an honest answer.

*   *   *

Times have changed since those days of winged collars and part-time officials immune to criticism — although the basic fabric of the game of cricket in Australia still remains with volunteer administrators. However human nature doesn't change and there linger a few who hold office for the wrong reasons. They can usually be found in State Association boxes, set high in the cricket stadiums of the nation, occasionally looking at the game below, while their table host pours them another chardonnay. 'McGrath's bowling well. Good drop of plonk, this.'

Yet when all things are taken into consideration, I believe cricket is now administered in a far more professional manner than it ever has been. Over the last few decades the game has been challenged by changing lifestyle patterns, other sports and different recreations. Despite all these problems, the game has not only survived but has strengthened. Cricket is still an important part of Australia's way of life, although some of its finer traditions appear to be at worst, lost or at best, denigrated. (The over-emphasis by players on sledging and dissent are examples of this.) For the present healthy state of cricket, some of the credit must go to the Australian Cricket Board.

Going back to the days of Monty Noble, Australian cricket was directed by a group of amateur officials known as 'The Board of Control'. Control they did — with an iron fist and the tightest purse since Ebenezer Scrooge decided to embark on an economy drive. However, around the time of World Series Cricket, those in charge, and under siege, felt that the word 'control' implied too much ... well ... control! So the name was changed to 'The Australian Cricket Board' (ACB). This title is a misnomer and leads to complications.

We now have the Australian Cricket Board administering an organisation called the Australian Cricket Board, when actually the ACB board is set up to govern Australian cricket — it's not there to look after itself! Complicated, ain't it? Still, don't expect this to change! There has been so much money and exposure invested in the ACB logo, and it is now so implanted in the public's mind that sponsors and potential sponsors see real value in being associated with such a motif.

The ACB board is comprised of 14 members, all of whom are elected by their State Associations (three each from NSW, Victoria and South Australia, two each from Queensland and Western Australia and one from Tasmania). The numbers are based on history and tradition. NSW, Victoria and South Australia were the first three states to play in the Sheffield Shield and all had equal voting rights. When Queensland was invited to join after World War I, Western Australia after World War II and Tasmania in 1977, there was no way that the 'old' States were going to give these 'johnny-come-latelys' full voting rights. Indeed, there was a clandestine arrangement among the original three to vote together and take it in turns when it came to the appointment of the chairman. This 'wink, wink, nod, nod' arrangement often meant that the best man was not chosen.

[To quote the famous Hollywood mogul Samuel Goldwyn, 'This verbal agreement wasn't worth the paper it was written on.' In 1995, Denis Rogers of *Tasmania* was elected chairman of the ACB. To the best of my knowledge, nobody will openly admit who broke the arrangement between the three 'old' states.

Denis Rogers turned out to be a tough, hard-driving chairman who was often controversial and occasionally, in my view, bloody-minded — but in the long run, history will probably judge him as successful. He was the first chairman to lead Australian cricket into the truly professional era — although during Rogers' tenure there were some tense times between the ACB and the players.]

Traditionally, with a few notable exceptions, members of the Board of Control (and later the ACB) were renowned for a type of impassive conservatism and an attitude of 'if it ain't broke don't fix it'. World Series Cricket changed all that! Though conservatism dies hard within the panelled walls of the ACB boardroom, businessmen with cricket backgrounds are moving into positions once held by various non-achievers, diehards and 'blowhards'. So far, no women have been appointed to the Board and, to be honest, they don't seem likely to be in the foreseeable future. Nonetheless, most of the present ACB board members seemed to be quite happy to enter the 21st century without kicking and screaming for the past. There is even talk that people such as Mark Taylor and Allan Border will continue to play a role in sustaining and improving the game that made them — this time as Board members.

Before World Series Cricket, the State Associations performed most of the day-to-day work for the Board of Control, and then later the Board of Control appointed Alan Barnes as its first full-time employee. (Barnes was the much-respected CEO of the NSW Cricket Association, who had done a sterling job for the game in his beloved State, as he did later in his position as Secretary to the Board of Control).

Thirty years on, the paid employees of the ACB number around 60 and administer the game from Melbourne. Notwithstanding the number of well-paid 'Indian braves' on the reservation, the Board 'chiefs' control finances and policy, and despite a few nice lurks and perks continue to remain volunteers. The ACB board may have spruced itself up and endeavoured to be more democratic and egalitarian than it was in days of yore, but in reality it is still a board of control.

So let us take a look at a newer breed of administrators; at one of the younger brigade, whose responsibility it is to see that cricket moves strongly into the future while still remaining faithful to its past.

*　　*　　*

Jack Clarke doesn't look like your typical ACB board member. Though intelligent and perceptive, he radiates a 'one of the boys' attitude, which in the past has not always gone down well with the staid 'Establishment' members of the board, especially those from Victoria. In his professional life, Jack is a partner in Hunt & Hunt, a large and distinguished legal firm, well respected within both the time-honoured walls of judges' chambers and the less salubrious bar rooms of advocates' drinking houses. Although Jack's slightly overweight figure is inclined to give the impression that he would be a very good judge of a cold beer on a warm day, his attractive eyes stare out from a good-looking face, greeting the world and those in it with a smile. In the dour world of legal briefs and cricket budgets Jack would be the resident optimist in a room full of fault-finders. He is the type of person who would not waste time in long discussions of the problem itself; he would move straight towards finding the solution.

It is probably fair to say that Jack had an upbringing similar to that of many South Australian kids. Jack's father worked in a bank in the days when bank branches in the bush meant something, and lived in a number of outback towns with his wife and their daughter and son. When he reached high school age, Jack was sent to Adelaide to board at the famous St Peter's College — regarded as one of the top boys' schools in Australia. Jack enjoyed his days as a boarder and was a talented and extremely enthusiastic sportsman. On leaving school he would have loved to have tried for the 'big time' in cricket or football, but he was studying for a law degree and could not devote the necessary time to training. Modestly, Jack says he was never good enough anyway. Instead, he opted to play cricket in the Adelaide Turf competition.

Actually, the Adelaide Turf comp is not just a hit and giggle Saturday afternoon get-together of would-be flannelled fools with insatiable thirsts. It is a very strong second division competition played by some fine players who like their cricket competitive but do not want to go any further in the game. Jack played with the SPOC Club, which mainly consisted of St Peter's old boys. The SPOCs were a tightly knit group and Jack greatly enjoyed his days in their company, both on and off the field. In Jack's time with the club, the members somehow obtained access to a broken-down old dwelling which they turned into a clubhouse. This clubhouse was situated in a back street of one of Adelaide's less fashionable areas. The club members brought in a bar and a couple of old fridges, hammered down the loose floorboards and returned to this run-down building each Saturday evening in summer to discuss the day's play, tell yarns, drink beer and talk tactics for the following week. (The discussions on the day's play were cynical, the yarns hilarious and the beer plentiful, but to the best of his knowledge Jack can't recall the players ever getting around to talking tactics. And whether or not a liquor licence was obtained for such an enterprise is veiled in the mists of time!) The building has long gone — probably condemned by the local council and bulldozed.

One of the members of the SPOC Cricket Club was the famous yachtsman Jim (later Sir James) Hardy. Because of his summer yachting commitments Hardy didn't play much cricket, but that mattered naught to the members of the SPOCs. Once a member, always a member! It was during the America's Cup races in 1970 that the SPOCs became particularly incensed. Hardy was captaining the Australian challenger, *Gretel II*, against the New York Yacht Club's (NYYC) boat, *Intrepid*. The NYYC had never been beaten in the America's Cup and they did not intend to start now. *Gretel II* was first past the post in the second race but was disqualified — the win was given to the American boat. Despite wrath from Down Under, the NYYC, the most elitist of all elite clubs, celebrated once again. A win is a win and the faces of the NYYC members gleamed like the gold buttons on their navy jackets! However, they reckoned without the SPOC Cricket Club. One of the members owned ES Wigg & Sons, a well-established Adelaide printing firm. The club had no letterhead, so the full resources of ES Wigg & Sons were 'hijacked' to design and print some 'official' club stationery. As soon as this was done, a formal letter was sent off from the president of the SPOCs to the president of the NYYC. In no uncertain terms, the letter stated that the members of the SPOC Cricket Club were appalled at the treatment meted out to fellow SPOC member Mr James Hardy during the recent America's Cup race. The letter went on to say that Mr Hardy was not only a yachtsman of unblemished record but also a gentleman, a respected citizen of the City of Adelaide and a handy lower-order batsman. Thus, henceforth, all reciprocal arrangements previously enjoyed by both clubs would be cancelled.

When Jack was 20 he met a girl he now calls 'Suse' — she was 18. They were instantly attracted but they let the romance cool; each went off in different directions, then they would come back and see each other again. How these circumstances didn't split them apart only the Good Lord knows. Take, for instance, the time Jack took Suse and a couple of her girlfriends to a Test match at the Adelaide Oval. 'What's happening?' said one of the girls after the game had been going 20 minutes.

'Look at the scoreboard,' said Jack.

'Where's the scoreboard?' asked the girl. Jack immediately retired to the Chappell Bar to recover. He returned seven hours later to escort the girls home. A form of resolve that most red-blooded male cricket followers would regard as only right and proper.

Suse and Jack went out with others, but somehow it was pre-ordained that eventually they would be together. After a courtship of 13 years — almost Bradmanesque in its length — they were married. The union of Jack and Suse later brought about two lovely daughters, Georgina and Lucy. Life is hectic in the Clarke family, but it is good.

In 1983 Jack captained a happy band of Aussie cricketers who came together to tour the British Isles, play some friendly matches against the lower-rank club and village teams and watch the World Cup that was being played in England that year. To call this group 'cricketers' was technically correct if you were referring to their sporting apparel, equipment and the game that they played at. If you were describing their ability, the term 'cricketers' was very loose indeed. While playing a match in Dublin, this journeymen team of Aussies was given some local press coverage. The next day Jack received an invitation to dine in the Guinness Brewery boardroom, with the Chairman of the Guinness company and other VIPs from Dublin's fair city. [They say in Dublin that 'most Catholics genuflect when going past the Cathedral but *all* Catholics genuflect when they go past Guinness Brewery'.]

While being wined and dined in a manner that only the Irish can accomplish, the Chairman of the Guinness organisation leant across and asked Jack if he would mind speaking to the gathering. Jack was surprised, but boosted with confidence from his host's product he replied that he would be happy to do so. The Chairman patted him on the shoulder and said, 'It's not every day that we have a captain from Australia to speak to us.' Hell, thought Jack, he reckons I'm either Ian Chappell or James Cook.

Jack was a member of the SPOC committee, but other than that had never thought of going into cricket administration. However, in 1986, Jack's mate, well-known Adelaide identity John Selth, mentioned that the South Australian Cricket Association (SACA) was about to revamp its constitution and suggested that as Jack was a lawyer and loved the game, perhaps he'd be willing to help. Former Test umpire and ACB member Col Egar was introduced to Jack and eventually Jack was co-opted to help guide the new constitution through. Soon afterwards, a vacancy occurred on the SACA committee. Egar approached Jack to stand and he was appointed to the position. After a dozen years on the SACA, witnessing the manoeuvres and machinations of cricket politics, Jack stood against Des Rundle, one of the incumbent ACB reps from the SACA. Jack won the spot, and threw himself into the position with gusto.

Now, almost four years on, Jack is ready to stand back for a moment and reflect upon the situation of Australian cricket from his own and an ACB point of view.

*   *   *

Jack Clarke believes that Australian cricket is travelling well at present. In place at the ACB offices in Jolimont Street, Melbourne, he sees a top management team which, he feels, is working in an efficient and harmonious way. There is sufficient money in the coffers to handle the ever-increasing demands of wages, player payments and development, and the icing on the cake is that the national teams are world champions in both Test cricket and the limited-overs game. Despite the fact that the number of employees has been growing considerably over the last decade, Jack does not see any sign of empire building within the walls of the Jolimont Street office, pointing out that the Board's budgetary provisions restrain such practices.

[This may be so, but the powerful empires of both Rome and Britain also had fiscal constraints and they always found a rationale for expansion.]

To defend the ACB against such accusations, Jack points out that in the last seven years, the income from Australian cricket has grown by over 400 per cent and the game has moved ahead in all areas. For example, 'Development' under the auspices of the innovative and dedicated Ross Turner has tilled previous barren fields and the playing numbers throughout the country appear to show that more people than ever before are engaged in the game. On some days, television ratings have been extraordinary and overall they continue to remain high throughout the summer. Channel Nine and the ACB should be regarded more as cricket's commercial partners rather than as clients, and pay television has brought an additional dimension to the game. Talent spotting of the top young players is becoming far more refined and the tactics from grade cricket upwards have become fundamentally more attacking — some credit for which, according to Jack, should be given to Rod Marsh and his influence on the Australian Cricket Academy.

In my view, if criticism for empire building is to be levelled at any organisation, it could well be at the International Cricket Council (ICC). The ICC, based at Lord's, has proved to be a paper tiger in its handling (or non-handling) of a series of horrendous problems which have beset world cricket, and the numbers of people it employs far outweigh the results it has achieved. Former ACB boss Malcolm Speed has now been placed in charge of this body and from his record with the ACB, appears to be the type of person who will directly face the challenges of world cricket. Jack Clarke feels reasonably confident that the ICC will become a genuine leader and gain the confidence of its member nations. Let's hope he is proven right, for it is time that this world body put some 'runs on the board' — and quickly. So far, the ICC doesn't appear to have broken its duck.

The first Board meeting that Jack attended was the meeting in which the Sheffield Shield was replaced by a carton of milk as the symbol of Australian cricket. To many, this is a day that will live in infamy. The reason for such a controversial decision was purely fiscal. The Sheffield Shield remained the strongest domestic competition in the world, although over the previous few years it had been weakened slightly by the fact that the Test players were competing in fewer games than they once had. The fact that it had been a losing financial proposition for a long time, and a running sore in the side of the bean counters on the ACB eventually led to the change. Tradition was pitted against money. Money eventually won — outright, by an innings!

Imagine how Jack Clarke must have felt as he walked into his first meeting and saw that the main item on the agenda was a decision on whether Australian cricket's holy grail should be, metaphorically, placed in the wheely bin, left out for the 'garbo' and taken to the tip! It was a hard day for the novice member — and for all the other members as well. Yet although he was struck with a sense of disquiet, Jack consoled himself with the fact that because of the decision more millions of dollars would go into youth development.

[Oh well, some scavenger at the tip has, by this stage, picked up a valuable piece of memorabilia. I hope they understand its significance and cherish it, because its owners didn't.]

Something that has heartened Jack in his time on the ACB board is the popularity of cricket with potential sponsors. A few years ago, those in charge of the game were worried at the forced loss of Benson & Hedges as major sponsor. However, Carlton & United Brewery and Ansett were soon signed on and everything went well for a few years. Then out of the blue Ansett collapsed and the ACB were short a major sponsor. Within days, other parties showed interest and eventually Hutchinson, the telecommunications firm behind the 'Orange' mobile phone brand, won the contract. In times when the sponsorship dollar is decreasing in many areas, cricket appears to be the type of 'product' that large sponsors are still seeking. Cricket's status as Australia's truly national game was a major factor in Hutchinson's decision to become a major sponsor.

One of the problems that faces the governing body of any organisation is when to move forward and when to consolidate. Jack feels that the ACB cannot sit back. He believes that although many good things are happening, the Board must do more in our multicultural society to bring Australians of Asian background into the game. So far little has been done in this regard, although if the precedent of European migration is anything to go by, this will happen with the second and third generations. On the other hand, there is some progress being made in the area of indigenous Australians. To date, Aboriginal people who live outside the cities have had little exposure to cricket. The AFL footballer Gilbert McAdam is a sports development officer for the Aboriginal and Torres Strait Island Corporation in the north of Australia, his area of responsibility stretching from Wyndham to Broome. In discussions with Jack and the ACB, McAdam has told of the unbelievable ball skills and hand-eye coordination of the youngsters from the north. Money is being put aside and competitions are being organised for these kids. There is also a great opportunity for a sponsor to come in on the ground floor to help such a project. These potential champions must not be lost to Australian sport, and to cricket in particular.

Although a large part of the ACB budget is being poured into development, Jack believes that the game is for all Australians, and that money should not be spent on developing only the gifted and talented. Jack's ambition is to eventually see a situation where there is an outlet for every kid in the nation to get a game of cricket if he or she wants one. Played as it should be, cricket produces quality people and good citizens who come to understand the advantages of teamwork.

In looking to the future of cricket, Jack accepts that we should correct some of the mistakes of the past and resurrect some of the tried and true customs that appear to have been forgotten. True sporting values must remain. The saying 'It's not cricket' has real meaning, and should not be used in a derogatory way, as if it were only a cliché from a bygone era. There must be no hint of corruption in Australian cricket — anyone who is in any way connected with such contemptible behaviour must be charged with 'cricket treason' and banned from any form of the game forever. Jack is 'as confident as I can be in Australian cricket that this is not happening and will never happen'. Let's hope he is right, and that other cricketing nations can say the same!

In a perfect world, Jack would like to see Australian international cricketers able to play more interstate cricket. And he would be delighted if extra money could be passed on directly to the clubs which are doing such a great job in encouraging junior development. However, Jack's greatest wish is to see more ex-first-class players move back into the ranks of the lower grades and (preferably) captain or (at least) coach the youngsters on the way up, instilling in them the virtues of the game as well as the tough Australian way of playing it.

In many ways, the popularity of sports in this country is based around the success of its national teams. When the Australian cricket team is performing well, the crowds at international games are large, the television and radio ratings boom and more kids play the game. This was so back in the time of Warwick Armstrong, Bill Woodfull and the Invincibles, and it has been the same in the Taylor/Waugh eras. However, in the last decade another dimension has come into cricket. Whereas in past times even Don Bradman had to have another job, now cricket at an international — and even interstate level — is a full-time occupation. Players are playing round the calendar and the money is big. This changed state of the game concerns cricket people such as Jack Clarke.

Jack sees the danger of international cricketers living in a false world, as many tennis players have done for years. There can be a cocoon surrounding them as they travel the world from cricket stadium to cricket stadium; a danger of a man losing his sense of reality and then, when suddenly his form slumps and he is dropped, finding his future lying desolate before him. Most players have managers who advise them off the field. Some of these managers can set players up for life, others can be fair-weather friends. Everybody needs a mentor, and sportspeople need one more than most. Not just somebody who can advise them about their game or their finances, but a person who can keep their head out of the clouds and their sprigs planted firmly in the outfield of life. Jack does not see the ACB as filling that role of mentor, but he is convinced that it is part of the ACB's job to provide education and access to advice for talented young cricketers who can bowl and hit a ball.

Over the generations, those controlling cricket have been a mixed crew. Some have understood the game but had little knowledge of running a business. Others have known the business side but couldn't tell an on drive from a bumper. In Jack Clarke we have a man who understands both these aspects, and who also understands people. He is a genuine allrounder. In all facets of the game, Australian cricket badly needs allrounders!

*   *   *

Since the days of my first AGM, the game of cricket has changed enormously. Those charged with the responsibility of protecting and enhancing it would do well to remember (as sometimes those in the past forgot) that they are there for cricket — not the reverse. What hasn't changed since the 18th century is that cricket is about hitting a ball with a bat and having a drink and a yarn afterwards. Cricket may have become an entertainment, an industry and a product, but first and foremost it is a game — only a game!

SIXTEEN

An Icon and a Gentleman

Of late, Arthur Morris, the cricketer, is having a resurgence. I guess this can be put down to the publicity from the 50-year anniversary of the Invincibles side, the death of Sir Donald Bradman in 2001 and the fact that Arthur was chosen as a member of Australian cricket's 'Team of the Century' in 2000 and Bradman's posthumously announced 'greatest team ever' in 2001. This is not to say that Arthur hasn't had a wonderful reputation as a gentleman and a personality in the game since well before he buckled up his pads to play his very first game for New South Wales, in which he scored a hundred in each innings. Yet as Arthur grows older, he gets closer to becoming a national icon — if he is not one already.

Nowadays, Arthur is greatly sought after by the media and is an entertaining and humorous guest of honour at high-profile dinners. He has a fund of stories, is a great ad-libber and his one-liners are apt and pithy:

> *Question*: Arthur, you have a wonderful record and a reputation second to none as a fair and popular sportsman but what would you say you got out of the game of cricket?
> *Answer*: Poverty!

As a team player, Arthur was uncomplicated. He was never one for psyche-up lectures or for verbose diatribes on the baggy cap the like of which we often hear from jingoistic journalists and fringe candidates trying to impress captains and selectors. Arthur realised he was just one of 11, so he did his best as an individual and helped his teammates if they needed it. When I read stories and articles about Arthur Morris, I am always surprised at how rarely the sporting writers of the time mentioned his ability as a fielder. From the moment I was released from kindergarten until I crashed through puberty, I saw most of the games that Arthur Morris played on the SCG and I cannot recall him ever missing a catch — indeed, I can't recall him misfielding. (Mind you, as I look back on that golden decade, I can't remember it raining either.) Perhaps the reason for the critics giving little attention to Arthur's fielding prowess is that, on the field, Arthur Morris was almost anonymous until the ball came to him. Furthermore, Arthur never seemed to be required to field in what could be described as the 'glamour positions' — unlike the brilliant and flamboyant Miller at first slip, Harvey, the panther, in the covers, or the colourful, confident and controversial Barnes, who often parked himself closer to his opponent's hip pocket than was the batsman's wallet. Being of average height, of sturdy but not bulky build, and also due to the fact that he always wore his baggy cap, Arthur was less noticeable than, say, 5 foot 4 inch Lindsay Hassett or Ian Johnson and Richie Benaud, all of whom seldom wore head cover.

Notwithstanding his other skills, it was for batting that Arthur achieved his fame. He was a batsman with a speed of footwork that quickly guided him into the correct position and always seemed to allow him that most important of all batting gifts — time. In defence, his bat was perpendicular and wide, and although he understood that his job was to wear the shine off the ball, he didn't care if he achieved this aim by careful defence or by hitting the ball against the pickets. If the first ball of the match was loose, Arthur would crack it for four. He may not have been quite as deft a cutter as Barnes, as fierce a puller as Bradman, or as elegant a driver as Harvey; he didn't hook with the ferocity of McCabe and perhaps Hutton may have been tighter in defence, but Arthur could play all these strokes, and others of his own. He had a whimsical ease about his batting, a laconic power which gave the impression to those watching that he didn't really want to hit the ball so hard and would like to apologise to the bowler, in his gentlemanly way, after each ball struck the palings. 'Sorry, dear boy, but I'm only doing my job.'

Ted Dexter once wrote: 'The only time I played in the same game as Arthur Morris, I had the dubious distinction of bowling to him. He proceeded to dispatch my offerings to every part of the ground with the least possible effort and the maximum of bonhomie. Anybody who still thinks that all Australians are rough and ready, beer-drinking Pommy bashers should meet Arthur Morris, who is quietly spoken and companionable. He always enjoyed scoring runs against [whomever] he played, which is not to say he did not also enjoy the occasional glass of an appropriately comforting liquid.'

In the Australian summer of 1953–54 there were no international teams touring the country. Therefore, as the season was a domestic one only, Sheffield Shield teams were at full strength for every game. For lovers of Australian cricket it was a great year and those who were lucky enough to watch games at the SCG saw Morris and Miller at their best, and on many occasions batting together. The contrast between the style and approach of the two batsmen was interesting. Miller always seemed nervous as he walked out to bat, flicking his shirt and brushing his cheek, while Morris gave the impression that he had just enjoyed a hearty breakfast and was walking down the front path to pick up the morning paper. Morris sighted the ball very early in its flight and seemed to be debating with himself where on the field would be the most productive place to hit it. Miller often seemed to make his mind up late (particularly playing forward to spin bowling) and at the last minute would jab the ball away. Morris hooked and pulled the bouncers, Miller just ducked his broad shoulders under them. Morris would mentally chart the gaps in the field and then, with the constancy of a metronome, hit the ball along the turf into these gaps. Miller looked upward: 'Where will I hit the next one? Into Moore Park or the Showground?'

For those who were lucky enough to witness these two great players in partnership, it was a season to savour: Arthur Morris, cap over the ball, directing it like a guided missile through the covers to the fence and Keith Miller, slamming the ball straight and high, hair flying as he did so. In my mind's scrapbook of cricket memories these two pictures take pride of place.

Cricketers sometimes suffer the same fate as singers — they are classified. People never called Bing Crosby a singer; they referred to him as a crooner. Pavarotti is known as a tenor. As fine a batsman as he was, Arthur Morris is generally called an 'opener'. Perhaps this is right and proper, because for an Australian supporter there was no more comfortable sight, on the first day of a Test match, than seeing this square-shouldered left-hand opener walking to the crease. His green cap perched on his head at a jaunty angle may have caused those who did not know him to believe that there was a touch of arrogance in his character and his splay-footed gait could have had others believing that Morris lacked athleticism. They would all be wrong! Arthur was certainly determined, but he was as far from arrogant as a third man is from long-on. As for his athletic ability, Arthur Morris represented the Combined High Schools and the Combined Services at rugby. (Playing for the Services, against a Combined Sydney team, virtually a State side, Arthur scored three tries.) Arthur went on to play first-grade rugby for the St George club in Sydney. He was also a top-grade tennis player until well into his seventies. Yet, above all, Arthur Morris was the quintessential opener, a man born for the task. In my late teenage years I recall attending parties (in the days before twist tops), where somebody would reach for a bottle of beer and, in the Aussie vernacular typical of the time, say, 'Pass me the Arthur Morris.'

In the early period of Arthur's career, he was almost two people. For unlike all other batsmen, an opener never walks out on his own; he must have a partner. Arthur's partner was the enigmatic Sid Barnes. 'Morris and Barnes': what memories those three words evoke! Yet somehow they weren't three words, they were really one — 'Morrisnbarnes'. The word denoted solidity and purpose; front-line tanks going in first to soften up the enemy while the infantry waited back in the trenches to mop up later. When 'Morrisnbarnes' was followed by three more words, 'and then Bradman', the Australian sporting public was able to sit back calmly and comfort themselves with the knowledge that their cricket team was an impregnable fortress, and no matter what those wily Poms tried, it wouldn't work. God was in His Heaven, the world was as it was meant to be, and the Ashes would remain with us and be handed down to our children and our children's children!

Like so many of the great players of that era, Arthur spent some of his best cricketing years in the army, mostly in New Guinea. Despite this, it could be said that in his postwar career, which spanned nearly a decade, the outstanding highlight was the 1948 Invincibles' tour of England. It comes as a surprise to some to discover that Morris topped the Test averages on that tour (87), forcing Bradman into second place. Yet Arthur's place in history will surely be remembered, if only for one thing. You see, Arthur was at The Oval, standing up the other end, when *it* happened. This incident gives rise to one of cricket's most often repeated but best yarns:

Question: Arthur, what was the best innings you ever played?
Answer: My 196 in the Fifth Test at The Oval in 1948 — but nobody remembers it because up the other end there was a little bloke who got bowled for a duck in his last game.

[Sid Barnes' biographer, Rick Smith, tells another story which followed this most famous of noughts. Barnes opened with Arthur and was out for 61 when the score was 117. Sensing history in the making, as it seemed almost certain that this would be Bradman's last innings in Test cricket, Barnes headed straight for his bag, pulled out his movie camera and began filming 'history'. As all the world knows (well, nearly all), on the second ball, Bradman was bowled by Hollies for a duck. When the great man walked back into the Australian dressing-room, nothing could be heard but his sprigs on the floor and the whirring of a camera. Then Sid Barnes' voice broke the silence, as he said reassuringly, 'Don't worry, skipper, I've got your complete innings on film.']

Arthur Morris can always see the funny side of things, whether circumstances are with him or he is on the blind side of fate. The clash with Tom Goddard is a case in point. It is now history that during the '48 tour, the Invincibles swept all before them. With batsmen such as Morris, Bradman, Barnes, Hassett, Brown, Miller and Harvey, the English first-class attacks were plundered as never before. The English selectors were in a quandary. Who could they pick to bowl to these super batsmen? Jim Laker was supposed to be the best spinner in the country, but in the Lord's Test Arthur had made a century and smashed him all round the 'Home of Cricket'. So the press, as is their habit, began calling for Laker's scalp and for the inclusion of an off spinner — Tom Goddard, from Gloucestershire, who hadn't played a Test since 1939. The public followed the 'leaders' from the press and everyone was waiting expectantly for the clash of Australia v Gloucestershire, to be played at Bristol: Superbats v Goddard. Tom would show 'em!

The day of the Australia v Gloucestershire game dawned, and Arthur Morris was feeling good and ready for the challenge. Actually, he was feeling so good that he made a hundred before lunch, a hundred before tea and would have made his third century before stumps had he not hit a full toss back to the bowler when he was on 290. When Goddard first came on to bowl, Arthur jumped a third of the way down the wicket and smashed him through the off side. If Goddard dropped the ball short to compensate, Arthur pulled him through the on. Arthur showed no mercy to the Gloucestershire spinner, and Goddard had no respite from the other batsmen. In its innings, Australia managed to 'scrape' together 774 and the unfortunate Tom Goddard was never spoken of as a potential Test bowler again. England's selectors stuck with Jim Laker.

In 1956, Arthur was covering the Ashes series for a newspaper, and watched at Headingley as Jim Laker picked up 19 wickets for the game, humbling Australia by an innings and 170 runs. In the press box that day, Arthur could not prevent a wry grin from crossing his countenance as he thought: I really should have gone a little easier on dear old Tom Goddard.

Colin McCool was a teammate on the 1948 tour with Arthur. McCool was a good allrounder who had succeeded against England in Australia with his well-flighted, big spinning leg breaks. He was of the ilk of Mailey, Philpott and Jenner rather than the Benaud/Warne type, who depend as much on nip and bounce as on spin.

The first time Morris met McCool was when they were playing in a Poidevin-Gray Shield (club under 21) game between Paddington and St George at Trumper Park. As a teenager, Arthur was regarded by the St George selectors as a left-hand spin bowler of great potential and an average batsman — the selectors were wrong on both counts. So in the St George Poidevin-Gray team, Arthur was batting down the list. This particular day, the young Morris came in, took guard and looked around the field. Noting the gaps, he faced up to Paddington's Colin McCool, who was causing devastation at the top of the St George batting order. Then from behind Arthur came a voice, 'Jump down and hit him on the full.' Morris pulled away from the crease and turned around to see who had spoken. The voice had come from the wicketkeeper, a good-looking young man of Chinese origin. (His name was Geoff See who later went on to become an excellent first-grade keeper and at one stage was close to being chosen for interstate cricket. In the years to come he and Arthur were to become good friends.)

'Sorry, what did you say?' asked the batsman.

Geoff See smiled. 'I told you that the best way to play McCool is to jump down and hit him on the full.'

'Jump down at him, you reckon?' repeated Morris.

'That's correct. All your batsmen have been tied up by playing him from the crease.'

'Thanks for the advice,' said Arthur. 'I'll give it a go.'

Geoff See nodded and said, 'Good on you, son. Now remember, jump down as far as you possibly can.'

In telling the story of his first meeting with Colin McCool and Geoff See, Arthur is straight and honest, but shows no embarrassment as he explains. 'You guessed it! The scorebook read: *A. Morris — stumped See bowled McCool*. So I fell for Geoff's three-card trick. Oh well, you live and learn.' Then Arthur continues, 'Mind you, I'd scored 115 before I fell for it.'

Like all who have played the game, Arthur Morris has had his triumphs and failures. As Jim Burke, one of Arthur's former opening partners, used to say, 'Cricket is the great leveller.' After his triumphs of 1948 and in South Africa 18 months later, Arthur had a run of failures, and when Alec Bedser dismissed him for a string of dismal scores, the Australian opener was dubbed 'Bedser's bunny' by the press. It reached the stage where there was talk that the great Arthur Morris would be dropped. In the midst of this trot, Arthur's implacable opponent, and close friend, Alec Bedser, gave him a present wrapped in gift paper. Opening the paper, Arthur found a cheap little paperback book entitled, *Cricket Coaching Series — How to Bat*.

When Arthur came to the Adelaide Oval for the Fourth Test of the series against Freddie Brown's English team, there was little doubt that he was fighting for his position and possibly the rest of his career. As he walked out to bat on the world's most beautiful Test ground, the pressure must have weighed heavily on Arthur's mind and his nerves must have made their presence felt as well — but nobody would have known it. Arthur made 206.

The bunny had returned as a lion. The next evening Alec Bedser received a gift-wrapped book entitled, *Cricket Coaching Series — How to Bowl*.

There were other disappointments in Arthur's career. His being dropped as captain of New South Wales after a couple of successful seasons must have been hard to bear. Arthur later heard that one influential State selector had been heard to say that he would never vote for any man who wore suede shoes as captain of the premier State team in Australia. (This sort of comment from selectors is not unusual, as a few belonging to this species are inclined to look at the game from the lofty heights of arrogant self-aggrandisement. Meanwhile, their often limited knowledge of cricket is known only by those who sit with them behind locked doors, where 'cabinet solidarity' is ingrained and sacrosanct.)

Still, minor setbacks and affronts don't really matter to a man who has fought in a war and who has experienced life's triumphs and tragedies. Arthur's ability to look at life through a window of humour has made his time easier and certainly more pleasant for those around him. Arthur can always come up with a funny yarn when the time is right. Like the one about Bill O'Reilly and Denis Compton's dog.

In 1956, Arthur, Jack Fingleton and Bill 'Tiger' O'Reilly were in England covering the Ashes tour for various media outlets. One Sunday they were asked out to Denis Compton's place for lunch. After the three Aussies arrived, their English host quickly invited them into the living room for a drink — a pastime of which all four were devout exponents. Soon afterwards, Mrs Compton entered the room carrying a little Maltese terrier under her arm. After the formalities had been completed, she walked up to Tiger O'Reilly, pushed the terrier forward and said, 'Doggie, say hello to nice Mr O'Reilly from Australia.' Nice Mr O'Reilly hesitatingly pushed his hand forward to pat Doggie, when, without warning, the little canine growled and bit the great bowler viciously on the finger. Blood spurted everywhere. Mrs Compton put the dog down and, accompanied by Denis, rushed out to find some ointment and bandages for their guest's injured finger.

As soon as the Comptons disappeared from the room, Tiger O'Reilly scooped up the still growling dog and with perfect timing drop-kicked it across the room. Arthur Morris, once a very capable rugby five-eighth, could only watch in awe as the dog seemed to fly through the air, hang for a moment and then crash into the opposite wall, tilting a landscape painting sharply to the left. If the kick had been made at Cardiff Arms Park, the dog would have sailed between the goalposts and over the black dot with inches to spare. Whimpering, the dog crawled back to where O'Reilly was standing and grovelled at his feet. For the rest of the day, the dog followed the big man around, trying to lick his boots. When the time came for her guests to leave, Mrs Compton was under the impression that the 'biter' and the 'bitten' were getting along famously. Arthur was under no such delusion. Tiger O'Reilly liked Doggie about as much as he liked batsmen!

In the era when Arthur Morris played, the game was not strictly amateur — as rugby union and athletics then were. It was, however, only a few measly quid short of being so. All players had to have a job that would allow them time off to play. Today, in the era of cricketing millionaires, Matty Hayden would earn twice as much money in one Test as Arthur Morris made in his whole career. The great players of Arthur's time don't begrudge this state of affairs. After all, none of us chooses when we are born. Nevertheless, many of the old-timers hold the view that some of the personnel who are now regarded as vital adjuncts to the game would not have been tolerated in the past. The idea of coaches at interstate and international level, for instance, is anathema to the older generation of players. Indeed, the players of earlier times have an unqualified fear of over-coaching at every level, believing that flair and individuality can be coached out of potential champions. Some years ago, I was in the Cricketers' Club of Sydney, having a drink with the popular and highly regarded Max Shepherd, who was then the Chief Development Officer for the New South Wales Cricket Association. Arthur came into the club and walked over to join us. I introduced Max and explained his job with the NSWCA.

'Does that mean you're a coach?' Arthur asked.

'Yes I am,' Max replied.

Arthur grinned as he said, 'Excuse me for saying this, Max, because you seem a nice sort of fellow, but if I had my way I'd scoop up you and all your colleagues, put you in a box, tie it with a ribbon and drop you in Sydney Harbour.'

Now in the late afternoon of his years, Arthur and his vivacious wife Judy have lived for many years in the Hunter region of New South Wales. He has recently had to give up his beloved tennis and although not as spry as of yore, Arthur is still interested in life and cricket and continues to drink his red wine on a daily basis with the pleasure of a connoisseur — which he is.

Question: Arthur, have you ever thought of joining a bowling club?

Answer: Yes, I've thought about it but I decided not to. I don't think I'd be able to afford the wreaths.

When Arthur claims that he received only poverty out of cricket, his tongue is well and truly stuck in the left side of his cheek. Fame, satisfaction, travelling the world and pleasant days under cricket's sun cannot be measured in pecuniary terms. Just to be 'up the other end' at The Oval, playing the greatest innings of your life, while nobody notices, would have been enough for most of us.

Yet it is in friendships and people that Arthur is rich. For Arthur Morris meets people the way he batted — with an effortless charm and a disarming grace.

SEVENTEEN

Room, but Never Bored

He works harder than a spinner into the wind, covers more ground than the keeper, sweats like an opening bowler, dries towels and clothing with the efficiency of a hotel laundry and opens more cans and bottles than a publican on Anzac Day. He has broken up fights, found stowaway fans under lockers, abused caterers and listened to confessions that should only be heard by the parish priest. His principal brief is to smoothly control the home team's locker room. His official title is 'Room Attendant' but to all in the world of cricket, he is known as 'the roomy'.

As well as being a security guard, packhorse, finder of missing articles, autograph collector, nurse and 'gofer', the roomy is also a shoulder to cry on, a bloke to abuse and a friend in need. The roomy is the heart of the locker room, and a part of its soul as well. The roomy can never be glum, for when he is down the game is as good as lost. However, when the team is victorious, he is the life of the party, the teller of yarns, the supplier of sustenance and stimulants, an ever-moving hail-fellow, part teammate, part servant, part vaudevillian. Conversely, when the game is over and the team *has* been beaten he must never crack a joke; just open the drinks, bring out the sandwiches and occasionally pat the defeated players softly on the shoulder. Next to the captain of the team who is having a run of outs, the roomy has the toughest job in cricket.

Like most sportsmen, cricketers can be fragile. So when things go wrong, and with wives/girlfriends/mothers excluded from the room, who can a bloke turn to? They turn to — and sometimes turn upon — the reliable old roomy! This has been going on since Charlie Bannerman ran his first overthrow and generation after generation of roomies have copped it. This begs the question: why does the roomy do it? The money isn't much … I guess the answer is that they love the game. This and the fact that despite everything, a roomy becomes mates with the players and part of a special scene. The roomy is privy to some of the most closely kept secrets of the game. They know the players' peccadilloes and habits. They know where the players went last night, hear the words that the players call the selectors when the selectors leave the room (always nasty), and have hordes of other information that the tabloids would pay five-figure sums to obtain. Indeed, it is astonishing that there has never been a roomy who was a mole. Never have we seen the blazing headline: *Roomy Tells: WG Grace And The Barmaid* … (or) *From Inside The Room: Can Star Opening Batsman Beat The Demon Alcohol?*

The good roomy is a contradiction. He is abused and loved (though nobody would ever use that word). Above all, he is a precious cricket commodity. The roomy arrives early and leaves late. He is more than just a faithful servant; he is an obedient slave. Yet the future looks bleak for these men. There is no union to represent them, no budding Lincoln to release them from bondage, and, knowing the way the lousy State Cricket Associations operate, I doubt whether they are even covered by 'compo'. Eventually, the heavy loads they are forced to carry and the mental pressure of their vocation will catch up with these willing vassals and they will break down physically and mentally. The roomy will be then shunted away to a back ward of some public hospital, where he will be visited by his young cricketing mates who come armed with raunchy get well cards, contraband booze and spend their time in another ward chatting up the nurses. If he's lucky, the roomy will have his hernia operation and psychiatrist's consultations covered by Medicare — but don't count on it! Then, against doctor's advice, he will return to the room in time for the vital game against Queensland and it will start all over again.

Despite all this, if you rove around the country and speak to roomies, you would find that not one of them would give back a minute of the time they have spent in the dressing-room with cricketers. It was all worth it, for the experience gained, stories told and friendships made. Roomies may be the butt of jokes and the plough horses of the game, but at the end of it all they have a tremendous amount of fun and are envied by many who, on the surface, regard themselves as superior.

*   *   *

Nobody has ever written a manual for roomies, but if an apprentice room attendant wanted to learn the job, he could do a lot worse than accompany Merv Seres on his rounds for a couple of days, take notes and then emulate Merv to the letter. For Merv Seres (rhymes with terrace) is the quintessential roomy, a man for whom nothing is too much trouble, a true professional in his sphere. He is a confidant, servant, motivator and best (or worst) of all, Merv is a teller of jokes. Jokes are Merv's specialty, although 'original' is not a word that would trip lightly off the tongue when explaining Merv's one-liners. They are jokes that vary in style. They can be risqué, politically incorrect, irreligious and corny, but they all have one thing in common — they are all *old*. Merv's jokes are so old that they have died, gone through reincarnation and come back for a third time.

[Merv joke: from his 'Very Early' period.

A bloke, leading a crocodile, walks into a pub in the outback of NSW. 'Do you serve Catholics in this pub?' he asks the man behind the bar.

'Of course we do,' says the publican.

The bloke nods and replies, 'Good, then I'll have a schooner of beer and my croc will have a Catholic.']

Merv is one of those men who likes to make other people happy and for 16 years he has done just that at the SCG, in the home locker room of NSW and Australia. To say that Merv was 'loved' by his teams is not an exaggeration, nor a phrase used lightly. Around the walls of Merv's den in his home in a northern seaside suburb of Sydney are photos of Merv with some of the great cricket teams of history and individual portraits of distinguished players, all with an inscription for Merv.

'Best wishes, Merv, Don Bradman.'

'My mate, Merv. Enjoy your smiling face but hate your jokes — Deano [Jones].'

'Merv, thanks for your support and love — your mate, Whit [Mike Whitney].'

'To the best roomy in Australia — Tugga [Steve Waugh].'

During his time in the home room, Merv has found himself facing many problems, mostly of the players making. Some cricketers are well organised and neat, while others have lockers and bags in such a mess that they are struggling to find their pads, let alone their wallets. When the latter situation is the case, you will hear the famous words, 'Hey Merv, somebody's pinched my transistor' or 'pinched my cricket shoes', etc. Of course the missing article is always found in quick time, under the seat or in the bag itself, but it always starts out as being 'stolen'. Merv handles this situation with aplomb, makes the appropriate comments and returns to doing his real work. Even though it is not really part of his brief, one of Merv's hardest tasks is finding the right words to say to a batsman who has just got out for a duck. Silence is usually the best way to handle it, yet often it's the batsman himself who speaks. 'I stuffed that up didn't I, Merv?'

Merv puts himself in the batsman's place and does his best to make the man feel better. Kind-hearted people always do!

One of the nicest things ever said to Merv came from Mike Whitney. The two had been talking together and Whitney placed his hand on Merv's shoulder and made the comment, 'Merv, you have the great knack of knowing when to talk and when not to talk. That's a gift.' Merv was moved by the remark, then as Whit walked away he laughed and continued, 'Except for your bloody jokes.'

[Merv joke: from his 'Multicultural' period.

A bloke bursts into a Chinese restaurant brandishing a gun. He walks straight up to the lady sitting at the cash register. 'Give me all your money,' he demands.

'Certainly sir,' she replies. 'Do you want to take it away or count it here?']

* * *

Merv Seres was born and bred in the Newtown district of Sydney and sport was in his genes. His father was 'Sailor' Billy Seres, the welterweight boxing champion of Australia. Merv didn't take up boxing as a sport — although around the Newtown area in those days, a young man had to know how to handle himself. In his early days, Merv proved to be very proficient at rugby league and cricket — particularly rugby league. In 1949 and 1950 he played five-eighth for the Newtown club. Newtown was particularly strong in those days and Merv could only manage a few games in first grade, when injuries to others allowed him to move up.

In 1951 Merv's mate, international second-row forward Bernie Drew, moved to Queensland. Merv decided to try his luck there as well. He played four seasons in Queensland and was chosen in the Queensland State team on four occasions. One of these games was against Puig Aubert's fabled French team. Merv marked the irrepressible Jacques Merquey, one of the greatest backs in the history of rugby league. 'Jacques scored three tries that day,' Merv recalls. 'I couldn't lay a hand on him. He was a will o' the wisp, a wonderful footballer. Jacques also had a wonderful combination with scrum half, Jean Dop.' Then, as an added compliment to his French opponents, Merv states, 'Dop was as good as Merquey but he had the added advantage of playing real dirty when he set his mind to it.'

There was no money in any code of football in those days. In his first year for Newtown, Merv made 13 pounds and 10 shillings. Later on, Merv was on a contract of 500 pounds in Queensland, to be captain/coach of a club team in Rockhampton — a princely sum indeed! Unfortunately, the club went broke halfway through the winter, after the club president absconded with both his secretary and the club funds, and though Merv played out the rest of the season, he received nothing for his trouble. I should have settled for 13 pounds 10 from Newtown, Merv thought as he left the Rockhampton club for the last time.

In his first year in Queensland, Merv was approached by a young centre named Noel Hazzard, who asked, 'Merv, do you reckon I could make it in Sydney rugby league?' Merv replied, 'To be honest, Noel, I don't reckon you'd make second grade in Sydney.' The following season, Hazzard played three Test matches in Australia and was chosen in the Kangaroo squad to tour Britain. A few years later Merv returned to Sydney and at the instigation of the great Wallaby winger Eddie Stapleton, played rugby union for a short while with the St George club. After a couple of games, a thin little fullback came up to him and in a lilting Welsh accent said, 'You've played rugby league, boyo. How do you think I'd go if I switched over?'

'Mate, you're far too small, they'd chew you up and spit you out in league.' Nowadays, when Merv meets 'Golden Boots' Keith Barnes, former captain of Australia and a rugby league legend, Keith never fails to remind Merv of this advice. In his playing days, Merv was a pretty handy footballer, but clearly was not much of a judge.

[Merv joke: from his 'Religious' period.

An old nun comes bursting out of a doctor's surgery and rushes down the stairs, yelling, 'I can't be, I can't be.'

212 ~ **Great Australian Cricket Stories**

The doctor's receptionist watches the nun rush by and then quickly goes into the surgery and asks the doctor the obvious question. 'What did you say to Mother Superior?

'I told her she was pregnant,' replied the doctor.

Astounded, the woman says to her boss, 'Oh doctor, how dare you tell dear old Mother Superior that she is pregnant!'

To which the doctor replied, 'Why not? It cured her hiccups, didn't it?']

*   *   *

After his return from Queensland, Merv got a job as a welfare officer in the Manly-Warringah district of Sydney (he eventually rose to the position of Chief Welfare Officer for the Northern Area Command). At the same time, he gained his diploma as a trainer and masseur. Because of his football experience and ability as a trainer, Merv was appointed by the Manly Rugby League club to help with their training. Meanwhile, Merv had married the love of his life, Olga, and was raising six children (a seventh child died when a baby). So he had very little spare time on his hands, holding down a responsible job, raising a family and working evenings and weekends with the Manly football team.

Merv took early retirement from the Welfare Department in the 1980s but continued to work for the Manly RL club. At around this time, Dave Price, one of the room attendants at the SCG, had to go to hospital and retired from the job. A mutual friend then arranged for Merv to meet Bob Radford, the CEO of NSW Cricket, to discuss the vacant position. Merv, having 30 years' experience with a well-run organisation — the Manly RL Club — was just what was needed. And Radford, a shrewd man, quickly saw that Merv Seres would bring not only that experience but also another dimension to the dressing-room. So, in the typical no-nonsense manner for which Radford is famous, he appointed Merv to the job. He gave Merv only three instructions. 'Keep the boys happy, the bloody beer cold and make sure there is a bottle of Black Label whisky ready for the CEO when he comes in at the end of each day's play.' For the next 16 years Merv obeyed his boss's instructions to the letter, and over that time a mutual respect grew between these two professionals.

It was 1985 when Merv began his time as roomy for the 'home' room at the SCG. Though his time there was not without some drama and trauma, it was for Merv mostly a time of interest, fun, challenge, laughs and friendship. And a few jokes as well.

(If you listen closely to Merv's jokes, though most people don't, you'll find that they normally start off with a bloke walking into a pub. Why this is so, I know not. Perhaps it comes from his youthful days in Newtown, where every second building was a pub and Merv walked into most of them.)

[Merv joke: from his 'Politically Incorrect' period.

A blind man walks into a pub, being led by his seeing-eye dog. The man tells the dog to stop and then leans down, grabs the dog by the tail and whirls it round his head three times.

The barman jumps over the bar, grabs the man and shouts, 'What the hell are you doing?'

'Nothing,' says the blind man. 'Just looking around.']

* * *

From the moment he entered the hallowed portals of the home room at the SCG, Merv was welcomed by all. It was not just his breezy personality that impressed those concerned — that can only go so far, and becomes tiresome if overdone — it was Merv's work ethic and happy team spirit that were the real cause of his popularity.

Merv also quickly noticed the difference between the 'cricket' room at the SCG and the 'football' room at Manly. Although the footballers were all friendly and likeable athletes, good for a laugh and a yarn, Merv was not included in the informal team get-togethers. This was certainly not deliberate. Manly club had a squad (with officials) of over 100 people and, because of the numbers, was not as close-knit as the NSW cricket team, with its match-day component of about 16 people and a training squad of around 30. There was an ethos in Blues cricket which automatically assumed that Merv would be part of any social function in which the team was engaged. Merv was taken into the fold and in time became part of its heart and soul.

Yet what surprised Merv even more was that when the Australian team took over the room each season for Tests and one-day internationals, the same rules applied. As a man who in summers past had sat on the Hill under a hot sun and with only a few beers to keep him comfortable, watching everyone from Bradman to Border, Merv was now an integral part of the scene. He was the driver of the engine room, as well as the driver of the drinks cart.

Coaches may have a part to play in the running of first-class cricket teams, but as it has been since before the first ever Ashes Test, the captain owns the room. What he says goes and not the Chairman of the ACB, the President of the NSWCA, nor even the legendary Bob Radford can overrule the skipper in this domain. If Sir Donald Bradman and Queen Elizabeth II had walked into the room and the captain of the team had said, 'You two, get the hell out of here', The Don and the Queen would have been escorted to the door. (To the best of my knowledge, no such incident has ever occurred.)

If it is not exactly blue blood that runs through Merv's veins, it's at least the blood of the Blues. Metaphorically and literally, Merv has shed it for his beloved NSW team. He was with them when they won three Sheffield Shields and though this is not a large number compared with the triumphs of the distant past, those three were all the more welcome because of the years of disappointment between them. His happiest moment was when the Blues won the Shield final at the SCG in 1992-93, under the captaincy of his good friend Phil Emery, while their international players were away playing for Australia in New Zealand.

On the other hand, one of Merv's most melancholy moments was the Test in which Australia were chasing 117 to win in the final innings against South Africa in 1993–94. The batting collapsed under pressure and some superb bowling from the visitors, and Australia lost by five runs. Merv recalls the atmosphere in the room as the most depressed he has ever experienced. Heads were hanging lower than the floor. If some do-gooder had come in and said, 'Don't worry, fellas, it's only a game,' he would have been thrown out the window.

Merv has been roomy under three Australian captains (Border, Taylor, Waugh) and his admiration for them is unbounded. His intimate comments about each are interesting:

Sometimes 'AB' has had bad press — you know, the Captain Grumpy thing. This is absolute garbage. Sure, during the game he was dedicated and sometimes intense, but when play was finished he loved a beer with his mates, and often with the opposition as well. Early in my time in the room, somebody found out it was my birthday and AB told me that the team was taking me out for dinner. They took me down to The Rocks to celebrate. We had a great time and AB paid out of his own kick.

'Tubby' was a little more laid-back than AB but he was a great captain and a terrific bloke; intelligent but always level-headed. We were playing a game up in Newcastle and Tub brought Judi and the kids up. I had gone to get some items from the chemist in the morning and in the shop there was a battery-operated train engine on special. So I bought it for three-year-old Jack Taylor. The next morning Tub came to me and said, 'Thanks for nothing, Merv. Jack kept us up half the night with that bloody train. When we eventually took it away from him, he spent the rest of the night waking up and going "Whoo-oo, Whoo-oo". From then on, if Tub ever wanted something in a hurry I'd say, 'You wait until I'm ready, otherwise I'll buy Jack another train.'

'Tugga' is a tough and dedicated player, and he's the same as a captain. We've been good mates for quite a while now — he's a great bloke! The Waughs' mother, Bev, was a Bourne before she got married. I have relations named Bourne, so I keep telling the twins that I'm related to them — although whether we are,

*I haven't got a clue. I remember once, sitting next to Tugga, I told
a joke to the others in the room, which went over like a lead
balloon. As I copped a sledging from every corner, Tugga leant
across and said out of the corner of his mouth, 'Merv, do me a
favour. In future, don't ever tell anybody we're related.'*

[Merv joke (this is the worst yet, and what's more, no person
under the age of 45 would understand it — and even a majority
of those over 45 won't. It comes from Merv's 'You've Got To Be
On My Wavelength To Comprehend It' period):

Sign on Police Station door: WANTED — Joseph Groves, who
once lived in the town of Tooting, England, where he played the
flute in the local orchestra. His widowed mother has recently left
Tooting to join an order of nuns in Barcelona. Joseph was last
seen in the city of Haifa, where he was working for a short time
ploughing fields before he went on a rampage of looting in the
central business district of Haifa.

Police are looking for: a Haifa looting, Tooting fluting, son of a
nun from Barcelona, part-time ploughboy Joe.]

*   *   *

As Merv looks back at his 16 years in the room, memory plays
funny tricks. He can recall the good, the bad and the embarrassing,
and although some of the incidents were high dramas at the time,
when looked at in hindsight, Merv sees all of them as memorable
and most as fun. He remembers with great pleasure the personal
triumphs of his mates; the look on Mike Whitney's face after
Australia won the World Series final in 1991–92 and the excitement
in the room when, on the last ball of the night, Michael Bevan hit
that four straight past Roger Harper to beat the West Indies. Nor is
it only the home team's triumphs that Merv remembers. The
greatest innings Merv ever saw on the SCG was Brian Lara's 277 in
early 1993. Merv rates this as even better than the innings played
by Bradman and Sid Barnes against England in 1946 — every ball
of which Merv saw — when they each scored 234.

One of the things that Merv regrets is the nasty injuries he has witnessed. He has seen smashed teeth, broken limbs and bloodied faces. All of it is part of the game, but seeing your mates with busted bodies and potentially ruined careers certainly doesn't make a roomy happy.

A game never to be forgotten

There are games of cricket played and won that nobody remembers, but every now and then there comes a game that is so packed with action and incident that Hollywood would reject the script as too far-fetched. Such a game was played in Newcastle in 1989, between NSW and Queensland, and Merv has cause to remember it well — nobody who played that game will ever forget it.

Actually, the events began a few hours before the game, when the NSW team members were driving their cars up the M3 freeway to Newcastle. [I remember this occasion well myself, as I was driving up for the game, in my capacity as a NSW selector, accompanied by Herself. I happened to be both a spectator and participant in an incident that occurred on the freeway.]

The Queensland team had arrived in Newcastle the day before, with the exception of Allan Border, who had stayed overnight at Mosman with his in-laws and thus drove up at about the same time as the opposition. At this stage of its construction there were parts of the M3 that had not been completed, one of these being the section between the turn-off to Gosford and the town of Wyong. There is a steep hill dropping down to the Gosford turn-off, three lanes each way where the legal limit was 110 km/h. Cars zipped down the hill at speeds anywhere between 110 and 135. However, on this day, two-thirds of the way down, behind a thick bush, the RTA had placed a speed sign which read 80. It was impossible to see this sign unless you were coming the other way or had a third eye up your exhaust pipe. Down at the bottom of the hill was a police radar van and about three police cars. 'Like shooting fish in a barrel' I believe is the appropriate analogy. The wallopers hadn't had so much fun since the Commissioner got drunk at the Policemen's Ball!

As I reached the bottom of the hill, a cop waved me to the side of the road. Cars were lined up as if they were at a toll booth in peak hour. In front of me I saw Allan Border, reaching for his papers and about to be booked by a female member of the Police Department. While I was giving details to my own 'personal' policeman, I noticed the lady cop walk over to the police car next to mine and I heard her call back to headquarters. 'Bob, we could have a bit of a problem,' she said.

I listened as a voice came back, 'What's the matter?'

'We've got Allan Border,' she replied. 'Will I charge him?'

'You a fan of his or something?'

'I admire him, yes.'

There was silence for a moment. Then over the crackling radio the voice said. 'No, bugger it, book him, just like he was an ordinary person.'

This is going to be an interesting four days, I thought — and it was.

It began with the announcement that Greg Matthews had been made 12th man for the Blues — quite a shock to the media, not to mention to 'Mo' Matthews.

On the first ball of the game, Craig McDermott knocked Steve Small's middle stump out of the ground. The crowd roared but the umpire had called 'No ball!' As 'Billy' McDermott walked back, seething, there was a commotion in the second row of the grandstand as a man slumped forward and fell to the ground. The paramedics arrived five minutes later and play was held up while the man was taken away, but he died soon afterwards. Obviously this tragic happening created a pall over the game for a time and put things into perspective.

NSW did not bat well, but there was a large cheer from the crowd when the popular figure of Mike Whitney walked onto the ground. It wasn't that Whit was expected to make many runs — the cheers just showed that the fans appreciated the fact that he was trying to win his way back into the Test team. (Earlier in the year, despite having taken 7-89 and 2-60 against the then mighty West Indies in the last Test Australia played before the 1989 tour of England, and despite being the leading wicket-taker during the 1988-89 Australian first-class season, he had been left out of the Australian party for the Ashes tour.) McDermott charged in, and let fly a bouncer. Whit put up his arm to protect himself. The noise that the ball made as it hit the forearm was like the sound of a bullwhip cracking the early morning air. Bones were broken, Whit's season ruined — his fightback on hold yet again.

For two days the match ebbed and flowed and by the end of the third day it could have gone either way, although Queensland would probably be the slightest of favourites.

The night before the final day's play, most of the NSW party went out to dinner together. We arrived home between 10.30 and 11:00. By about 2am toilets throughout our hotel began to flush and the unique sound of vomiting echoed from floor to floor. By next morning the NSW group could be split into two — those who had it and those who didn't!

Queensland needed 164 to win in the last innings and somehow NSW managed to get 11 players on the field. Then, like the green bottles on the wall, those in the team who felt quite well before the game suddenly began to switch camps! The NSW room became a casualty ward — it looked like a scene from *Gone With The Wind*. Moreover, it was not only the players. There were also wives and girlfriends and selectors scattered around the locker room and in the dining area. Sick people were lying on massage tables, benches and stretched out on pads. The Newcastle Cricket Association doctor was doing his best to cope with this epidemic but he was fighting a losing battle. (The fittest man in the NSW team at that moment was Mike Whitney, and he had a number of busted bones and his arm in a sling.) Then, to make matters worse, Ian Thomas, one of the umpires, sprinted off the ground and headed for the toilets in the umpires' room, to lie there for the rest of the match. The sights and sounds at Newcastle that day were awful to behold and be heard.

Merv, who had never worked harder in his life, was everywhere. His room attendant duties had multiplied tenfold and he was now also a combination of Florence Nightingale and Sadie the Cleaning Lady. Then Merv began to feel queasy himself.

Meanwhile, out in the centre, the battle continued apace. Players were running off and on the field in turns and showing an amazing amount of courage in adversity. Two of the sickest were keeper Phil Emery and fast bowler Wayne 'Cracker' Holdsworth. Emery knew that, as keeper, he couldn't come off, so he stuck it out, but it must be admitted that the slips were giving him a fairly wide berth. Cracker kept hurtling into the crease with his smooth action and express deliveries, although at the end of each over he wasn't so smooth, retching into the gutter at deep fine leg. 'Bags not field at deep fine leg,' said 'Jack' Small.

To make matters worse, the other umpire, Graham Reed, now on his own, was required to umpire from bowler's end to bowler's end, supported by a local grade umpire from Newcastle, standing at square leg. As the game became tighter, poor Graham was under constant pressure and there was no relief for him. Then there were a couple of controversial decisions, one concerning Border (who seemed displeased when given out lbw), and the tension out in centre became volcanic. The teams were into each other like two fighting cocks, with Graham Reed in the middle, no doubt feeling like a rabbit in a nest of pythons.

Down to the wire it came and eventually NSW were the winners. There were no hugs or high fives from the Blues, nor handshakes with the opposition (not that they would have received any in return). As soon as the last man was dismissed, all the fielding team ran to the sheds to attend to their own particular needs. However, as it turned out, there were two pieces of drama still to come. Firstly, as the NSW team were tramping through the area between rooms, a Queensland player challenged one of the them to 'step outside' (or it could have been the other way around). Then they decided, why step outside? Why not settle it here? As the crowd began to gather and the press reached for their pencils, wiser heads prevailed and pulled them apart. Just when we all thought nothing else could happen, Merv collapsed with a suspected heart attack and was rushed to hospital.

Actually, Merv didn't have a heart attack at all, he just had a more severe attack of the food poisoning than did the rest of the NSW party — which would have made it pretty nasty indeed. Though he was allowed to go home from hospital that night, the Sydney press reported next day that both Merv and his heart attack were still under observation in Newcastle Hospital. Before he was released, Merv recalls lying on a bed waiting for the result of the various tests that he'd been given. Suddenly a large nurse appeared. She was carrying his chart and looking very serious indeed. 'Tell me the worst, nurse,' said Merv.

The nurse replied, 'You're tied up with the Manly Football Club aren't you?' Merv said that he was. 'Do you know [she named a second row forward]?' Merv said he did. Throwing Merv's chart on the bed she snarled, 'Well, you tell the big bludger to pay the alimony he owes or I'm comin' after him.'

When the rumour got around that Merv had had a heart attack, the phones ran hot in the cricket community. Merv's mates thought the worst and plans were soon under way for the wake. There was even a feeling of guilt among the NSW team members that they had treated Merv badly in the room; if he survived, they swore they would not be such a burden to him — they would even laugh at his jokes. However, when it was realised that Merv was not in a serious condition, the good intentions were forgotten and Merv soon returned to his packhorse duties and to having his jokes sledged.

[Merv joke: this comes from Merv's first book, entitled *Regurgitated Jokes And Sickly One-Liners I Have Known*. (The book has not yet been published. Any publishers who are interested should contact Merv Seres, c/- NSWCA, Moore Park.)

A bloke walked into a pub in Manly. 'What's your pleasure?' asked the publican.

The bloke answered, 'My greatest pleasure is a double malt whisky, 18 years in the vat.' The publican poured it out, the man drank it down, then walked out of the pub.

'Hey wait a minute, mate, that will be $16,' said the publican.

'Why?' said the man. 'I didn't ask for the drink. What I did was answer your question: "What's your pleasure?" My greatest pleasure in life is a double malt whisky. All I came into this pub for was to pick up a box of matches.'

'Oh, a conman, are you!' yelled the publican. 'Well get out of this pub and never enter it again.' The man strode out, smiling.

A few days later a man who looked exactly like the bloke who'd conned his way into the free scotch walked in. 'Get out! You've been ordered out of here forever,' yelled the publican.

'Why?' replied the customer. 'Upon my honour, I've never ever been here before.'

'Well I can't understand it. Are you a twin?' asked the publican.

'No, I'm not,' replied the customer.

Shaking his head, the publican said, 'Then you must have a double.'

'Thank you very much,' answered the customer. 'Malt, 18 years in the vat. And while you're at it, mate, could you get me a box of matches?']

*　　*　　*

A man can't work 16 years in a room in close contact with young athletes without, occasionally, something going wrong. Thus, embarrassment and Merv are old friends For example, the $100 a head luncheon.

The players have lunch in the annex off the locker room. The food is brought in in warming trays and left for the players to serve themselves. Normally, they have the choice of fruit, salads, vegetables, fish, chicken, pasta, cold cuts and perhaps a mild curry or a casserole and for dessert, pears and ice cream. Apparently one particular day the NSWCA and the SCG Trust were having a 'VIP day'. Vice-regal personages, political notables and 'heavies' from the CBD end of town were all invited to wine and dine and, if they felt so inclined, watch the cricket as well.

For such functions all the stops were pulled out — the meal laid on was fit for a Queen (or at least some of the Queen's representatives). However, there was a mix-up, and the caterers brought the lobsters, prawns, oysters, and fancy entrées to the cricketers' room, while the VIPs received some pasta in a creamy sauce and a few limp lettuce leaves. Panic swept through the ivory tower of cricket's castle! Quickly realising their mistake, the caterers rushed down to the home room — but the food had gone. It was explained that the cricketers had suffered a hard morning in the field and thus did not notice the change in their menu. Apologies were duly extended to the Governor-General, the Governor, the Prime Minister, the Cardinal, the Archbishop and the Chairman of Westpac.

Outside the door of each locker room there stands a man in a green coat whose duty it is to protect the players from intruders. Over the years, these men have done their best, but their record isn't quite up to that of the Swiss Guard in the Vatican. One particular day, the usual doorman was ill and another man was sent to replace him. Merv explained the duties to the new man; the do's and don'ts of who is allowed in and who is not, emphasising that this day the cartoonist, Tony Rafty, was going to be drawing caricatures of the players for a magazine. Merv explained to the doorman that Rafty would be coming and going all day and to take no notice of him. About 10 minutes before play started Alan Davidson came down to the room to wish the team good luck for the game. Now 'Davo' was one Australia's great allrounders, and if he is not the best-known man in the city of Sydney, he would certainly make the semi-finals. To add to that, Davo had been president of the NSWCA for three decades. As Davo went to walk into the room the doorman stepped in front of him, saying, 'You can't come in here.'

'But I'm the president of the Association,' Davo gasped.

'I don't care who you are. Merv Seres said you can't come in and he's the boss.'

Hearing what had occurred, CEO Bob Radford came rushing down, screaming for Merv. He found Merv out on the balcony in front of the room. In no uncertain terms Radford told Merv what he thought of the doorman. Merv knew nothing of the incident and was very embarrassed. 'Well, I want to speak to him,' said Radford. However, when they went round to the door, the guard had disappeared. Radford's purple comments reverberated around the Members' area and he stormed into the locker room. What he saw made him stop dead and caused even the explicit Radford to be lost for words. There, wearing his green coat and sitting under the window in the Australian locker room, was the missing doorman, having his portrait drawn by Tony Rafty — best side to the light!

Merv has received a minor sort of fame by driving the drinks cart onto the SCG. When the big games are on, there are as many people watching Merv tootle onto the ground in his golf cart as watch Michael Schumacher in the Australian Grand Prix. Recently, Channel Nine requested that a camera be placed on the cart to give a different view of 'drinks' to the viewers. On the back of the cart this particular day was Channel Nine producer and former NSW allrounder Brad 'Buzzard' McNamara. It was fortunate that Merv was at the wheel of the cart because Buzzard's record on 'road trips', driving the team's bus from the hotel to the ground and back, is not one of which you would be proud. Though Buzzard is quick to point out that he never actually wrote the bus off and, anyway, what's a few little scrapes between friends?

When drinks were over, Merv headed for the room. Buzzard, a renowned practical joker, was standing at the back of the cart. 'Well, that went well,' Merv muttered to himself as the cart reached the gate. Suddenly, Merv went blind! From somewhere behind him, a pair of hands covered his eyes. The drinks spilled everywhere, the cart swerved left and took out two seats in the Members' enclosure. Fortunately, the members who were previously sitting on them had gone up to the bar for a drink. The cart was knocked around a bit, but as Buzzard blithely pointed out, 'There is no way you could call it a write-off.'

Merv's most embarrassing moment occurred recently during a Test match. The day's play had been over for about 30 minutes and the players were settling down for a drink. As they usually do at the end of a day, the caterers had delivered sandwiches, party pies and nibbles to the room. Merv had already taken the sandwiches around to the players and guests in the room and had gone back to get the pie plate to do the same. Picking up the pies, Merv walked along in front of a group of lockers, not noticing the handle of Steve Waugh's bag sticking out. Merv's foot became tangled in the bag, and he stumbled forward trying to keep the plate from falling — to no avail. At that precise moment the Prime Minister, John Howard, was walking towards Steve Waugh to have a yarn. CA-RASH! Pies, sausage rolls, tomato sauce and the Prime Minister of Australia came into violent contact with each other as Merv tumbled to his knees and stared at leaking pie on the Prime Minister's shoes. The room fell deathly silent for a moment. Then Adam Gilchrist called out, 'I know you didn't vote for him, Merv, but you didn't have to go this far!' Then everybody roared with laughter, none louder than John Howard.

* * *

Recently, Merv had a stint in hospital, and though his health is improving immeasurably, he is now talking about retiring. Olga believes the time has come and that there is no way he can continue his packhorse duties of the past. Yet Merv's experience is invaluable — perhaps there is a spot for him as a 'consultant' to fledgling roomies. Moreover, it would certainly be a great pity if young cricketers missed the opportunity of knowing and being in a room with Merv. After all, though his jokes are not getting any better, they're certainly no worse. Whatever happens, the NSWCA and ACB should make sure that above the home room's door there is a photograph of Merv Seres, beaming down on all. Cricketers come and go; characters are a lot harder to find!

There is an aura about the home room of the Sydney Cricket Ground. It's not a spooky thing, just a feeling of the past; a nostalgic journey to yesterday. From here many Wallaby sides, and the great South Sydney and St George rugby league teams of the 1950s and '60s, ran onto to the field. Here Victor Trumper padded up and Bradman strode with confidence. This was the place where players wearing baggy green and baggy blue caps returned in triumph. Yet it's not just a room for champions. It's also a room for fun and friendship. It's a room for banter, booze and bloody awful jokes:

'This bloke walked into a pub and said to the barmaid ...'

CLOSE OF PLAY

1945

I know this is a book of Australian cricket stories, but I want to end with a story that is based in England, and was told to me at the funeral of a great New Zealand batsman. However, there is an Aussie connection, albeit a slightly tenuous one, for the funeral was held in Sydney, the Kiwi cricketer had lived in Australia for many years, and the match that is the basis for the tale did feature some notable Australian players, including a very famous one — my favourite player of all-time, Keith Miller.

* * *

You know, I reckon that England would have been a great place to be in the summer of 1945. Although many of those who lived through the last months of the war, who were forced to dodge doodle-bugs and had to survive food shortages would, no doubt, disagree with me. Yet when I read about the period and watch old films on television, it evokes in me a feeling of latent nostalgia, as I muse about a place which for a split second in history stopped to gather its breath and celebrate the good fortune of its recent triumph. This was the interval between the ages, the metaphorical 'half-time' between a simple world and a complicated one, a special God-given instant to plan for the future. As it turned out, it was a false dawn, the time of the 'Phoney Peace', and plans didn't really mean much. In the cold, hard light of the years that followed, it would be seen that there were no spoils to the victor, no laurel wreaths, no riches and rewards — only debt, and the knowledge that the sun *had* set on the once great British Empire. Nonetheless, for a few euphoric months in 1945, the sun shone down on a people who had awoken from a nightmare, a people who had *won* and who looked out on a world which they thought was, almost, as it used to be. Admittedly, there was rationing of everything except fresh air (which isn't always fresh in England, anyway), public transport was unreliable and the weather remained as uncooperative as always, with the rain still coming down regularly and at the most inopportune moments. Yet for those who can still remember, it seems that the days were warm and golden and harmony pervaded the land.

Recently, in the eulogy at the funeral of Martin Donnelly, I heard a simple story about cricket in England in 1945 (later confirmed by Martin's wife, Elizabeth). As the little tale unfolded, a shiver slid down my spine and nostalgia grabbed me in its warm and comfortable clutches once again.

*   *   *

Martin Donnelly was one of New Zealand's greatest batsmen. He was chosen to play Test cricket at the age of 19 and toured England with the New Zealand side of 1937 and again 12 years later with the strong team of 1949. Nuggety and strong, Donnelly also played rugby for Oxford as five-eighth while completing a postgraduate course and made such a strong impression in the 15-man game that he was selected to play for England against Ireland in 1947. During the war, Martin Donnelly became a tank commander and at war's end he was seconded to play for the 'Dominion Cricket Team'.

The Dominion XI was comprised of a group of non-British servicemen who were top level players before the war. The idea to quickly revive first-class cricket was said to have been encouraged by Winston Churchill and the players' brief was to help bring back a feeling of normality to a battered Britain.

The greatest match played during the summer of 1945 was an England v The Dominions encounter played at Lord's. The England team was captained by Wally Hammond, one of England's greatest cricketers. (Aloof in social contacts and enigmatic in personality, Hammond's reputation is enlarged or tarnished depending upon whose opinion you seek.) The home team contained players of the stature of Bill Edrich, Doug Wright and Eric Hollies, a leg spinner who did not have much of a record but who has carved out his place in cricket's eternity because of one ball he bowled to Bradman at The Oval in 1948.

In the Dominion Team were Australians Cec Pepper and Keith Miller. Pepper, now almost forgotten in Australia, was well named. He was a hot and fiery allrounder who once sledged an umpire in a Shield match for giving Bradman not out after Pepper had struck him on the pads. Rumour has it that the 'great man' was also included in the sledge. Potentially one of the world's best allrounders, Pepper was not chosen in Bradman's 1948 side. On the other hand, Keith Miller *was* chosen! Though Miller, the handsome, swashbuckling airman, was also little known in 1945, he eventually became a 'larger than larger-than-life' character whose legend increases as each new generation of cricketers learns of the game's folklore. The Dominions XI was captained by the West Indies' Learie Constantine, the greatest allrounder of his generation and a man who was to West Indian cricket what Victor Trumper was to the game in Australia.

The match was played over three days in perfect weather and is regarded by some cricket historians as the greatest game of cricket ever played at Lord's. For the duration of the match Londoners flocked to the Home of Cricket and officials were forced to bring the boundary ropes onto the field to allow the overflow crowd to sit inside the fence. There was a total of 1241 runs scored (more than 400 per day) and 16 sixes were hit. After a pulsating contest that continually ebbed and flowed, the Dominion team came out victorious. Yet it was not the result or the closeness of the game that captured the public's imagination as much as the individual performances. The deeds of some grand old names plus the uninhibited flair of new heroes pointed the way to a bright future and brought cricket back to the consciousness of the British people after five sports-starved years.

For England, Doug Wright (the man with the windmill Bill O'Reilly action) claimed 10 wickets and Wally Hammond made a hundred in each innings. For the Dominion XI, Martin Donnelly made 133 and Keith Miller blasted 185, including a number of huge sixes. King Cricket had returned to its home with an entourage of splendour and a blaze of glory. Meanwhile, further afield, on the picturesque village greens of the English countryside, willow and leather took up their time-honoured battle once more.

*   *   *

Kitty James and her husband Jimmy were keen followers of cricket, so they attended all three days of the great contest at Lord's. They did, however, have an extra incentive to be at the game, as their daughter Elizabeth's boyfriend happened to be Martin Donnelly.

After three days of euphoric cricket, Kitty and Jimmy walked out of Lord's and headed for the nearest pub. When they arrived, the place was crowded but they collected their drinks, eventually found themselves a table and settled back to reflect on the game and what life would hold for all in the postwar world. A few minutes later a frail, elderly man entered the pub, walked up to the bar near where the James were sitting, and asked the barman for a scotch. The barman reached for the bottle behind him. 'You wouldn't have a single malt, would you?' asked the pale old man.

'Sir, there's been a war on, you know. You're lucky to get a blended scotch,' the barman replied.

'Sorry,' answered the old man, 'just thought I'd ask.'

The barman grinned, 'Well, perhaps this time. Let's see what's under the counter.'

'You couldn't make it a double, sir, could you?' asked the insistent customer.

'You're making it hard, sir, but I suppose so,' answered the kindly barman, pouring out a large whisky and handing it to his aged customer.

The old man thanked his benefactor, placed his money on the counter and then reached across the bar and rang the ornamental bell which was part of the olde worlde decor of the pub. 'May I have your attention, please?' called the man. The room became instantly quiet. All looked towards this thin and pale person as he lifted the whisky to his lips, took a sip and began speaking.

'Ladies and gentlemen, over the last three days I have watched cricket come back to Lord's. I have followed the game all my life but never have I witnessed a match like this. I saw Doug Wright take 10 wickets with his spinning leg breaks and googlies and I saw Martin Donnelly make a majestic 133. I watched with nothing short of awe as Hammond scored two superb centuries and then a tall Aussie named Keith Miller came in and belted the bowling all around the ground, hitting the biggest six I've ever seen at Lord's. The sky was blue and the war has ended. God bless you all.' The man raised the glass to his mouth and drank the contents in one gulp.

The old man placed the glass back on the counter, turned and began to walk to the door, when suddenly he clutched his chest, staggered and fell. He was dead before he hit the floor.

Cricket and single malt whisky — there are worse ways to go!